MENTIONED
IN DISPATCHES.

To Bob and Lee,
We think
of you as family!

Matthew

Greenland

Anchorage

North

America

Greenwich

Rochester★
Cooperstown★ ★ Exeter, M.E.
★ Sands Point, L.I.
Kansas City★
★ Centreville
Charlottesville

Mexico City●

South

America

FIGI

Buenos Aires

● Italic and underlined text – Cities mentioned in
Matthew Stevenson's previous book "Letters of Transit"

Please visit the book's Website:
www.lettersoftransit.com

MENTIONED IN DISPATCHES

The Travel Essays
of an Expatriate American

by Matthew Stevenson

Matthew Stevenson

Princeton

ODYSSEUS BOOKS

MENTIONED IN DISPATCHES
Copyright©2005 by Matthew Mills Stevenson

ISBN 10-digit 0-9709133-3-8   13-digit 978-0-9709133-3-3

paperback edition ISBN 10 digit-0-9709133-4-6   13-digit 978-0-9709133-4-0

For information, address: Odysseus Books c/o Pathway Book Service, 4 White Brook Road, Gilsum, New Hampshire 03448. Toll free: 1-800-345-6665. Fax: 1-603-357-2073. E-mail: pbs@pathwaybook.com

Please use the same contact numbers for special or direct orders, group sales, or special promotions, for example, those available to book and reading clubs.

Please visit the book's Web site: www.mentionedindispatches.com

To contact the author on any matter, such as to arrange a speaking engagement, please use: matthewstevenson@freesurf.ch.

To contact Odysseus Books use:
www.odysseusbooks.com

Some of these essays first appeared in *Harper's*, *American Scholar*, *American Spectator*, *Global Vision*, and *American Enterprise*, in a somewhat different form.

This book was printed on acid-free paper in the United States. It was edited by Sandra Costich. Jacket and book design by Albert M. Cetta. Patricia Tobin Fein drew the map.

Library of Congress Cataloging-in-Publication Data

Stevenson, Matthew Mills, 1954-
Mentioned in Dispatches / by Matthew Mills Stevenson.
p. cm.
Includes bibliographical references and index.
ISBN 0-9709133-3-8 (alk. paper)
1. Stevenson, Matthew Mills, 1954—Travel. 2. Voyages and travels. I. Title.
G465.S7445 2005
910.4—dc22   2005018244

10 9 8 7 6 5 4 3 2 1

This book is dedicated with love and devotion
to my children:

Helen Stevenson, whose smile radiates the warmth
of her grandmothers;
Laura Stevenon, who has her grandfather's
drive and charm;
Henry Stevenson, a natural at all he tries,
and he tries hard at everything;
and
Charles Stevenson, whose fine mind is alive with
numbers, words, and wit.

Your mother and I salute you.

(And don't forget: *"there's no parking in the white zone."*)

Acknowledgments

In September 2001, I published *Letters of Transit: Essays on Travel, History, Politics, and Family Life Abroad*. The book made its way to some bookshops, amazon.com posted its high-digit rank on the Internet, and I made the rounds of readings and radio shows. The book had some chapters that were essays that I had written during the past ten years. When the articles were being published in magazines, I remember receiving only a handful of letters from readers, mostly to correct my patchy spelling. Hence when I was publishing the book, I gave no thought to the correspondence I might receive. But since *Letters of Transit* was published, I have received hundreds of messages. I have files in my computer labeled "Comments on book." I have Christmas cards held together with rubber bands, and I have e-mails and letters from friends as far-flung as my high school class and people I met casually on long-haul flights. I did my best to answer these messages—Stevensons having been raised on thank-you notes. But I never expected to receive such an exchange of generosity. To this day I remain grateful and touched that so many friends, family members, and strangers would take the time both to read my book and then to write me a few lines. Which isn't to say that the book was a best-seller or that I was featured on the *Oprah Winfrey Show*. Far from it. The book was a collection of personal and political essays, and it sold modestly by word of mouth among friends and family. But for me it became a connection to a world of readers and justified the many long nights that it takes to write a book. Thus I want to begin this introduction to the new book by thanking so many of you for your kind thoughts on the last one.

It would give me great pleasure if I could list the names here of everyone who helped make *Letters of Transit* a success. But I would regret omitting a name. The same is true for the help that I have received with *Mentioned in Dispatches*. (The title comes from a phrase used mostly in England to connote heroism in battle. In World War I, for example, it would be said of someone serving bravely that he had been "mentioned in dispatches.") But I do want to single out some of the stalwarts who helped get this book ready for its readers. My biggest thanks go to Sandra Costich, the associate editor of *The American Scholar*, who not only edited the manuscript but also handled every challenge with professionalism and endless good cheer—two of her many fine trademarks. Sandra is the best at what she does, and it is an endless pleasure for me to see her thinking on every page. The book's graceful design is the handiwork of Al Cetta, who in 1984 made Connie's and my wedding cake and who in 2004 set this book into type—although here I am less eager to eat my words. Patricia Tobin Fein sketched the map at the front, no doubt bewildered why a rendering of the world had to include Sands Point, Exeter, and Laconnex. But as T. S. Eliot said: "The end is where we start from." Once again Tom Wallace has stood behind the book as an agent, friend, and counselor. My friendship with Tom dates to the 1970s, when I discovered that he both liked professional ice hockey and had cable television—qualities that pulled us together more than our conflicting loyalties for the Islanders and Rangers pulled us apart. Ernest Peter and his team at Pathway Book Service are wonderfully responsive in their approach to distribution and sales. Lisa Guida and

Alistair Layzell have handled the publicity in the United States and the United Kingdom, respectively, and I never spoke to them on the phone without feeling a sense of excitement and gratitude.

Some of these essays were published in magazines, in a slightly different form, and thus they have had the benefit of editorial eyes other than those of Sandra's or mine. For that professional scrutiny, I am indebted to many, including: Wlady Pleszczynski, managing editor of *The American Spectator* and editor of several lively Web sites, whose gift to magazines is that he encourages writers to write about their passions; Jennifer Szalai and John Sullivan, both of whom have edited the review section at *Harper's Magazine*, which has benefited, as I have, from their strong sense of language and love of books; Karl Zinsmeister, editor of *The American Enterprise*, who, in addition to raising a family and editing a magazine, found the time and the courage to advance with American troops on their 2003 march to Baghdad; Anne Fadiman and Jean Stipicevic, of *The American Scholar*, who demand editorial excellence, be it with the galleys they pore over or the issues they publish; Dick Wilson, executive editor of *Global Vision*, who encouraged me to write a column as though I were writing letters to my friends; and Michael Martin, another American in Europe, who publishes *Hogtown Creek Review* and whose lively mind and affection for, among other things, baseball reminds me of several great and enduring friends—Winthrop Watson, Tom Leonard, John Wiebe, and John Russell—whose friendship shapes much that I do.

I try to bring to my writing what I have learned from the editing and writing of Joseph Epstein, my friend who edited *The American Scholar* longer than Walter Alston managed the Dodgers and who, in my mind, has posted more wins than Brooklyn and Los Angeles in the summer game of American letters. I also have gratitude and deep admiration for Lewis H. Lapham, who has served as editor of *Harper's Magazine* for thirty years. For most of that time we have been colleagues and friends. Archaeologists may someday discover that my library in Switzerland is a duplicate of his in New York, because I have been working off Lewis's reading lists since 1977. Still I never quite feel that I am ready for the exams. Like so many around Lewis, I benefit not only from his own writing and editing but also from his courageous convictions that bond him with a vast circle of readers and writers. I wish my family friend and godfather, Robert Lubar, were still with us, so that I could give him a copy of this collection. Bob, a college friend of my father's, was managing editor of *Fortune* for ten years, and from an early age he instilled in me the sense that magazines and books matter.

For the last thirteen years, I have lived overseas near Geneva, Switzerland. Thus on most days I am far from some of the people mentioned here—a source of regret that dampens the pleasures of expatriate living. At the same time I have made new friends in Europe, and some of them have helped make this a better book. My friend David Haettenschwiller proofread some of these pieces. Although he and I worked together in banking, he has a wonderful editorial eye and improved a number of my dangling phrases. I also had the great pleasure to spend my workdays in the company of Inger Olofsson, who came to Switzerland from Sweden, where she spends some of her summers on the Baltic coast. Anyone who dealt with me professionally in the last decade also had contact with Inger, and they always remarked on her wonderful qualities of warmth and steadfast professionalism—something I saw every day. I wrote these essays at night and on the weekends, and one reason I could switch gears was that Inger made my work life go so smoothly. I also want to take note of another work-related Geneva friend, Matthew Cooper, who is both English and Swiss, and whose career—to use a phrase of Yankee pitcher Jim Bouton—is "to teach people to love their work or to work at what they love." Like everyone on the job, I have my good days and bad. But I have noticed that Matthew is always there on the bad ones. When I had a good one, it was probably because I was applying some of his passion for excellence. Alas, my good friend Rob Schmoll has heard all of the jokes contained in this book, and probably more than once. But who else in Geneva appreciates the philosophical ruminations of Joe Namath?

In these acknowledgments I want to express my love and gratitude for my parents, who in the last five years moved from our hometown on Long Island to a retirement community in Princeton, New Jersey. At age 85, my father still commutes to an office in New York, something he sometimes calls "hitting the line"—a whimsical connection between his responsibility for the Association of Macular Diseases and his earlier occupation as a combat officer leading men up Pacific beaches. My mother remains at the emotional center of many lives, including those of her children and grandchildren, with the same qualities of empathy that she brought to her career in social work, which began in 1941 and, professionally anyway, ended in 1994. Together they remain my most devoted readers. One way to undertstand the enclosed essays is to think of them as letters home—a habit that has kept us close despite the separation of an ocean in our lives. My father tirelessly travels the United States to help those with impaired vision. At the same time he contributes high energy and frequent-flyer miles to spread the word about my writing— another unexpected bond from *Letters of Transit*. Likewise, some of the stories here capture the lives that I share with my sisters, Nanette and Julie, who have devoted a large portion of their lives to books and teaching. As I write this, Nanette, two years older than I am, is on the North Slope of Alaska, instructing Eskimo children on how to sew the binding of a book. Julie, our younger sister, is bringing her gift of words and energetic presence not just to her own children but also to the many classrooms that feel her inspiration.

In closing, I want to thank my wife, Constance Fogler, with whom I have now spent more than half my life and who has shared most of these stories first hand—if not my devotion to the Yankees, Islanders, and Jets. When I was promoting *Letters of Transit*, I was often asked how I am able to work, raise four children, and write books. When I answered the question honestly, I would say it was because of Connie and her unflappable devotion to me, our children, the house, and our lives together. Traveling and writing are not always pastimes that go well with domestic simplicity. But never once in our time together has Connie blinked or complained when I retreated to my desk or purchased plane tickets to a place like Albania. (In terms of washing dishes, however, I tend to be what in baseball is called a "spot starter.") More than a few letters I received on the first book inquired how I managed to convince my wife to take vacations to places like South Africa or the West Bank. I still can't answer that question, although not long ago we celebrated Easter vacation by taking the children on the overnight train from Zagreb to Belgrade, an excursion that tested Connie's holiday deployment of chocolate rabbits. To be fair, Connie's daydreams dwell on old wooden alpine chalets, while mine tend to drift to coastal ferries in Papua New Guinea. But most of our dreams still overlap, and in some of those we are tramping in the Alps, even if, at the summit, I am singing her the feint praises of Port Moresby.

MATTHEW STEVENSON
Laconnex, Switzerland
December 9, 2004

Contents

Contents

MENTIONED IN DISPATCHES

Book Tourism

On many days I think I published a book of essays so that I could have a reason to travel across America with my children.

For most of the year I live in Switzerland, in the vineyards and winter fog that surround Geneva. Although my family and I are American, we have lived abroad since the four children—now ranging in ages from fifteen to six—were small. On weekends we walk in the Swiss Alps or ski in nearby France, and, idyllic as that sounds, I daydream about taking my kids to the Everglades or Valley Forge, perhaps to recall my own childhood excursions to the Mississippi or Harper's Ferry.

Letters of Transit was published in autumn 2001, in the haze rising from the abyss of the World Trade Center. As if a primer on homemade cruise missiles, the cover featured an airplane emerging from the clouds, which dampened what little enthusiasm there was, at that time, for a book of travel essays. The collection included chapters titled "Traveling the Afghan Archipelago" and "The Playing Fields of Terrorism"—neither of which needed any promotion after that black September.

Undaunted, and often in the company of one of my children, I set off on a series of American book tours, which I spliced between work and family obligations. During the past year, I visited (in order of appearance) New Paltz, Woodstock, Albany, Williamstown, Amherst, Northampton, Concord, Beverly Farms, Boston, Worcester, Greenwich, New York City, Princeton, Chicago, Rochester, Miami, Washington, St. Louis, Palm Beach, Key Largo, Naples, Gainesville, Atlanta, Washington, St. Louis, Brunswick, and Bangor—feeling at times like lost luggage on a discount airline. Along the way I gave readings, talked on the radio, and made what Willy Loman would have known as "cold calls" on neighborhood bookstores.

I can't say I sold a lot of books on the strength of my smile and a shoeshine. Small independent bookstores may be charming places to browse and have afternoon tea, but in my experience, they rarely buy into the portrait of the author as a door-to-door salesman. Nor do most readers purchase books after hearing an author chat on drive-time radio. They buy because they feel a personal connection to the writer or his stories. Done right, a book tour should resemble an endless Tupperware party. But as Loman knew, it isn't always easy to set your table. Still, with one of my children in tow, my travels included a visit to Martin Luther King's boyhood home in Atlanta, fishing off the Florida Keys, and a night at Yankee Stadium. Even if I didn't sell a lot of copies, who can say the book business is all bad?

I had never been to Woodstock, New York, except in the lyrics of Jimi Hendrix. Thirty years on, the main street is a pastiche of scented candles, designer coffee, and antiques that only the Jefferson Airplane can afford. After a stop in the Golden Notebook bookstore, we should have driven directly to Albany, where the next morning I was to be a guest on public radio. But this was a Sunday during the World Series, and I was with my nine-year-old son, Henry. So we strayed from our flight path and made an improbable detour—along the tracks of the Delaware & Hudson Railroad, for which my grandfather may have worked—to Cooperstown, New York, and the National Baseball Hall of Fame.

Cooperstown remains the perfect American town. The outskirts are untouched by malls. It nestles at the end of a beautiful lake, has an opera house and stately Victorian homes. Instead of Gap and Pottery Barn, the main street is lined with baseball memorabilia. I still regret not buying a replica of Babe Ruth's forty-two-ounce bat and a first edition of Lawrence Ritter's *The Glory of Their Times*, a splendid oral history of early baseball with narratives from the likes of Chief Meyers, Goose Goslin, and Smokey Joe Wood. Sam Jones, for example, remembers that the Babe "could hit a ball so hard, and so far, that it was sometimes impossible to believe your eyes. We used to absolutely marvel at his hits."

We arrived too late to visit the Hall of Fame that Sunday evening, so we had hamburgers and fries in the Abner Doubleday Café, where the waitress gave us free refills on our root beer and recounted how Pete Rose often sat behind a card table on the sidewalk to stake his claim for admittance to the Hall. The next morning we paid homage to the Babe's uniform, compared the Mick to Willie Mays, and hummed the first verse of "We Are Family" in front of Willie Stargell's plaque. My only book obligation was to telephone Susan Arbetter at WAMC at 12:15 P.M.—something I felt more comfortable doing after recalling a few Casey Stengelisms. (On Marv Thronberry: *He's twenty now and in ten years he has a chance to be thirty.*)

We left Cooperstown at 11:00 A.M. and rolled through apple orchards and dairy farmland until I began to realize that finding a land line for the book interview would not be easy. Upstate New York may be long on the elegance of the Hudson River School, but it is decidedly short on telephone booths suitable for radio interviews—known in the trade as "phoners."

Minutes before the call deadline, I followed signs for what I thought would lead me to a Holiday Inn. When one did not appear, I ran breathlessly into a remote family courthouse, where those slated for "interviews" sometimes arrived in chains. Fortunately, I was wearing a necktie, which made the security officers think I was there to cop a plea. An amused judge let me use a conference room, and I connected to Albany's public radio with a minute to spare. Then for the next hour, I gave elaborate, floral answers to simple questions—never admitting that itinerant authors can tell the same fanciful stories as deadbeat dads. Nor was I able to work in a quote from that non-Hall-of-Famer but noted author, Pete Rose, who remarked: "The only book I ever read is the one I wrote, and that one I didn't finish."

From Albany, Henry and I drove to Amherst, a book-buying Mecca in central Massachusetts. But before crossing the Berkshires east of Williamstown, we tarried at Saratoga to walk the remote battlefield that saved the American Revolution from a stillbirth along the Hudson River. On a perfect autumn day there were more deer than tourists in the national park, and we had the visitors' center to ourselves.

Overlooked in American history is George Washington's record as general, which was 2–11, his only real victory coming with French assistance at Yorktown. But when General Horatio Gates trapped Burgoyne's redcoats on the heights at Saratoga, he secured the French alliance for what otherwise would have been a lost cause. The British defeat took Washington by surprise, as Tom Paine wrote: "So totally and unconnected was the latter [Gates] of the authority of the nominal Commander-in-Chief that the two generals did not so much as correspond, and it was only by a letter of [American] General [George] Clinton that George Washington was informed" of the victory that secured the faltering revolt. But when it came time to choose a father of the country, Washington had a better agent.

Wanting to show Henry an American university, I took him to the Williams College campus where we played catch (as if cutting class) and leafleted Water Street Books, the college bookstore. Amherst was a delight in many ways. Atticus Books bought five copies of *Letters of Transit*; and I found the street where, in October 1963, I had seen President John Kennedy dedicate the Robert Frost Library and then ride through town on the back of an open convertible—Prince Hal in search of a homecoming queen. I also reconnected with my best childhood friend, Nick Seamon, owner of the Black Sheep Café. That evening we watched the Yankees steamroll the World Series opposition as we had so often seen them do with Maris and Mantle in the 1960s. (Before he died, the Mick said during one of his own book promotions: *If I had known I was going to live this long, I would have taken better care of myself.*)

From Amherst to Boston, Henry and I decided to meander along Route 2—hardly one of William Least Heat Moon's "blue highways." Much of it appears as tarnished red brick, more vacancies of the fading industrial revolution. But it put us in position to visit the distinguished stacks of Concord Bookshop—those browsing should be called "Hourmen"— and then track the footsteps of the British "lobsterbacks" who were ambushed by Minutemen. In the Lexington visitors' center I found a quote from the Earl of Sandwich, of the English aristocracy that squandered its colonial inheritance. Before the war, he scoffed: "Are these men to fright us from the post of honour? Believe me, my Lords, the very sound of a cannon would carry them off . . . as fast as their feet could carry them," words that, come the Revolution, could have described the British retreat to Boston.

Outside Boston, in keeping with the revolutionary theme, Henry and I tried to visit that famed frigate *Old Ironsides*, but a park ranger stopped us from boarding her. "Sorry, sir," he said, "due to September 11, the *Constitution* is closed"—something I had already inferred from the speeches of Attorney General John Ashcroft.

My talk that afternoon was at Boston University. As we checked into the Algonquin Club, with its aura of William Dean Howells and Henry Adams, I discovered that my son planned to wear his new Derek Jeter jersey to the speech—something that would have been as inflammatory in Boston as additional taxes on tea. In less than an hour, we managed to get him a fitting at Gap Kids and to stop at the Kenmore Square Barnes & Noble, where, when I asked to meet the buyer, I was led by mistake to the office of the president. Michael Gore received me graciously, if unexpectedly—perhaps hoping my book revealed an affair between Princess Diana and Pedro Martinez.

Here I digress on American bookstores in a year when I have visited about fifty in eleven states. In the current wisdom, small independent bookstores represent the best hope for American literacy, and the encroachments of the national chains threaten their survival by dumping books into living rooms as if they were imported steel or stock items at Wal-Mart. Certainly Boston has a near endless supply of charming bookshops—The Globe Corner, Harvard Book Store, and Wordsworth are among those where I tried to get my foot in the door. And on my tours, a number of store owners gave me a gracious hearing.

I recall warm welcomes from Susan Novotny, owner of Albany's Book House, Pam Price, who runs The Book Shop in Beverly Farms, Jeff Krauth, the engaging owner of Northampton's Beyond Words, and Gary Lawless, who mans the desk at Gulf of Maine Books. Tom Rider at Goerings in Gainesville and Trudy Chambers Price at Maine Coast Book Shop in Damariscotta were equally enthusiastic. But from Bangor, Maine, to Naples, Florida, I have also pressed the flesh with numerous independent booksellers for whom books and authors are one of the annoyances of the trade, like shoplifters or teenagers at the magazine rack.

By contrast, despite their reputation for ruthless marketing and bland coffee, the national bookselling chains are open to unknown authors, stock everything, work hard at promotional readings, and treat the writer-as-salesman as a potential customer and thus someone to be cultivated. I have only praise for Marcella Smith, the buyer of small-press books at Barnes & Noble. Admittedly, the chains rarely have an orange cat sleeping in the window, as you find at Gotham Book Mart in New York. But Amazon and the other behemoths do sell books. As Brendan Francis remarked: "What an author likes to write most is his signature on the back of a check."

During my year on tour—as part of my wholesaling—I went twice to book fairs, first in Frankfurt, and later in New York City. Each is held in a huge convention center filled with booths that represent publishers, agents, presses, bookstores, libraries, and remainder houses. As if it were Halloween, everyone walks around with a favor bag and at each booth casts an eye for free books, if not UNICEF money. For my part, I tried to trick-or-treat the distributors—Ingram and Baker & Taylor actually fulfill bookstore orders—and to cause mischief with buyers.

In many senses, visits to the Frankfurt and American book fairs are like a day at the mall, although wandering the aisles in New York, I was surprised to find, instead of books, a booth lined with sofas and the kind of sultry women who the author Joe Willie Namath, in his memoirs, refers to as "tension easers." Further investigation informed me that the book under promotion was *Pandering*, the memoirs of Heidi Fleiss, procuress to the stars in Hollywood. The line was too long for me to get a photograph with the author, and it's not a book where you want to appear in the index. But I did think about what I could do with such a sales force.

In making the rounds at the trade shows, I found it helpful to have what insiders call a "selling review," meaning praise from a large magazine or a national newspaper—although to succeed at that often requires efforts along the lines of pandering. In my case, the book had sympathetic words from *Publishers Weekly* and *Library Journal*. But the big fish had eluded me. At one moment my publicist, Booknote's Lisa Guida (who is terrific), told me that the editor of the *Times Book Review* had the galleys "on his desk." But then fate and September 11 intervened, and the radar went blank.

On another occasion Lisa reported "some interest" in a review from *Playboy*. For purposes of marketing research, I purchased the latest issue. During my survey—spent wondering if the "Girls of the Big Ten" would buy a book that included essays about Serbia and the Russian economy—I came across a column titled "Hanging with Hef," snapshots of the septuagenarian swinger on the arms of adoring Playmates. Who needs Oprah asking all those personal questions, I decided on the spot, when you can hang with Hef? Alas, in no future issue did a Playmate-of-the-Month list among her turn-ons, "Spending a quiet evening in front of the fire reading *Letters of Transit*."

There were other tours, if not one to the Mansion. With my twelve-year-old daughter, Laura, I drove around Florida, where we logged one thousand miles in a white Lincoln Continental (thanks to a mix-up at Avis and then an upgrade), as if we were trying to sell books on the set of Miami Vice. Between engagements we saw Flagler's private railroad car, drank coffee at The Breakers, counted alligators in the Everglades, and walked the ramparts in St. Augustine. I also pitched the book in several retirement villages, where I found the residents—with both time and money—to be an ideal audience. I also tried my hand again at broadcasting.

The easy calories in book promotion are radio interviews—talking away on the phone as if wasting time at your desk. Most such interviews last a few minutes, preceded by the host, off air, asking what the book is about. In my case all the questioners wanted to hear about was my trip to the Afghan frontier in the 1980s, an essay almost deleted from the book because I thought no one now wanted to read about earlier Afghan wars. I had written about a day I spent with Abdul Haq, a *mujahidin* leader subsequently in opposition to the Taliban. After September 11 he was sent (by the CIA?) into Afghanistan to rally opposition forces, and he was killed. For several weeks in October 2001, I was billed on-air in Las Vegas, Madison, Chicago, Memphis, and Minneapolis as an Afghan expert, based on my travels in 1983. I obliged listeners with long descriptions of the Hindu Kush, my thoughts on the geopolitics of Kashmir, and asides that explained the Uzbek influence in the Northern Alliance, which for contenthardly rose above Garrison Keillor's ten-minute *Hamlet*. Perhaps if I had stayed another week in Peshawar, I might have been invited to join the war cabinet?

My only television appearance took place in Boston, where Smoki Bacon and Dick Concannon host a weekly book program at the Park Plaza Hotel. I was told that the interview would be filmed over lunch, so when a waiter came for my order, I had a moment of panic, fearing all of Boston would tune in to see me grapple with linguini. But the book chat aired away from the luncheon table, although still in the lobby where vacationing Shriners stood watching my seven minutes of fame. Nobody has worked harder for the cause of good books than Smoki and Dick—in television, we're all on a one-name basis. But even they were amused when I kept dropping my Web site and 800 number into the questions about a chapter on the battle for Guadalcanal.

Of course, like most authors, even those who tell you they shun publicity tours, I daydream about seeing my book in airport stalls or chatting with Larry King. But, to be truthful, the rewards of publishing a book are the readings, which I have given in places as far-flung as Rochester, Minnesota, home of the Mayo Clinic, and the Saint James Club in Paris. Usually I read aloud from the five sections of the book and then retreat to a card table to sell copies as fast as I can sign them. (Calvin Trillin said that new books have a shelf life "somewhere between milk and yogurt.") Sometimes I think I am reading bedtime stories. But a great event was in Greenwich, Connecticut, where six wonderful listeners caught every joke and bought twenty-five books, a ratio that is hard to beat.

If I have a favorite appearance, it was in Gainesville, Florida, at the home of my friend Bob Chambers, a former college president. At the time he was new to the city, but he still managed to round up forty friends. I showed up in the Lincoln with my parents and Laura, who ran the cash box and collected extra books from the car. Until that visit, if I thought of Gainesville at all, it was as a football factory. But the intellectual warmth and diversity of the city appealed to me. After the reading, Hank Conner invited me to appear on his well-respected book program, *Conner Calling*, and that was among the best radio interviews I have had. And I have never had a better setting for a reading than Bob Chambers's house, which is literally book-lined and has a shelf of inscribed first editions, including a number from his friend Robert Penn Warren and others from Philip Roth.

Leaving town the next day, we made a brief tour of the campus, on the theory that it is never too early to start visiting colleges. Gainesville is the Sparta of America, a phalanx of stadiums, tracks, golf courses, and swimming pools, capable of hosting the Olympic games at twenty-four-hours' notice. We cruised past the Swamp, the home of the Florida Gators, and drove around a residential neighborhood where the "old houses" date to the 1960s. We also stood on the banks of Hogtown Creek to pay a small tribute to *Hogtown Creek Review* and its editor, Michael Martin, whom I had met and very much admired in Amsterdam. Like many streams that run through the American imagination—Antietam comes to mind—Hogtown Creek, as it meanders through the university, is barely a trickle. That is true of many headwaters. Moreover, I was pleased to see the magazine's source, knowing that the current was strong enough to connect me with many new friends on both sides of the Atlantic.

[2002]

Notes
from the State of Virginia

If you want to know what the world is really doing to any good purpose, pass a winter at Samarcand, at Timbuctoo, but not at Washington. Be a bank-clerk, or a journeyman printer, but not a Congressman. Here you will find nothing but wasted effort and clumsy intrigue.

—Henry Adams, *Democracy*

During several childhood springtimes in the 1960s, I boarded the train with my father in New York, at the now-departed Pennsylvania Station, and arrived some hours later among the flowering dogwoods of the Virginia countryside. Selling sugar to what he called "the trade," my father busied himself with meetings in factory boardrooms while I played handball against a brick wall or flipped through homework in a barren waiting area. Some hours later another train would depart— for Richmond, Charlottesville, or Alexandria—and we would repeat the experience of mixing his business with my pleasure, sometimes making a detour to Mount Vernon or the battle-fields around Fredericksburg, so that back in school I could share some newly learned facts about early America.

Last winter, as if to recall those Appalachian springs, I started planning a family trip to Virginia, beginning with a tour of the White House in Washington, D.C., and ending with a tour of Colonial Williamsburg. For ten of the years that my four children have been growing up, we have lived in the Swiss countryside outside Geneva. As I imagined the trip over the family dinner table, we would picnic along Bull Run and spend the day at Thomas Jefferson's home, Monticello. My wife was skeptical that we needed to fly eight hours to find late-winter sun, when Mediterranean beaches were just two hours south. But we had courted at, among other places, Antietam; besides, North Africa seemed a compromise with the Barbary pirates. As Jefferson wrote: "Avarice and Fear are the only Agents at Algier."

THE WHITE HOUSE: *"an unsuccessful hotel"*

We began the grand tour in a long line beside the White House fence—the one that Eugene McCarthy had pledged in 1968 to take down upon his election to the presidency. It was before eight in the morning, and because we had withdrawn VIP passes from the favor bank, I assumed that we might sweep to the front, as if the Clintons were awaiting us at the East Portico. Symbolic of America in 2000, everyone in this long line had VIP tickets. In our collective importance we inched forward in the rain and half-light until a Secret Service agent took charge of a group near the downstairs library—"a favorite of President Franklin Roosevelt for evening cock-tails"—and started us on our appointed rounds.

In the Green, Blue, and Red rooms, I can't say that the gifts to the nation from Dolly Madison or Eleanor Roosevelt made much of an impression on the children, who fidgeted with the velvet ropes and yawned with jet lag over accounts of the War of 1812. On such a public tour it becomes the extent to which the White House remains a work-in-progress, as changeable as its tenants' politics, not unlike Nathaniel Hawthorne's house of the seven gables: "The aspect of the venerable mansion has always affected me like a human countenance, bearing the traces not merely of outward storm and sunshine, but, expressive, also, of the long lapse of mortal life, accompanying vicissitudes that have passed within."

Lincoln called the White House "an unsuccessful hotel," and most changes of government have included a tag sale of the previous first lady's dreadful furniture. Benjamin Harrison thought the White House should be remodeled into an American Louvre. The Theodore Roosevelts gave it a modern appearance and scattered pelts on the floors. Harry Truman went down to the foundations. Jacqueline Kennedy wanted the White House to be a showcase for American art, and her collection, which rises to many ceilings, includes views of pilgrims landing, the Rockies, winter farmyards, and Shinnecock Hills—a "romantic view of America's un-contaminated origins," as was said of Jefferson's political philosophy.

Before cascading out the main entrance, we stood in the front hall before a portrait of John F. Kennedy—arms folded, obviously brooding about Cuban missiles. I told the children of seeing him in October 1963, a month before his assassination. Dedicating a library in Amherst, Massachusetts, he had come down the main street sitting on the back of an open convertible, as if part of a homecoming parade—a setting as innocent as his wife's art collection. But my earlier promise to buy Washington T-shirts abbreviated the memoirs, and we left thankful that we hadn't paid the rack rate then on offer for the Lincoln Bedroom.

We spent the day touring the capital—the Mall, the Lincoln and Roosevelt memorials, and the Smithsonian—and following the station-wagon wheels of countless earlier Americans, most of whom were probably more successful than we were at finding parking. Heavy spring rains kept us from walking, so we darted from presidential memorials to the Spirit of St. Louis, like Lindbergh, running ever lower on fuel and trying to make it across the ocean on five chicken sandwiches. Lunch and the souvenirs were the last best hope for a new birth of freedom.

HENRY ADAMS:
the education of Hillary Rodham Clinton

On the flight from Europe to America, I had read Henry Adams's political novel, Democracy. As we slid into a booth at a Pennsylvania Avenue luncheonette, I wondered what he would have made of the present political climate, which consigned the president to wear a scarlet letter and encouraged his wife to stand for federal office. Adams, the grandson of John Quincy Adams, is remembered for his autobiography, The Education of Henry Adams, which involved diplomatic service in London, grand tours of the Continent, stints for the press in New York, Washington, and Boston, and an ability to describe politics in the context of his family's oral histories and his own observations. ("The progress of evolution from President Washington to President Grant, was alone evidence enough to upset Darwin.")

Adams, like Tocqueville, believed the strength of American democracy lay in the inability of mediocre men to undermine the durability of its constitutional origins. But he saw the intrigues for power in Washington only in terms of romantic comedy, much like the evening news that we were fed on hotel television. His heroine in *Democracy*, Madeline Lee, is a woman of ambitious grace—like Clare Booth Luce, Jacqueline Bouvier, or Hillary Rodham—who trawls the capital's drawing rooms, unsure whether she is after love or power, allowing Adams to cast her, a bejeweled Huck Finn, adrift in the political currents:

But, in truth, her notion of legislative bodies was vague, floating between her experience at church and at the opera, so that the idea of a performance of some kind was never out of her head. To her mind the Senate was a place where people went to recite speeches, and she naively assumed that the speeches were useful and had a purpose, but as they did not interest her she never went again. This is a very common conception of Congress; many Congressmen share it.

Adams also wrote an eight-volume account of the administrations of Jefferson and Madison. "I have never yet heard of ten men who had ever read my History," he remarked. I took a break at the halfway mark, after the second Jefferson administration, which Adams summarizes this way:

> The great issues of 1776 and 1787 had dwindled into disputes whether robbery and violence should be punished by refusing to buy millinery from the robbers, and whether an unsuccessful attempt to purloin foreign territory should be redeemed by bribing a more powerful nation to purloin it at second hand.

Jefferson's affection for the Rights of Man, he notes dryly, "had acquired the flavor of French infidelity." But a conclusion in *Democracy* speaks similar volumes on the last administration: "The capacity of women to make unsuitable marriages must be considered as the corner-stone of society."

First Bull Run: *"a charge of light brigades"*

The next morning we escaped the Washington beltway orbit on a westbound interstate. At Manassas, we put gas in the rental car and filled a plastic bag with root beer, cream soda, and other snacks of convenience, which was what remained of my Civil War picnic dream.

Ground soaked in blood, the battlefield at Bull Run

survives as a peaceful no-man's-land in the otherwise angry development wars of northern Virginia. High-speed county roads bisect parts of the national park, and every few years a Virginia builder threatens to envelope the lines with a strip mall or scatter-site housing. But the broad field around Henry Hill, where the confederates broke the hollow squares of northern optimism, remains faithful to its 1861 moment in history. In rolling Virginia farmland, opposing rows of Union and Confederate cannons define the ranks that stood almost at attention moments before nineteenth-century fusillades cut gaps of twentieth-century casualties into the hastily formed armies. Herman Melville described the innocence lost at Bull Run:

> *In Bacchic glee they file toward Fate,*
> *Moloch's uninitiate;*
> *Expectancy, and glad surmise*
> *Of battle's unknown mysteries*

Unknown even to his loyal readers, Melville went several times to the front lines of the Civil War and later published *Battle-Pieces and Aspects of the War*—his bid to become the American Homer. Alas for Melville, the uneven verse faded into English-department obscurity, even after his sea stories were resurrected. Not an epic so much as epigrams, written after the fighting, the poems connect the struggles at war that, not long before, Melville experienced in mortal combat with the whale. He recalled Gettysburg, as he could have Bull Run:

> *Before our lines it seems a beach*
> *Which wild September gales have strown*
> *With havoc on wreck, and dashed therewith*
> *Pale crews unknown—*
> *Men, arms, steeds. The evening sun*
> *Died on the face of each lifeless one,*

And died along the wind marge of fight
And searching-parties lone.

In many respects First Manassas was a charge of light brigades, a battle that Union General Irvin McDowell thought he could win almost just by showing up with polished brass on his uniform. But the more than one thousand casualties taken early in the fighting broke the northern units, which then fell back on Washington in flight. Laurie Robertson-Lorant, a Melville biographer, describes a scene that rarely gets into the histories: "When survivors of Bull Run who did not need hospitalization reached Washington, they drowned their grief in alcohol and smothered their fear in desperate sexual encounters. The Union Army's respite from Hell turned into an orgy, and the war-torn capital resembled Pandemonium."

As our two boys imagined cannonballs in the air, I thought about the District of Columbia's unrequited romance with war. Many of those of who fled Bull Run were affluent Washingtonians who had watched the battle from nearby heights, after lavish picnics—not unlike the CNN wars of Iraq and Kosovo that played to Washington cocktail parties. Nor were the sons of Washington well represented in the tattered regiments, as the likes of Chester A. Arthur, Grover Cleveland, J. P. Morgan, and the fathers of Theodore and Franklin Roosevelt all hired working-class substitutes to take their places on the rosters—a solution less complicated than six years in the national guard or an Oxford regiment.

Melville turned to poetry, at Bull Run and elsewhere, to rescue a writing career that, by the 1860s, had among its critics his wife and close friends. He had gone to sea in his early twenties and, before the age of forty, had written nearly all of his great books. Only *Typee* and *Omoo*—semi-autobiographical accounts of paradise found in the South Seas—earned any money, and the rest, including *Moby-Dick*, left him in debt to his publishers. Before his career vanished into a New York customhouse, Melville applied for jobs in Washington, D.C., where his family had political connections.

During one round of interviews, he met the new president, Abraham Lincoln, at a White House reception. Melville wrote: "Old Abe is much better looking [than] I expected & younger looking. He shook hands like a good fellow—working hard at it like a man sawing wood at so much per cord. Mrs. Lincoln is rather good looking I thought. The scene was very fine altogether. Superb furniture—flood of light-magnificent flowers—full band of music &c." Lincoln never knew that he had met someone who would become known as a great American novelist, but as Melville's biographer observed: "The two men shared a love of literature and a philosophy of history formed by Shakespeare, the Bible, and the Greek and Roman classics, and the rivers of tragedy ran deep enough to break their hearts."

JEFFERSON AT MONTICELLO:
"my family, my farm, my books"

The drive between Manassas and Charlottesville is a hundred miles, leaving the suburban front lines to the southwest and traversing spectacular horse country as the road dips and rolls through Orange County. We paused briefly in Culpeper, where Melville interviewed General Grant, but were too late to tour Montpelier, James Madison's plantation. At dusk we arrived in Charlottesville, where Jefferson lived and founded the University of Virginia.

I had notions of staying at a colonial inn, where the themed entertainment would include the guests debating constitutional questions (the Presidency, Jefferson once wrote, *"seems a bad edition of the Polish king"*). But since arriving in Washington, we had seen mostly rain, and the children needed something to consume their backseat energy. Thus we checked into a mock-Tudor motel with a fetid indoor swimming pool and, before dinner, watched them wade into the murky waters, as if seeking ablution in the River Ganges.

Despite Hollywood's interpretation, Jefferson—in Paris or Washington or at Monticello—was, at times, a remote and conflicted man. He embraced political liberty, yet he rarely freed his slaves, even at his death. As president, he spent an average of nine hours a day at his writing table. During two administrations he gave only two public addresses. In the last thirty years of his life, he never visited a northern city. But to my mind Monticello, Thomas Jefferson's plantation, is as close as America comes to Periclean Athens, and it remains as I first saw it in the seventh grade, a Parthenon to the Age of Reason.

Even if from some angles Monticello can look like a savings bank, it still has the Lewis and Clark maps of exploration in the front hall and the sense of the lives within that embraced words as easily as concertos. The tour covered his heat-efficient bedroom, the scientific inventions, and the Revolutionary busts in the dining room. But nearly all the tour questions addressed the matter of Sally Hemmings, and what for me started as a morning at the Agora ended in the audience of Jerry Springer.

Hawthorne wrote of the Pynchons, owners of the seven gables, that "life is made up of marble and mud." So, too, it must now be with the Jeffersons. My wife spent much of the tour whispering to the children the meanings of words like *affair*, *DNA*, and *scandal*. The guide was an elegant woman with gray hair, and she answered the Hemmings questions respectfully, but with the weariness of a witness yet again being asked where she was on a night in 1802. But no one wanted to hear about the library sent to Congress or the early drafts of the declaration until we had cleared up how the back stairs led to the slave quarters.

I heard later that Joseph J. Ellis, Jefferson's objective

biographer in *American Sphinx*, has changed his vote on Jefferson's innocence to that of guilty of miscegenation or, at least, of loitering with intent. But I have never thought it diminished Jefferson if he did find solace with Sally Hemmings, who was likely the half-sister of his deceased wife, Martha, a young woman of grace and charm who died shortly after they were married. Many of the Hemmingses were likely descended from Martha's father, John Wayles, and it is easy to imagine the romantic widower at Monticello—drawn to what he called "my family, my farm, my books"—glimpsing the paradise that he lost in his sister-in-law's familiar expressions.

AMERICAN AURORA: *"kings, queens and knaves"*

On Jefferson's tomb, which is between the house and the visitors' center, he is remembered for his 1776 declaration, his essay on Virginia, and his founding of the University. He omits from the epitaph any mention of the presidency, which he called "a splendid misery." It was raining too hard to visit the gardens or the plantation. We retreated to the souvenir stands, where one of the books I pulled from the shelves is my favorite from the 1990s—American Aurora, 988 pages of small type by Richard N. Rosenfeld, which tells the story of revolutionary politics through a history of the Alien and Sedition Acts. It also presents Thomas Jefferson less as an American icon and more as a founding father of factional politics.

Aurora was a Philadelphia newspaper, edited by the grandson of Benjamin Franklin, that infuriated President John Adams ("*His Rotundity*" to the editorialists) to the point that he had passed into law acts meant to silence the opposition and a disrespectful press. To Jefferson and his allies, the Federalists wanted to mortgage the American Revolution to the English aristocracy. Only Jefferson's election in 1800 saves free speech from Adams's laws of libel and deportation.

On the flap jacket to *American Aurora*, Rosenfeld is described as an "independent scholar," with connections to Yale, Columbia, and Boston University. Among his heroes are Jefferson, Tom Paine, and Benjamin Franklin Bache, who defeat such pretenders to a throne as Adams, Alexander Hamilton, and George Washington (*"fit only to command a regiment"*). Paine, for example, writes of Adams: "his head was as full of kings, queens, and knaves as a pack of cards."

What makes Rosenfeld's history such a pleasure is that the narrative of political intrigue is presented as extracts from letters, diary entries, newspaper columns, and editorials written between 1777 and 1800, to illustrate that politics, as played among the founding fathers, used the sharp edges of slander, wit, and cronyism as the contested precincts so required. For example, in trying to tilt the 1800 election away from Jefferson, Hamilton writes to John Jay: "In times like these in which we live, it will not do to be over scrupulous."

Henry Adams said politics is the "systematic organization of hatreds," a phrase that both his great-grandfather and his enemies would have understood. Followers of Jefferson and Franklin wanted the chief executive to be a rotating federal council, chosen annually by the congress, not a watered-down Polish king. They were grateful to France for its help during the Revolution and vigilant against any form of monarchy. As Jefferson wrote: "If any of our countrymen wish for a king, give them Aesop's fable of the frogs who asked for a king; if this does not cure them, send them to Europe . . . the best schools for republicanism are London, Versailles, Madrid, Vienna, Berlin, &c."

In the pages of *Aurora*, Jefferson is routinely denounced as a "pensioned tool of the French" or a "Jacobin," a reference to his affection for the French and presumably its revolution. In *Democracy* Henry Adams elaborated: "The democrat had no caste; he was not respectable; he was a Jacobin—and no such character was admitted into a Federalist house. Every dissolute intriguer, loose-liver, forger, false-coiner, and prison-bird; every hair-brained, loud talking demagogue; every speculator, scoffer and atheist—was a follower of Jefferson; and Jefferson himself the incarnation of their theories." A hostess of the period drew the lines more distinctly: "There was no exclusiveness, but I should as soon have expected to see a cow in a drawing-room as a Jacobin."

Nobody quite excited the *Aurora* contributors so much as Alexander Hamilton, the "amorous general" to his enemies, who, it was rumored, had financially defrauded the republic with one Dr. James Reynolds and then, as part of his inside trading, had cultivated the favors of his wife, Mrs. Maria Reynolds. Hamilton responded with a twenty-eight-thousand-word pamphlet on the pleasures of adultery—the founding fathers' Starr report or, in *Aurora, The Cuckold's Chronicle*. His accuser, James Callendar, analyzed his confession: "The whole proof in this pamphlet rests upon an illusion: 'I am a rake, and for that reason I cannot be a swindler.'" This is an edifying and convenient system of logic. Rosenfeld adds a quote from Benjamin Franklin (Poor Richard): "Dally not with other Folks' Women or Money," and asks, "So was Hamilton fooling with the wife or the money?"

WASHINGTON AT YORKTOWN: *"founding stepfather"*

Before leaving Charlottesville, I floated the idea of a visit to Ash Lawn, the nearby house of James Monroe, whose diplomatic expulsion from Madrid in 1805 was only slightly chillier than the call paid by our children to his mansion. We had lunch in the historic Michie Tavern, where everything from the waiters to the beer is supposed to look like Sam Adams. We ordered the "hearty midday fare," which included fried chicken, biscuits, ale, and pie, and I embarrassed the children by drying my shoes and socks near the fire. Then we marched on Richmond.

Everything about the state capital evokes the war between the states. In the rental car, we cruised Monument Avenue, with its bronze phalanx of the Confederate cause, and drove past the capitol, which Jefferson designed and for which Grant bled his armies at Cold Harbor and Petersburg. I told the children about Lincoln's anonymous visit to Richmond after the surrender in April 1865, when his carriage rolled past the houses of generals Lee and Pickett, and he swiveled in the abandoned desk chair of Jefferson Davis. I could have lingered among the dogwoods, to smell the petals of my childhood visits, and dropped hints about swinging past the Edgar Allan Poe Museum. But as the weather still had the air of the house of Usher (*"a pestilent and mystic vapor"*), we pushed toward Williamsburg, bypassing the city that Grant took straight on.

We decided to proceed to the battlefield at Yorktown, a strategic reckoning as foolish as that of the British general, Cornwallis. Detached from my supply lines, I turned the car into something called the Yorktown Victory Center, a stockade of gifts shops, organic farm animals, time lines to the Revolution, and an Adult Resource Room—at least one with more discretion than those we passed on Virginia's state highways. All I had wanted to do was glimpse the trenches of the Revolution's last battle and then find hearty fare for lunch. But as the Victory Center admission cost was seventy-five dollars, we felt obliged to pause reflectively at the Powhatan Indian dance circle.

In received American wisdom, George Washington won the battle at Yorktown and thus the Revolution. But a different portrait of the general emerges in *American Aurora*, one of the few contrarian portraits I have encountered. "He is the most amiable, obliging, and civil man," wrote a source close to the founding father, "but as a General he is too slow, even indolent, much too weak and is not without his portion of vanity and presumption. My opinion is that if he gains any

24

brilliant action, he will always owe it more to fortune or to the faults of his adversary than to his own capacity."

Prior to the surrender of General Cornwallis, Washington had lost nearly all his encounters with the British, having been absent when the minutemen won at Saratoga. He was crushed at the battles of Long Island and Brandywine, crossed the Hudson in flight, and limited his strategic contributions to letters to the Continental Congress—pleading for men and material, and excusing defeats. Even his unctuous subaltern, Alexander Hamilton, had threatened to sensationalize the general's shortcomings. Only a British march of folly let the American colonies slip away. As one British officer observed: "Our generals and admirals don't seem to be in earnest about this business."

By the time we reached the actual battlefield, not many in the car were keen to follow the "tour tape" that I purchased in the gift shop. We did stand atop the inner trenches, which give a fitting European cast to what was largely a struggle between Continental armies. A Yorktown dispatch is quoted in *American Aurora*: "There are approximately 32,000 French soldiers and sailors at Yorktown, four to six times the number of George Washington's army, and more than twice, if not three times, the number of all Americans at Yorktown, including militia. The entire blockading force at sea is French." During the course of the Revolutionary War, the French monarchy sent 47,000 soldiers, 3,668 cannon, 63 ships of the line to assist the cause of rebellion, not to mention imperial retribution.

In *The First Salute*, Barbara Tuchman writes about how, during the Revolution, the British transferred regiments from Philadelphia to the Caribbean—the sugar islands meaning more to London than to the American wilderness. Incompetence at the admiralty also allowed the French fleet to checkmate Cornwallis while relieving English squadrons were still off station. Short of supplies, cut off by the French and the Americans, the English surrendered and marched out of their earthworks to the tune of *The World Turned Upside Down*, thus sparing George Washington from ending his career as a colonel.

Henry Adams also had his doubts about Washington: "What I most wonder at in him is not his military or political genius at all, for I doubt whether he had much, but a curious Yankee shrewdness in money matters. He thought himself a very rich man, yet he never spent a dollar foolishly. He was almost the only Virginian I ever heard of, in public life, who did not die insolvent."

WILLIAMSBURG: *"Remembering, we forget"*

Club sandwiches in Williamsburg are named after revolutionary heroes, so I was not surprised that our motel was called the Patrick Henry Best Western Inn. But it had the virtue of proximity to the historic district, where the cost of admission tickets for a family of six feels as unjust as the Stamp Act.

The boys drilled with the minutemen, and the girls dressed for colonial games and chores. At the House of Burgesses, the presence of Jefferson and Patrick Henry—the patriot, not the motelier—hung in the air. Harvard and Yale were denounced as "seminaries of despotism." A printer was on trial for an earlier version of the Alien and Sedition Acts, but we returned an innocent verdict in less time than it took to free O.J. We cheered the delegates who departed for the Continental Congress, and only a silversmith exhibition at 5:00 P.M. kept us from tarring and feathering some wayward British tourists who dared to defend the King's own.

Lost in the street theater of Williamsburg or even in my beloved *American Aurora*, however, is the extent to which the rebels of 1776 became the imperialists of the 1800s. Jefferson, not Washington, coined the sentiment about avoiding "entangling alliances" and articulated the policies of "fair neutrality."

But in purchasing Louisiana from the French or quelling the Barbary powers, Jefferson presided over the greatest expansion of both national territory and federal edict. As Henry Adams writes in his history: "His ideas of Presidential authority in foreign affairs were little short of royal." Above all he wanted to keep the United States out of the Napoleonic wars, but it came at a cost: "The men who had abused John Adams as a despot because of the Alien and Sedition Acts were forced to pass acts far more restrictive in order to carry out the commercial policy which they hoped would keep America from war."

It was, however, in recalling the shores of Tripoli that we came to Williamsburg, where my father was attending a reunion of his World War II Marine Corps rifle company. I wanted to travel again with him through the landscapes of memory, as well as to show the children Colonial America.

The marines that survived the Pacific campaigns are now in their seventies and eighties. About twenty-five men, along with wives, children, and grandchildren, gathered at the Best Western, combining colonial tours with the somber business of reminiscence. A hospitality suite was available for the reunion. But in a town overflowing with admiration for the courage of minutemen, not one tourist in a hundred would have mistaken the older men sitting on motel sofas with the assault forces that cleared the Pacific of the Japanese Empire.

A few in the group wore Marine Corps caps or lapel pins, and a company flag of the Fleet Marine Force hung in the suite. But these were not veterans who in VFW hats would cheer rumors of war, any more than they believed in the search for Private Ryan. "War was a miserable, common experience," is how one marine put it, and it was to pay homage to what Melville called "the cannibal god of war" that the men got together every year.

No company was overseas longer than C Company of the First Marine Regiment, which fought the first American offensive action of the war in August 1942 with bayonets at the Tenaru River on Guadalcanal, and also the last action, among the flamed-out caves of Okinawa in June 1945. In between it fought in the jungle of New Britain and among the coral escarpments of Peleliu, where at one point the company of 230 men was reduced to several officers and 12 men. No company earned more congressional medals of honor in World War II. As Melville observed of other Pacific actions: "For every drop of oil, at least one drop of blood."

The men of C Company had done their jobs, survived, and moved on with their lives, for which they were grateful. I tried tape recording some of their war stories, but later, when I listened to the tapes, I heard only fragments about battle or strategy. ("*These men just win the wars, they don't have to figure them out,*" is an observation in James W. Johnston's *The Long Road of War.*) Occasionally some of them would stop me in the motel corridor, make the connection between my father and me, and say in the short, declarative sentences of older people: "You know, your dad saved my life." Kipling wrote of a similar encounter between the generations:

> *Hail and farewell! We greet you here,*
> *With tears that none will scorn—*
> *O keepers of the House of old,*
> *Or ever we were born!*

On the last evening a banquet was held in a motel function room. Lukewarm roast beef and fish were served from a buffet, and after dinner, in his remarks, my father, who commanded the company through three years of fighting, called the men of C Company "survivors," both in war and in life, for having navigated the shoals of battle and now those of old age. "You speak the language of the front lines," was his tribute to the bonds of their courage and endurance.

Then, as at a revival meeting, everyone present said a few words about their lives since the last gathering: of regrets lingering from the war, of buddies killed in the shadows of Shuri Castle or Bloody Nose Ridge, of the pleasure of seeing new or familiar faces. Across the street, war was part of the glorious Revolution; here, the bloody shirt had yet to dry. The World War I poet Siegfried Sassoon remembered his company reunion in this verse:

> *To stand in some redoubt of Time,—to share again*
> *All but the actual wetness of the flare-lit rain,*
> *All but the living presences who haunt us yet*
> *With gloom-patrolling eyes.*
> *Remembering, we forget*

After breakfast the next morning, we packed the rental car and drove north through Virginia for our flight home to Europe. Even on an Interstate, it is inspiring to cross the Rapidan, Chickahominy, Rappahannock, and other streams that flow through the American imagination. As we needed a rest stop, I chose Chancellorsville, having never seen the place of Stonewall Jackson's hour of triumph or death. As Melville recalled Lee's lieutenant:

> *A Modern lived who sleeps in death,*
> *Calm as the Marble ancients are*

I might have lingered in the bookstore or set out on the self-guided walking tour to see where Jackson's men cut down their last best hope for victory in a forest and fog of war. But I had lost my audience. We had spent too much time in the rain and the car, and sedition was in the air. The children refused to budge from the car, and my wife's thoughts had switched to our European lives—that which Americans turned upside down when Jefferson wrote about the course of human events.

Near Washington we dropped my parents for a northbound Amtrak express, the faint whistle of my boyhood trains. The roads around Manassas, near Dulles Airport, were grid-locked, yet another retreat toward Washington, and the size of the suburban houses made me think America has become a nation of great Gatsbys. With the skies still gray, I wondered if anyone in the family would have the patience for another of my colonial tours or if, in thirty-five years, would any of the children lead their own families on a forced march across the Potomac? But later that afternoon, a Swissair jet lifted us into the first Virginia sunshine that we had seen in nine days—that which had prompted my travel daydreams and to which, come other Geneva winters, may return my thoughts, or those of the children, to the pursuit of happiness.

[2000]

Some Damn Thing
in the Balkans

Until it became an international controversy, Albania had been a terra incognita—a remote labyrinthine confusion of ragged chiefdoms. To guarantee such a country under such a mbret [i.e., the Albanian leader] meant to conjure it out of a plumed hat.
—Frederick Morton
Thunder at Twilight: Vienna 1913/1914

In the weeks that preceded President Clinton's decision to wag the Yugoslav dog, I made a trip through the federation's two republics, Serbia and Montenegro, wondering if American politics might reduce itself (not to mention the Balkans) to pulp fiction. The Yugoslav army, in the guise of local police, was then cracking down on Kosovar irredentists, and in Washington the drummer boys of war were suggesting that Belgrade might listen more carefully to Albanian declarations of independence if a few laser-guided bombs came down Milosevic's chimney.

Everything about Belgrade suggested a city under siege. In the brave old world of the Hotel Metropol, I seemed to be the only guest. A poster near the elevator hinted at a floor show of women accented with feathers, and it was easy to imagine Tito's new class celebrating here on New Year's Eve. But the long rows of unclaimed room keys and the stillness of the breakfast room suggested nothing had been quite the same since the Marshal died the death of a salesman.

In most press accounts, not to mention the pronunciamentos of Madeleine Albright, Yugoslavia is a reminder of Europe's encounters with fascism. The country is said to have fought and lost wars of nationalist expansion, wielded the tools of genocide, and dispatched warlords to the rolling valleys of Bosnia, which a few years before had seen only tour groups. Certainly the Clinton administration is not alone in reviling Yugoslavia or its masters, the Serbs. What other people prompt easy association with ethnic cleansing, sniper fire into Sarajevo, the oppression of the Kosovar Albanians, the massacres outside Srebrenica, or the specter of "Greater Serbia," which evokes both *Lebensraum* and czarist dreams of a Slavic empire? What federation is more deserving of devolution than that which sacked its own city, Vukovar, as if it were Troy?

Few voices have questioned the logic of American policies dedicated to the disintegration of Yugoslavia. Since the early 1990s, the United States has supported independence for Slovenia, Croatia, Macedonia, Bosnia-Herzegovina, and, more recently, autonomy for Kosovo and greater independence for Montenegro. But would it support secession in Russia, which has the same patchwork of national aspirations as the former Yugoslavia?

While the European Community introduces a single currency to blur its overlapping ethnic passions, the U.S. advocates statehood for nations that even President Woodrow Wilson deemed unworthy of independence. Bosnia, for example, was an independent state last in the thirteenth century (if then); Kosovo has less claim to independence than Wales. But to make good on its policies of irredentism, the U.S., rather than just play a make-believe game of honest broker, has dispatched NATO war planes and trade sanctions, not to mention Iranian weapons on a scale of which Oliver North could only dream.

NOT-SO-GREATER SERBIA

One of my hosts that week in Belgrade came by the Metropol the first evening. We drank tea in the restaurant, an empty cavern of tables with white linen, where the only other customers smoked cigarettes in a distant corner (perhaps, I mused, in the midst of an arms deal). As with most Belgrade conversations, this one drifted to a remembrance of wars past.

During the war with the Nazis, 1.7 million Yugoslavs died, many at the hands of their own countrymen. In World War I, one-fifth of Serbia's population died fighting the Austrians and Germans. In both cases Serbia, or later Yugoslavia, sided with the Allies for which the reward, my host observed, was now economic isolation and the threat of air strikes. In the rush to condemn Serbia, he asked, who really cared that Croatia or the Kosovar Albanians had done Hitler's bidding?

When I asked the reason for the butchery in Bosnia or the current conflict in Kosovo, the answer was not Milosevic or the expansion of Greater Serbia, but a more familiar cause of war: "Borders." Admittedly, his was a Serb view of history. But it matched my own reading on the Yugoslav breakup, when nationalities found themselves isolated across fateful lines.

Tito (who was born in Croatia but whose mysterious ethnicity was redefined as often as party principles) revived the Yugoslav ideal after World War II. The borders he drew around the nationalities had a goal of redistributing the Serbs over four republics: Substantial Serb minorities were gerrymandered into Croatia, Bosnia-Herzegovina, and Macedonia. And the republic of Serbia itself was saddled with large Hungarian and Albanian minorities. Although Serbs dominated the ruling Communist party, Tito drew the country's constitutional lines according to the principle that a weak Serbia meant a strong Yugoslavia.

As long as Yugoslavia remained solvent, it mattered little that the internal borders were no more accurate than colonial frontiers drawn in African sands or that several million Serbs were scattered in a diaspora outside Serbia. But when Communism defaulted both on its debts and ideology in the late 1980s, Serbs realized that the dissolution of Yugoslavia would leave many beyond its boundaries: fuel for the fires of Greater Serbia.

When Slovenia and Croatia declared themselves independent in 1991, the Serb-dominated Yugoslav army skirmished briefly in Slovenia, but quickly withdrew, as there were few Serbs in Slovenia. The Serb presence in Croatia made that republic's independence more problematic, especially when the government of Franjo Tudjman adopted a new legal system that denied the Serbs the rights of a national minority.

Western powers crossed the Rubicon into the Yugoslav civil wars when Germany and then the U.S. pushed the recognition of Croatia and later Bosnia-Herzegovina as independent states. Just as Bosnian Muslims feared Serb domination in a Yugoslav federation without Croatia and Slovenia, so did the 1.4 million Serbs in Bosnia fear persecution under a Muslim government that had severed its ties to Belgrade.

In recognizing Bosnia-Herzegovina, the West validated borders that even Tito knew were fictional, sketched not to define nationalities but to enhance the control of the Party. The lines around Bosnia, for example, took in lands with historical claims from both Croatia and Serbia. "With us," Tito is quoted in Milovan Djilas's *Wartime*, "this will be more of an administrative division, instead of fixed borders, as with the bourgeoisie." Little did the Marshal know that the U.S. would come to believe in these borders as if they were the Maginot Line.

MILOSEVIC: *Hamlet of the Balkans*

The American embargo makes doing business in Belgrade impossible, so I spent much of my week meeting friends of friends, and when I got home it struck me how many I met had, at some point, known the Yugoslav president.

Most described Milosevic as pragmatic, but none respected his leadership; they made his current government sound like a junta. To stay in power, I often heard, Milosevic would betray friends, much as on his climb to the presidency he cast his mentor, Ivan Stambolic, to the wind. As Lord David Owen writes in *Balkan Odyssey*: "There is a ruthlessness and a pursuit of power for its own sake about Milosevic that underpins the pragmatism that otherwise seems so neatly to characterize Milosevic's political personality." Of his habit of trading regions of Yugoslavia for more time in office, one friend said: "He would stay on as the mayor of the Free City of Belgrade, if Yugoslavia is reduced to that."

I have no brief to defend Milosevic, a man of Balkan expedience. But foreign policy by storyboard demands a prime-time strongman—a Balkan Saddam—to explain why America has brought the blitz to the skies of Yugoslavia. And what is clear from a visit to Belgrade or a reading of Bosnian memoirs is the extent to which his demonization fits the requirements of American policies rather than a careful review of his record.

Milosevic speaks fluent English, understands the nuances of American politics, and participates freely in most negotiations even if, like the Serbian government in 1914, he rejects the ultimatum to accept the jurisdiction of foreign forces. At Dayton, to get peace, his break with the Bosnian Serbs made the crucial difference. Belgrade is absent a cult of his personality—I never saw his portrait anywhere—and people do not look over their shoulders before denouncing him in public.

Ironically, it was in the defense of a minority that Milosevic came to power. With its many Orthodox monasteries and the Field of Blackbirds, where Serbia lost its independence to the Ottomans in 1389, Kosovo is Serbia's spiritual heartland. Yet a constitutional change under Tito in 1974 granted the province autonomy (similar to what is sought today), which allowed the Albanian majority to persecute the Serbs, whose complaints in the mid-1980s drew Milosevic's attention. He traveled there in April 1987 and proclaimed, "No one will be allowed to beat you!"

Milosevic wraps himself in the cloak of Greater Serbia not out of nationalist conviction but to survive in office. Although he has a record of ruthlessness, he usually compromises in the end—qualities that the Americans now seek to exploit. He barely opposed Slovenian secession, carved up Bosnia in a deal with Tudjman, sold the Krajina Serbs down the river, gave up Sarajevo, and embraced the Dayton accords in exchange for an end to the economic sanctions.

A number of people I talked with described the Yugoslav president as someone who uses the public face of tyranny to mask Hamlet-like indecision. In Bosnia and Kosovo, Milosevic's temporizing squandered many advantages. In the end the champion of Greater Serbia found his people living in four independent, sovereign states. His brinkmanship seems that of a muscleman defiant of Western ideals; in practice he is a poker player who can never remember if a flush beats three of a kind.

Having run Belgrade's largest bank, Milosevic should have known an asset from a liability, yet he led his nation into bankruptcy. He financed the war with printed money, stripped banks of their deposits to raise cash, and reduced Yugoslavia's considerable history of international trade to that of a smuggler's den. Wallowing in inflation, his central bank once printed a billion-dinar note, which lost most of its value before the ink dried on the last zero. The economy today survives on the soft credit of Russian natural gas. Most of the people I met earned less than $150 a month and worked two jobs. Even Tito's widow lives without a state pension. "We're a banana republic," I was told, "without bananas."

MR. HOLBROOKE GOES TO WASHINGTON

Since returning from Yugoslavia, I have read a number of accounts of the Bosnian war and peace, including *To End a War*, in which former Assistant Secretary of State Richard Holbrooke stakes out the claim to the one great foreign policy success of the Clinton administration. With the U.N. and the European Community unable to stop the slaughter in Bosnia, Holbrooke orchestrated the shuttle diplomacy that ended with the 1995 Dayton peace accords. During the 1996 elections President Clinton could speak of peace in our time.

Holbrooke is a man of many talents, not to mention jobs. In recent times, while he was Clinton's nominee-in-waiting to represent the U.S. at the U.N., he was also a special envoy for the State Department in Kosovo and a vice chairman of Credit Suisse First Boston, an investment bank that, despite Holbrooke's connections and savvy, still dropped more than a billion in Russian bonds. During the Bosnian peace shuttle, he managed to find time to marry Kati Marton, the ex–Mrs. Peter Jennings, at the U.S. embassy in Budapest. Less felicitous diplomatic contacts, after he left government, cost him five thousand dollars to settle an ethics-violation claim brought by the Justice Department.

To End a War opens with an attack on Rebecca West, the author of *Black Lamb and Grey Falcon* (1941), for her "openly pro-Serb attitudes," as if she were huddled in Pale writing speeches for Radovan Karadzic. Throughout the book,

Holbrooke blames extreme Serb nationalism for the ills of the Balkans. He carefully remembers all of his *bon mots*—"The Serb view of history was their problem, I told Roberts later; ours was to end the war"—and confesses modestly that when he arrived on location "there was no more energy left in the international system."

As European history, however, Holbrooke's account lacks the depth of a downloaded, Internet term paper. German interests in the Balkans are trivialized ("Genscher . . . ignored warnings of his old friends . . . not to recognize first Croatia . . . and later Bosnia"), and five hundred years of Ottoman cruelty are summarized in exquisitely diplomatic terms: "Turkey had once shared a common history with Bosnia." But as a journey through the whaling grounds of Washington politics, Holbrooke's account compares favorably to *Moby-Dick*.

Clearly Holbrooke's ambitions are to be secretary of state, perhaps in a forthcoming Democratic administration. Toward that end his account of the Bosnian negotiations reads like the longest résumé cover letter in history. He recalls with fondness his former employers, including Clark Clifford, W. Averell Harriman, and Jimmy Carter. As references he lists Joe Klein, Bob Dole, Jacques Chirac, Sam Nunn, and Mike Wallace (many more available upon request). Among his accomplishments are simultaneous positions at State and on Wall Street—making him one of the few investment bankers who come to a closing with cruise missiles.

Knowing that Washington has more mine fields than the hills around Sarajevo, Holbrooke heaps praise on his colleagues in the Clinton administration, not to mention such foes as Henry Kissinger and Richard Perle. Men who might someday write his letters of recommendation—Warren Christopher, Strobe Talbott, Anthony Lake, and Al Gore—rate encomia that read like the lives of the saints.

Chasing the white whale of influence, Holbrooke saves

most of his sail for the president. He remembers the president's birthday, shows him around Berlin, sends him Cliffordesque back-channel memos, and describes the First Couple enjoying a tender waltz at a White House ball. "The president succeeded brilliantly," is a typical compliment when Clinton has the good sense to endorse Holbrooke's advice.

In one of the book's most dramatic scenes, Clinton orders an air attack against the Serbs and tells Holbrooke, in perfect Hollywood diction, "to hit them hard"; then Clinton resumes his vacation in Wyoming. At least Lincoln waited in the telegraph office for news of casualties.

Mr. Holbrooke Goes to War

The Clinton administration likes to claim that it plays the role of honest broker in the Balkan wars, but what is clear from Holbrooke's account is the extent to which the U.S. tilts in any direction as long as it opposes the government of Slobodan Milosevic, "the man who, in our view, bore the heaviest responsibility for the war." To lay waste to the faltering Yugoslav ideal, the U.S. deployed the range of diplomacy, deception, and violence familiar to great powers.

Throughout his narrative Holbrooke is repeatedly calling for air strikes, like one of the Bundy brothers during the early years in Vietnam. "Give us bombs for peace," is Holbrooke's plea to the Washington brass, foreshadowing the administration's later romance with air power. Without American peacekeeping troops on the ground, the U.S. could freely advocate bombing Serb positions. But as the U.N.'s General Sir Michael Rose wrote in *Fighting for Peace*, "Without such a commitment [to put U.S. troops into the peacekeeping], President Clinton was, in effect, playing with the lives of soldiers from other nations."

During the wars of the Yugoslav succession, as today in Kosovo, the Clinton administration had the luxury, in Lord

Owen's phrase, "to practice realpolitik and simultaneously preach moralism." Repeatedly, the U.S. chose war over peace plans that had not been drafted in Washington. In 1993, for example, the U.S. sank the Vance-Owen peace plan, which would have given the Muslims 33 percent of Bosnia, because it suited the domestic agenda to encourage the Muslims to hold out for better terms; at Dayton the Muslims ended up with 21 percent of Bosnia. In Kosovo, the administration bypassed either a U.N. resolution or a congressional declaration of war, preferring its own policies of ultimata.

To reverse the effects of Serb ethnic cleansing, the U.S. and its allies excused atrocities that, had they been committed by the Serbs, would have prompted calls for air strikes. Holbrooke is breathless in his enthusiasm for Croat-Muslim offensives: "In early August, the Croatians launched a major offensive to retake the Krajina. It was a dramatic gamble by President Tudjman— and it paid off. ... The Croatian offensive was valuable to the negotiating process." The attack, which bore hallmarks of American military or perhaps CIA planning, did not retake land but drove 150,000 Serbs from towns they had settled in the eighteenth century. Unapologetic, Holbrooke writes: "I told Tudjman that current Croatian behavior might be viewed as a milder form of ethnic cleansing." Holbrooke offers no hint that the American government might have helped Croatia overrun the Krajina. But he does mention Washington's indifference to Iranians and *mujahidin* who were present in Bosnia after 1993. And Lord Owen confirms that the Iranian weapons pipeline ran via Croatia into Bosnia. Holbrooke's gift to his prince is to dress such realpolitik in the guise of humanitarian rescue.

ALLIES OF CONVENIENCE:
The Bosnian Minutemen

Because it suited American interests to dress the Muslim Bosnian government in the cocked hats of Minutemen, few accounts have ever addressed its conduct in the war. To be sure, the Muslims often fell between two ruthless, warring parties—Serbs and Croats—and suffered numerous atrocities, much as innocent Kosovars are now being marched forcibly into Albania. But the Bosnian government also found ways to exploit its image as a victim, with the goal of entrapping the U.S. to fight its battles, a strategy that is not lost on the Kosovo Liberation Army.

General Rose is one of the few willing to speak out on "the danger for the USA in pursuing a foreign policy in Bosnia shaped by the propaganda machine of a clever, ruthless government." In his book, he tells of one encounter with a Bosnian officer: "His underlying strategy was familiar to me, as it was the one followed elsewhere by the Bosnian Army: 1. Attack on all fronts. 2. Retreat into the enclave amid scenes of appalling suffering. 3. Call on the U.N. and NATO to bomb the Serbs." It was Rose who collected evidence suggesting that one of the hideous shells fired on the Sarajevo market (for which the Serbs were blamed and punished with air strikes) might have been fired from Bosnian positions.

Certainly no aspect of war excites more despair than the fate of the so-called safe areas. They were set up as sanctuaries in 1993 by the French general Philippe Morrillon. In reality they were also used by each side in the fighting as safe havens—almost like Trojan horses. Nor did the U.N. allocate the troops necessary to protect the six enclaves. When the Serbs attacked Gorazde in 1994, the U.N. had only six observers there. At Srebrenica, equally vulnerable, the Muslim commander, Nasser Oric, used the city's civilians to mask attacks on nearby Serb positions. Then he withdrew his forces, leaving the enclave defenseless. When Bosnian Serbs attacked the city and later massacred some thousands of male Muslims, they came with a vengeance as old as the *Iliad*.

WILL KOSOVO'S FATE BE
THAT OF SREBRENICA?

In reading the war dispatches from Kosovo, I am reminded of the summer after I graduated from college, when I spent time traveling in Kosovo. I stayed on a farm near Pristina, a dusty provincial city, where horse carts jostled lurching trucks on the city's main streets.

On my first visit to Pristina, I got mixed up in a student demonstration. Standing on the steps of a drab socialist hotel, I watched waves of angry young men, most dressed in black, protest the lack of Albanian language in courses at the local university. When the streets cleared, my friends and I pressed on to Graçanica, a monastery as sacred to Serbs as parts of Jerusalem are to the Jews. In the late afternoon, we walked the Field of Blackbirds, also a shibboleth of Serb memory. It is a day I recall with words from Rebecca West: "Kosovo speaks only of its defeats."

Both Serbs and Albanians in Kosovo see themselves as step-children in a promised land. Some two million ethnic Albanians live in Kosovo, as opposed to two hundred thousand Serbs, who like Afrikaners cling to ancestral lands against a rising demographic tide. (After World War II the populations were equal.) As I was told in Belgrade: "We have the churches, and they have the people."

Most press accounts and Pentagon briefings that describe the fighting between Kosovo Liberation Army and Serbian military police imply that the Serbs are in Kosovo only as an army of occupation. Holbrooke refers to them as "Serb-occupiers." In a syndicated column, William Pfaff writes that Kosovo is "where the vast majority of the former Serbian population no longer choose to live," as if they had retired to Florida.

Alexander Dragnich, a former U.S. diplomat in Belgrade who has written several books about Kosovo, better understands the Serb exodus: "The holy ground of Kosovo was not regained until the Balkan Wars of 1912. During the intervening centuries, many Serbs fled Kosovo to escape enslavement, while the Turks sent in more and more Islamicized Albanians, who engaged in massive persecutions of Serbs, which today would be called genocide."

As the Serbs regained Kosovo in 1913, Albania was carved from the wreckage of the Ottoman Empire, not for reasons of human rights but so that Austria-Hungary could check Serbia's progress before it reached the sea. Yet half of the Albanian population lay outside the 1913 borders—not just in Kosovo, but throughout the southern Balkans—an injustice the U.S. now thinks it can remedy with Allied bombers. As my father, a combat veteran, wrote to me recently: "With our current distaste for using the bayonet, it looks as though bombs will be the weapons of choice. There's much more comfort at 30,000 feet than there is at six."

What is lost on the war dogs in Washington is that Greater Albania comes at great peril. British historian Miranda Vickers warns: "Before this could become a reality the Serbs, Macedonians, Montenegrins, and possibly Greeks, would need to renegotiate their borders with Albania. This could be the cause of catastrophic conflict throughout the Balkans."

Against the aerial onslaught, Milosevic clings to Kosovo for what might be called geosentimental reasons. His tactics are violent and primeval (although little different from Sherman's march to the sea) as, in his mind anyway, he fights to preserve an imperfect union. Like the U.S. at Hiroshima, he targets civilians as instruments of war. But in launching Tomahawk missiles against military sweeps in Kosovo, the NATO alliance has endorsed the principle that the future map of Europe should conform to its linguistic and religious contours a Holy Roman Empire held together by American stealth bombers.

The Radetzky
March of Folly

For reasons not clearly explained, while fighting a remote-control war against Islamic fundamentalism in Iraq, Sudan, and Afghanistan, the U.S. has championed the rights of Muslims in the Balkans. The objective of the undeclared war in Kosovo is that ethnic Albanians, also mostly Muslim, might have home rule, something they would never have if they joined Albania's impoverished anarchy.

Few in Washington have asked whether it makes sense for the U.S. to align itself with the goals of the Kosovo Liberation Army, whose soldiers in most sovereign nations would be deemed terrorists or invaders. In the wreckage of Yugoslavia, the Clinton administration wants to showcase a foreign policy in which Wilsonian ideals of self-determination are defended with Richard Nixon's B-52 bombers, even if war with Russia is risked for the vague principles of irredentism.

What greater success has this administration known than the peace Holbrooke brokered at Dayton, or the image of Madeleine Albright reading Milosevic the riot act over Kosovo? But by dismembering Yugoslavia, the U.S. has jettisoned a historic ally from two world wars, in Europe's most unstable region, to take up the Habsburg legacy of "teaching the Serbs a lesson."

Can anything but folly, to use Barbara Tuchman's catchword, explain why America is fighting a war to create a greater Albania? How many Americans are willing to die for Kosovo's autonomy? Does anyone in the Clinton administration remember this fateful toast?

> To peace! What would we get out of war with
> Serbia? We'd lose the lives of young men and we'd
> spend money better used elsewhere. And what

would we gain, for heaven's sake? Some plum trees and goat pastures full of droppings, and a bunch of rebellious killers. Long live restraint.

Or that it was the Archduke Franz Ferdinand, in 1914, who was raising his glass?

[1999]

It Takes a Stadium

The fact is, I've always been a Yankee fan.
—Hillary Rodham Clinton,
while campaigning for the U.S. Senate

Among my early memories is Bill Mazeroski's homer beating the Yankees in the 1960 World Series. Tony Kubek choked on that ground ball, and the next thing I remember is Maz stepping on home plate, in a sea of those awful Pirates uniforms. But we won two Series in a row before losing to the Dodgers and then the Cardinals. Yogi got fired, and Johnny Keane, the Cardinals' manager, took his place. Then Maris was traded to the Cardinals. Why didn't the Warren Commission look into that?

I felt so out of touch at Wellesley in the 1960s. First Whitey, then the Mick retired. I went to the war rallies and the teach-ins, but all I could think was: You can't get back to the World Series with Gene Michael and Horace Clarke up the middle. I missed most of the sexual revolution, at least until Fritz Peterson and Mike Kekich swapped wives. Then they traded Bobby Murcer, which for me was worse than Watergate.

I remember taking an interest in foreign affairs about the time that Clete Boyer went to play baseball in Japan. But I was radicalized when Bobby Richardson moved to his religious right and later ran as a Republican for Congress in South Carolina. *Et tu*, Bobby? My Bobby, who shut down McCovey and the Giants in the 1962 World Series. At Yale, after I heard that George Steinbrenner had given money to Nixon, I decided to take a job with the House Judiciary Committee.

The 1970s were a difficult time for me personally. I was newly married and living in Arkansas. No Channel 11, no Phil Rizzuto. My husband was either out working his budding political career or out jogging. The Yanks had Thurman Munson, but not much more. Because of Doc Medich, I started thinking about health-care reform. I was shocked when Ford pardoned Nixon, but Steinbrenner attoned by signing Catfish and Reggie, and my life finally had direction.

First Chambliss beat the Royals in 1976 with that homer in the ninth. Okay, we lost to the Reds in four straight. But 1977 was our year. Guidry came on to win sixteen, and Reggie hit three in a row in game six against the Dodgers. In 1978 we lost the first two in L.A., and Lasorda was talking dynasty. But I knew we had them when Bill Russell called the New York fans "animals." Hey, Steve and Cyndy Garvey, this Bud's for you.

This is probably the place to confess how much I hate the Red Sox. Boston gives liberalism such a bad name. At least the Kennedys knew you had to win. Every summer in the Vineyard, all I hear about is Williams hitting .400. But the Sox haven't won the Series since we got the Babe. Same old choke story in 1978. Up by thirteen games in July, they folded in August, and then in the playoff, Bucky Dent took Torres to the Screen, and the Goose jammed Yaz, and that was it.

I cried the night Thurman Munson crashed his jet in Ohio. By then Sparky was gone ("Cy Young to sayanara," as Nettles said), and Steinbrenner had just shipped out Mickey Rivers. Billy Martin hated Reggie, who hated George, who eventually swapped Mr. October for Mr. May, Dave Winfield, who should have played in Boston. George fired Billy a few more times, but Jill Martin taught me the lesson of standing by your man: "I don't care where he gets his appetite," she said, after Billy was pitched out of a night club, "I know where he comes for dinner." Both of them were true Yankees.

Anyone who has seen my billing records knows how hard I worked during the 1980s. Sure I made a little money in commodities, but a lot less than Willie Mayes earned in the casinos. We went into Whitewater because it was the only place in Arkansas that got Mel Allen on cable. When I told everyone "I think he should run," I was referring to Rickey Henderson, but by then Bill was in New Hampshire.

People don't believe me when I say I was devastated to learn there was another woman in my husband's life. But when Sam Donaldson asked me if I knew he was fooling around on the road, honestly, I thought he was talking about Wade Boggs. I was a woman in transition, but Paul O'Neill got me over Mattingly's early retirement, and the Straw's comeback with Dwight Gooden made me see a kinder, gentler Steinbrenner.

It took me longer than it should have to switch from Buck Showalter to Joe Torre. At first I thought: "What? Another Cardinal?" But then in 1996 we put the chop to the team of the '90s, Ted and Jane. People say I never looked happier than in 1998 when my husband was impeached or under grand jury investigation. But I could not let them steal our place in history. Bernie, Derek, and Cone were as good as the 1954 Indians, the equal of the 1927 Yankees. As Casey would have said, "You can look it up."

[1999]

Vienna at Twilight

A few days before the attacks on the World Trade Center and the Pentagon, I finished reading Frederic Morton's *Thunder at Twilight*, which ends with the assassination of Archduke Franz Ferdinand on June 28, 1914, another day that shook the world. Morton's portrait of Vienna from 1913 to 1914 was first published in 1989, but over the years the book's exquisite ragtime evocation of the Old World has stimulated enough interest to warrant a new paperback edition. By chance, I read it on an Austrian Airlines flight that went along the Balkan spine leading from Sarajevo to Vienna—those dark canyons that broke not just the Austrian empire but most of Europe's imperial claims.

Morton's curtain opens on the ball season in the winter of 1913. "On the evening of January 13," he writes, " ...Vienna's Bank Employees' Club gave a Bankruptcy Ball. It was the height of pre-Lenten carnival—in midwinter at its meanest. Ice floes shivered down the Danube, galas sparkled inside baroque portals, and the bankruptcy gambol really warmed the Viennese imagination." But not many waltzing to the strains of the Old World knew the names on the dance card of the new. Elsewhere in the city, Joseph Dzhugashvili, soon to be known as Stalin, was researching an article on Austria's nationality problem; Leon Trotsky was reading the papers at his café; Adolf Hitler was wallowing in poverty as a sidewalk artist; and Sigmund Freud was interpreting his patients' dreams.

In describing the end of Habsburg Austria as a masked ball, Morton develops a theme familiar to many historians. In *The Habsburg Monarchy, 1809–1918*, A. J. P. Taylor wrote that "Austrian Baroque civilization, like the buildings which it created, was grandiose, full of superficial life, yet sterile within: it was theatre, not reality." By 1914 the reign of Emperor Franz Josef was in its seventh decade, and he hoped that the pomp and circumstance of government could hold together a central European empire of Germans, Magyars, and Slavs. Morton returns often to the point that "Nothing but style underpinned the Empire-style and an army with the world's smartest uniforms." The writer and historian John Keegan describes, in *The First World War*, the shock that preceded the guns of August: "In 1914 . . . war came, out of a cloudless sky, to populations which knew almost nothing of it and had been raised to doubt that it could ever again trouble their continent." Almost six weeks of tranquillity passed between Franz Ferdinand's assassination and the mobilization of European armies.

This pause surprises us now. In the popular imagination, the Great War began immediately after the heir to the Austrian throne was killed. But in June 1914, instead of going to war, Europe's political elite went on vacation. As Morton recounts, Britain's foreign secretary, Sir Edward Grey, went trout fishing, and the first sea lord, Winston Churchill, retreated to the beach in Norfolk, to build sand castles with his children, while the Russian czar and his family spent a carefree July at Tsarskoe Selo, their summer palace on the Gulf of Finland.

"Every day," Nicholas II noted in his diary, "we play tennis or swim in the fiords." Even the protagonists in the looming Serbia crisis found it easy to ignore that the lights were dimming across Europe. To be sure, the Austrian foreign minister, Count Leopold von Berchtold, stayed close to his desk in Vienna, quietly drafting the ultimatum that would be delivered to Belgrade toward the end of July. But his emperor passed July at his summer residence at Bad Ischl, to take the waters and the mountain air with his inamorata, Frau Katharina Schratt.

One reason that world war was unimaginable in the summer of 1914 was that nearly all the European heads of state were related by blood or marriage. They met often at what we now call the summit and exchanged correspondence that began, for example, "Dear Cousin Nicky." The royal families of Austria, Germany, and England loved nothing more than to get together to hunt, and the image of conspicuous recreation runs through Morton's treatment of empire at dusk.

Yet however fit the kings of Europe were to take on lakes stocked with trout and forests overflowing with pheasant, they were no more ready to handle the affairs of state than would be an admissions committee at a suburban golf club. Kaiser Wilhelm was petulant, puerile, and thought of his armies as tin soldiers. H. G. Wells may have had him in mind when he wrote in 1913: "Little Wars is the game of kings— for players in an inferior social position." The personable tsar, Nicholas II, in the words of Hugh Seton Watson, "appeared to agree with the last person he had talked to." England in 1914, by all accounts, was a hunt club, with King George V riding the country to the hounds. By contrast, the style of Emperor Franz Josef was more that of a somnambulist, as Morton evokes when he describes the conversation between the emperor and his foreign minister on the ultimatum to be served on Serbia:

"Well, Berchtold, ever on the go?"

"Yes, Your Majesty, one has to be. These are fast moving times."

"Exactly, as never before. The note is pretty sharp."

"It has to be, Your Majesty."

"It has to be indeed. You will join us for lunch."

"With humble pleasure, Your Majesty."

Morton describes a similar scene in Berlin. The kaiser, after signing the order to invade Belgium, "sent a note to the British ambassador: Let King George of England be informed that he, Wilhelm, would never ever, as long as he lived, wear again the uniform of a British Field Marshal." Morton adds, "Coming from the Kaiser, this signified ultimate bitterness."

The assassination of Franz Ferdinand in Sarajevo has been rerun as often as the collapse of the World Trade Center towers. In June 1914, the archduke—along with his wife, Sophie, the Duchess of Hohenberg—was assassinated in Sarajevo by a member of a secret Serb nationalist group, the Black Hand. The archduke had come to the city in part to watch Austrian troops on maneuvers. Thus he was linked, in death, with Habsburg militarism, much as the Austrian government concluded that his assassins wanted to rid Bosnia-Herzegovina ofimperial occupation. Yet neither assumption withstands Morton's inspection, which provides a cautionary tale of the consequences of snap, ill-founded decisions in the wake of national tragedy.

As told by Morton, the road to Sarajevo began fourteen years earlier, on June 28, 1900, when Franz Ferdinand married Sophie von Chotek. At the morganatic ceremony, his less-than-royal wife renounced, for herself and for her children, any claim to the Habsburg throne. Franz Ferdinand was the nephew of the Emperor Franz Josef and had become the heir apparent in 1889, after Crown Prince Rudolph killed his lover and himself. The emperor never warmed to his nephew, and his courtiers took endless pleasure in humiliating the couple waiting. "During all court functions of all those years she had had to enter alone after the Emperor; he had had to wait for Sophie to creep in at the tail end of protocol, after the youngest Archduchess toddled by in diapers."

Only outside Vienna was Sophie accorded royal status. Morton believes that Franz Ferdinand's journey to Sarajevo, though made in the cause of saber rattling, was also something of a present to his wife (June 28 was the date of their anniversary), in that it afforded them both a respite from the humiliations of court. In Vienna, for example: "whenever Franz Ferdinand entertained a visiting sovereign there, she must remain invisible; Prince Montenuovo, the First Lord Chamberlain, decreed that on such occasions the existence of a hostess could be acknowledged—as a ghost: An extra place setting would be laid which would remain unoccupied."

Nor, according to Morton, was Franz Ferdinand as hawkish toward Serbia as his legacy suggests. Austria may have annexed Bosnia-Herzegovina in 1908, and he may have reviewed the troops on June 28, 1914, which was the Serbian day of remembrance for their defeat at Kosovo. But within Austrian government circles, Franz Ferdinand was the voice of appeasement. His principal rival was General Franz Conrad von Hötzendorf, who wrapped his personal and professional ambitions in a war with Serbia. To his coy mistress, the wife of a beer magnate, Conrad expressed his longings for "a war from which I could return crowned with success that would allow me to break through all the barriers between us, Gina, and claim you as my own dearest wife . . . [a war that] would bring the satisfactions in my career and private life which fate has so far denied me."

In the intrigues with Conrad for the ear of Franz Josef, the archduke had few opportunities to be heard. Sensitive to the slights against his wife and the emperor's formality, he kept his distance from court. To make the case that Bismarck had once made—that the Balkans were not "worth the healthy bones of a single Pomeranian grenadier"—Franz Ferdinand was reduced to letters and even toasts on state occasions, such as this one, given at the time of an earlier Serbian crisis:

> To peace! What would we get out of war with Serbia? We'd lose the lives of young men and we'd spend money better used elsewhere. And what would we gain, for heaven's sake? Some plum trees and goat pastures full of droppings, and a bunch of rebellious killers. Long live restraint!

According to Morton, "Franz Ferdinand intended to radically revise the constitution of the entire Habsburg realm. Under him 'Austria-Hungary' would be superseded by a 'United States of Austria.' With the Empire federalized, many present bedevilments would vanish."

Conrad and others despised the archduke for his compromises with the nationalism that would tear the empire asunder. But in death Franz Ferdinand became a martyr to the cause of imperial retribution. In his memory, the Serbs would be taught the lesson of subservience, just as today, in its wars against terrorism, the United States wants the Taliban and Iraq to atone for the attacks on American hegemony.

At neither Sarajevo nor the World Trade Center was it clear whether the violence was for internal or external consumption. Viennese authorities were able to link Gavrilo Princip (the actual shooter) and his band of Serbs to Dragutin Dimitrijevic, the leader of the Black Hand and the director of the Intelligence Bureau of the Serbian General Staff. Hence the murder of the archduke was seen as a Serbian attack against the empire, much as the Bush Administration has chosen to trace Islam's kamikazes to their protectors in Afghanistan. But Morton sees greater nuance in the Serbs' motives: "Decked out in Serb patriotism, they aimed at sedition against the Serb government. A murder of that enormity would cause an imbroglio convenient for the Black Hand—a chance to seize power."

Sadly for the rest of Europe, the best and brightest in Vienna ignored the complexity of the Balkan chessboard and instead focused their attention on making the world safe for imperial protocol. Morton masterfully describes the burial of the assassinated archduke:

> Vienna of the schöne Leiche, of the corpse beautiful, where paupers scrimped and schemed to be buried like princes, now had a prince reduced to an impoverished and furtive funeral. None of the nobility had been invited to pay their final respects . . . through the streets of the capital. . . .Near midnight a car coupled to a milk train took the dead sixty miles west along the Danube to the small town of Pöchlarn. There only a delegation of local veterans saluted, in old uniforms wetted down by a sudden squall.

In the aftermath, Sigmund Freud wrote: "If that Archduke had lived to sit on the throne, war with Russia would have been inevitable." But Morton believes "the truth was precisely the reverse," quoting from the satirist and writer Karl Kraus: "'He was not part of the fancy, dynamics of Austrian decay . . . he wanted to rouse our era from its sickness so that it would not sleep past its own death. Now it sleeps past his.'"

In describing the vanishing world of Franz Josef, Morton expands on Voltaire's epigram that the Holy Roman Empire wasn't holy, Roman, or much of an empire:

> This peculiarity has been a commonplace among historians: the Holy Roman Empire was hardly Roman. It was not holy (being a cauldron of profane ambitions). It was not an empire (being a mess of brawling princes beyond the

emperor's control). The Habsburg's practical power issued from the patchwork of their own huge possessions. As executive instrument, the title of Holy Roman Emperor was vapor. As mask of Christ's paladin it wielded incalculable force.

In Morton's words, Franz Josef was "the weathered centerpiece of a patinaed court." His empire embraced a patchwork of Slavs, Magyars, Italians, and Germans, but instead of devolving power to constitutional forums, wherever possible he chose to rule by fiat. "In 1913," Morton writes, "the Austrian Court Gazette used routinely the phrase 'by All Highest Decision' because direct reference to the Emperor might compromise his transcendence. . . .Through cloud or sun Franz Josef steered a policy that was mannerly, stately, steady, decorative. He directed it at a world of rude and enigmatic chaos." A. J. P. Taylor is less charitable: "It was a perpetual puzzle to him that he could not make his Empire work merely by sitting at his desk and signing documents for eight hours a day."

Franz Josef addressed the national problems of empire by ignoring them. Taylor dismisses his constitutional reforms: he "made concessions from fear, not from conviction," concluding that "they offered to a hungry man pictures of still life." By the early twentieth century, Austria was an anachronism, caught in middle Europe between the expanding empires of Russia, Germany, France, and Great Britain. In the board game of European politics, each player tolerated Austria only in order to deny potential rivals its holdings. As Taylor writes:

> The Great Powers were agreed that the fragments surviving from the Habsburg bid for universal monarchy were more harmless in Habsburg hands than in those of some new aspirant to world empire. . . .Unable to opt for either east or west, Austria remained thereafter in a state of suspended animation, waiting for extinction.

With the minority questions besetting the empire—the terrorism of 1914—Franz Josef retreated into a world of imperial solipsism. He continued to issue edicts, inspect troops on parade, and receive envoys. But his statecraft could well be said to have mirrored his unconsummated love for his mistress, with whom he shared his life after his wife, Empress Elizabeth, was killed by an anarchist in Geneva in 1898. As Morton describes it:

> Franz Joseph and Frau Schratt continued to be lovers in everything but raw fact. They never met between the sheets. Yet in Vienna or Ischl they practiced the entire range of stagecraft that surrounds the bed: all the ardent preambles of passion and the gallant postscripts, the avowals of desire, denials of indifference, impetuous confidences, embarrassed explanations, and the obligatory sulks and quarrels.

In the months leading to the Great War, the relationship that held the attention of Vienna was one known as the Redl Affair. Colonel Alfred Redl—like the C.I.A.'s Aldrich Ames or the F.B.I.'s Robert Hanssen—was a highranking counterintelligence officer assigned to watch Russia. In the years before the war, strategic plans for Austria's eastern front had been leaked to the Russians, and it was learned subsequently that they had turned Redl to their purposes. Redl had been made vulnerable by living a double life. According to Morton, Redl

> had been a secret homosexual debauchee. He had spent a small fortune on hair dyes, scents, cosmetics. He had filled his closets with women's dresses. He had bought his male paramour, a young cavalry officer named Stefan Hromodka, the most expensive automobile and gifted him with an apartment. He had financed his excesses by selling to Russia data on Austrian mobilization plans, army codes, border fortifications, military transport facilities, and supply structures.

In America, the Ames and Hanssen affairs cast both men in the dark light of individual frailty, their treason attributed to an excessive fondness for wine and women. But the sins under Redl's commission were assigned to the army and to the ruling class, which were deemed co-conspirators in a national disgrace. "So this is the new era?" Franz Josef asked rhetorically. "And that kind of creature comes out of it? In our old days something like that would not even have been conceivable."

Only a splendid little war would redeem the army's compromised image, and only the opposition of Franz Ferdinand kept Austria from venting its rage against Serbia. Instead, in 1913, the Habsburg monarchy moved to cleanse itself of the Redl Affair with a *Volksopera* in the Balkans. "It was an official, political, real life costume party that lasted much longer than one evening," writes Morton. "It was called Albania."

Austria had annexed Bosnia-Herzegovina in 1908 to bolster the frontier that lay on the fault lines between Islam, Orthodoxy, and Catholicism. But it remained suspicious of Serbian intentions, both along the River Drina and farther south in the banats of the crumbling Ottoman Empire. In the first and second Balkan wars, upstart Serbia had driven the Ottoman Empire from the Balkans, including the Muslim lands that we now call Albania. To Belgrade, Albanians were lapsed Slavs, and with their tribal lands Serbia would have an outlet to the Adriatic Sea—a possibility Vienna hoped to block. In such remote harbors (the Bay of Kotor is one) did the tides of war and peace ebb. For a time Austria chose to deal with Serbian expansion as if it could be solved by inviting another king to a shoot or a state dinner. (For example, in the second Balkan war with Serbia, Bulgaria had suffered 150,000 casualties and lost much of its Macedonian territory, but the imperial masquerade still required, in Freud's language, a belief in the future of an illusion. "In 1913," Morton writes, a London conference of Europe's leading countries (the Central Powers as well as the Western Allies) had awarded the Albanian Kosovo region to Serbia. Some snippets went to Greece. The rest of the territory, with the major part of its inhabitants and its anarchy, was to be an independent nation.

The nationhood of that nation did not exist. But Vienna guaranteed the integrity of the phantom. After all, Austria was the illusionist among the great powers.

Finding a ruler for this mountainous land proved no easier for the Austrians than it has for the NATO alliance. Various noblemen were approached, as was a London cricketer. Finally the royal castle at the Hofburg appointed William, Prince of Wied, a member of the royal house of Romania, to the position of *mbret*, a title that he was unable to pronounce. Morton writes that he had "no idea of Albanian customs, traditions, politics, vendettas, difficulties." But he was dispatched on a royal yacht with a wardrobe sufficient to establish sovereignty. On arrival, the Prince of Wied's first State Council "addressed three problems. (1) What were the best shoots in the most secure area? (2) What game was there to shoot? (3) What European princes should be invited to the hunt?" As Morton explains, "Until it became an international controversy, Albania had been a *terra incognita*—a remote labyrinthine confusion of ragged chiefdoms. To 'guarantee' such a country under such a *mbret* meant to conjure it out of a plumed hat."

Almost a century later, the NATO alliance went to war over the same dream of an independent Kosovo. Indeed, one of the pleasures of reading Morton's book is to learn how many of the problems of 1913–14 remain. Not only is central Europe still trying to conjure Greater Albania but, in other parts of the NATO realms, Redl-like affairs run daily in the newspapers; the American government is in the hands of an imperial archduke; anarchist terror strikes at random; heads of state still confuse shooting with diplomacy; and, despite gilded prosperity of the 1990s, there remains a longing for war.

Thunder at Twilight can be read today as a successful Broadway revival—with lyrics as fresh as they were in 1914; the Vienna that Morton describes is also, in countless ways, the city I remember from my own time there. I moved to Vienna in January 1975, as part of a junior year abroad in college, arriving on an overnight train at the Westbahnhof. I had shown up early for the semester and, thanks to a kindly dean of student housing, was given a room on the Ställburggasse, opposite the Spanish Riding School, in the apartments of a baroness whose husband had fallen with his sword in World War II. My small room was heated with a coal-fed porcelain stove, the bed was iron-framed, and a small desk overlooked an inner courtyard as bleak as the Viennese winter fog.

Even in 1975, Vienna was a cul-de-sac of the Cold War. On three sides were the pickets of the Iron Curtain. Although the Russian occupation had ended only in 1955, it was remembered with the fear that had accompanied the troops of Czar Nicholas I when he crushed the Hungarian rebellion of 1849. Vienna was the capital of a forgotten empire, the imperial head of lost dominions. Today it is the commercial center of a revived central Europe; then it was as threadbare as Freud's couch.

Our classes were held in the Palais Kinsky, which had belonged to a family that attended the Habsburg court. In turn, my courses were fit for the son of a nobleman. One afternoon a week we were taught to waltz. Other courses included classical music, opera, and the theories of Freud and Wittgenstein. The highlight of carnival was the Opera Ball, for which a dance floor was laid down over the orchestra seats. During the Second World War, the Americans had bombed in the roof, it was said, because none of the pilots could distinguish an opera house from a railway shed.

My favorite café was the Braunerhof, where most afternoons I nursed a coffee and waited for my friends Kim and Nancy Street, who with patience and humor steered me through a Viennese reading list that began with Joseph Roth's *Radetsky March* and faded into the works of Ernest Jones, Freud's faithful correspondent. On weekends we were free to wander in the nearby Alps, but more often we preferred the city's museums, where we would take in Beethoven's apartments, Kokoschka's art, even the car in which the doomed Franz Ferdinand rode through Sarajevo.

My grandmother, then in her eighties, wrote me letter after letter, many of which recalled the summer of 1914 she had spent in Vienna. She and her mother stayed several months at the Grand Hotel, where they had been stranded by rumors of war. She saw many of the wild demonstrations that followed the declarations of war described by Morton. She wrote in one letter:

> August 4th was to be our departure. When we reached the railroad station, there was high excitement. As we approached the departure gate, a railroad employee notified our Austrian friend conducting us that "the ladies should return to their hotel for the French were armed to prevent our train from starting." So we returned to the hotel and saw the pride and glory of Austria's armed might riding by on their magnificent horses. In the lobby tearful wives were saying good-bye to their heroes.

My grandmother, too, had fallen in love with a young Austrian officer, who gave her a ring and then disappeared in the cavalry charges that headed east, as if over the edge of a flat Earth.

Many of my books about Vienna came from my grandmother, who always inscribed them. On Christmas 1976, she wrote in Edward Crankshaw's *Vienna: The Image of a Culture in Decline*: "I value it greatly because it unites you and me in thoughts." In those years I was in graduate school at Columbia, and she lived on East Fifty-seventh Street. Most weeks we had lunch together, and inevitably the conversation returned to Vienna's fatalism. (As Crankshaw wrote: "If the city itself is the monument to the flowering of a people, the Ring [that surrounds the center of the city] is the formal admission of its decadence.") Although she had grown up on lower Fifth Avenue and had a doctorate from New York University, hers was a life that had turned on the guns of August in her twenty-fifth year. Her Austrian love had never returned, and later in the war, in New York, she married my grandfather, a Serbian exile who in escaping Balkan repression had himself passed through Vienna.

Not surprisingly, the city of dreams was a flickering shadow on the bedroom walls of my childhood. The only lullaby my father ever sang was:

> *Wien, Wien, nur Du allein*
> *Sollst stets die Stadt meiner Träume sein.*
> *(Vienna, Vienna, none but you,*
> *Can be the city of my dreams come true.)*

On our first family trip to Europe, we missed London and Paris, but described an arc through the lands of the Habsburgs, as if researching the sources of A. J. P. Taylor's claim that "old Austria . . . left two legacies to central Europe . . . the Austrian railway system and the port of Trieste." Two months after I graduated from college, I stood in Sarajevo at the Princip monument, which Morton, in his conclusion, notes was destroyed in 1997 as an ugly symbol of Serb nationalism. Karl Kraus wrote of the 1914 assassination: "No less a force than progress stands behind this deed— progress and education unmoored from God," to which Morton adds: "The Stalins, Mussolinis, Hitlers, Princips were the monsters of progress. Progress had abused and bruised them, but they could turn the sting outward and avenge the injury."

In an afterword to this new edition of *Thunder at Twilight*, Morton tells us that Franz Ferdinand's assassin died in Theresienstadt of tuberculosis in 1918. In Princip's cell, the following words were found:

> *Our ghosts will walk through Vienna*
> *And roam through the Palace*
> *Frightening the Lords.*

By then the Habsburg lands were in dissolution, true to the premonition in Oskar Kokoschka's great painting *The Tempest*, which a contemporary reviewer had called "a potent metaphor of collapse, dissolution, *finis Austriae*, the end of time." Some Saturday mornings, when I was living in Vienna and visiting the museums, I would pause before that painting, which shows the artist and his lover clinging to each other while caught in a vortex. The work is dated 1914, the year when the hopes of so many couples—from the emperor and Frau Schratt to my grandmother and her Austrian officer—swirled from waltzes into dust. Morton concludes that "The World War had come to the city by the Danube, dressed as a ball," leaving unsaid that, even in our own time, the monsters of progress continue to frighten the Lords.

[2001]

William H. Rodgers

1913-1997

To some of us, he was Bill; to a few of you, he will always be
Mr. Rodgers. He was born in Western Pennsylvania, outside
Pittsburgh, and died on March 26, 1997, in Chestertown,
Maryland, and in between he touched all of our lives in dif-
ferent ways.

At times like these, when we so wish that Bill were with
us—smiling underneath his red cap, clutching our arms,
asking us to speak a little louder—I think it helps to hear the
voice of the departed through his friends. Nowhere is Bill
more alive than among you.

Aside from fleeting childhood memories, I don't remember meeting Bill until August 1973, when he came to
our house in Sands Point. Some of us here today can remember those August dinners on the patio at Barkers Point
Road as if they were yesterday. We shucked corn in the growing twilight, made last-minute trips down the hill for more

coleslaw, grilled steaks on the barbecue, and then talked into the nights that were mixed with cicadas, laughter, and, for Bill, just one more beer. It was on such an evening that I told Bill about my college classes, my work on the student newspaper, and my January semester with the farm workers in California. To this day I remember his delight with my interests as if they were his own, and after that dinner we began a correspondence that, like the friendship it surrounded, lasted until the end of his life.

It was in that autumn of 1973 that I made my first visit to Centreville, driving my 1966 Volkswagen south, as I now reflect, on a course that traced Bill's own path from western Pennsylvania to the broad horizons of Maryland's Eastern Shore. I drove from Lewisburg along the banks of the Susquehanna River, east through Lancaster and the Amish farmlands, and finally south onto Maryland state highway 213, winding through the great fields of wheat and corn that mix with sky as in a Dutch landscape painting.

Bill and Katie were then living in the Captains' Houses—they did not divorce until 1978. The four Captains' Houses were joined on the outside front by a long greenhouse and inside by staircases and pebble gardens. A bathtub—usually empty—greeted visitors inside the front door.

In one house Bill had his writing studio, defined by a heavy IBM electric typewriter. Here he wrote his best-selling book about IBM and its founder, Thomas Watson, and was often critical of the company. But he never wavered in his love for this typewriter; over the years he had its motor rebuilt and the keys cleaned, and its heavy typeface lives on in the letters that Bill wrote to all of us.

At the other end of the house was Katie's sculpture garden. In between were their books and a marble table, where they took their meals. It was at that Parisian-style table that I first tasted Katie's cooking and Bill's equally consuming love of conversation.

Over the years Bill and I had many meals, some alone, others with friends and family. But we often returned to the subjects that we shared on that first weekend together in Centreville. Like the Roman writer Suetonius, Bill had his twelve Caesars; and during the 1970s and 1980s, rarely did the conversation stray far from the likes of Richard Nixon, J. Edgar Hoover, Ronald Reagan, or Nelson Rockefeller, whose so-called follies were the subjects of Bill's first book.

Bill had an innate distrust of political men in power, not that far from Lord Acton's remark about "absolute power corrupting absolutely." Where it came from, I was never able to decipher. But he expressed it many times in his writing. In 1984 he wrote:

> Ronald Reagan has, in his affable huckster fashion, in the style of the toastmaster of a thousand sales dinners and TV performances, insulted our America and the world. See Col. McCarthy's list of such insults in *The Washington Post* of October 21. In one, Reagan quips that we cannot know "for 35 years whether or not Martin Luther King was a Communist"—meaning, I guess, the national archives will provide the information. We know today that Reagan is a movie-lot trained man of shallow mind, ill-read, dangerously ignorant, dependent on bromides and platitudes, with a persona of form over substance, of screen presence over acumen, insight, and depth of character.
>
> There is about Reagan the mark of Elmer Gantry, of George Babbitt, of the Rainmaker who offers performance, an act empty of wisdom. It is probably too late in the day to reverse the trend. He will probably win. And before long we will live perhaps through one more debacle, as we did in 1972. And we'll have to repair the damage once again.

On that first weekend we were together in Centreville, Bill spoke about his friendship with Alger Hiss, who became another topic in our continuing conversation. Some years later, together with Bill, I met Alger Hiss on several occasions. I often reflected on what each saw in the other. Clearly they were friends, about the same age, who shared, among other things, both an early loss of their fathers and a love for the Eastern Shore. Bill wrote this about his relationship with Hiss:

> Just this past week he [Hiss] celebrated his eighty-second birthday with his wife, Isabelle, at their home in Easthampton, Long Island. He was fifty-two years old in 1956 when our friend, Elinor Ferry, brought him, his late wife, and their schoolboy son to our old Victorian country house along the Hudson River on land adjoining the vast Rockefeller estates at Tarrytown, New York.
>
> I had never met him, but had seen him occasionally in the area around my Manhattan office at Forty-fourth Street and Fifth Avenue, to which I commuted for 20 years. We had migrated upriver from Greenwich Village after I got out of the wartime U.S. Maritime Service and was married in 1945. I had also seen him often enough on that new monstrous wonder, television.
>
> Elinor, a writer, was then the wife of George Kirstein, publisher of *The Nation*, for which I later wrote. George's brother Lincoln—they were heirs to a fortune—was a founder and financial angel of the New York City Ballet Company. As guests at the ballet one evening, my wife and I were asked by Elinor if she could come up to our place with some friends to spend a day in the country. Elinor, a specialist in the labor movement, arrived one Sunday with Alger and Priscilla Hiss and their young boy, Tony. It was a meeting that made my life more focused and meaningful than I could otherwise have imagined.

Alger had spent some summers near Chestertown, and late in their friendship came to visit Bill in the Captains' Houses. They shared a mutual friend in Appy Middleton, a coach and educator who knew Alger at John Hopkins and later settled in Centreville. As Bill wrote on the occasion of Appy Middleton's death in 1983:

> This sense of revulsion over what occurred was a bond of sorts between Appy and me. We talked of it many times, especially after I'd met Hiss in New York and once a few years ago when Hiss came to Centreville to spend a day with me. There was no question that Appy and I, and perhaps Kitty, too, saw in Hiss, who still lives just off Gramercy Park in Manhattan, a surviving monument to an ugly aspect of our country. There was some vindication for us in the revelations that caught up with Nixon and J. Edgar Hoover, leaving them branded by their infamy.
>
> In an all-aftenoon colloquy one time, Appy told me he confronted two of the FBI spooks who often sought him out for ominous questioning of Hiss and his Eastern Shore connections.
>
> "Don't you want to hear any nice things about Mr. Hiss?" he asked the agents. I know him as a fine man, incapable of what you suggest."
>
> "We'll tell you what we want," one of them replied.

Leaving journalism and Greenwich Village in the 1950s, Bill and Katie moved up the Hudson, and Bill worked for twelve years for a paper trade association, in part, running a campaign to promote literacy and letter writing—Bill's "causes" long after he left the job in 1966 to return to writing.

In that year, Bill published Rockefeller's Follies. Several years later he wrote his biography of Thomas Watson and the founding of IBM, as well as another study of the power industry.

In 1969, Bill and Katie searched the East Coast, as he often said, from Georgia to Maine, for an area that offered access to a large city but also the serenity of a landscape painting. They chose Centreville and the four Captains' Houses.

Protecting the marsh, the wharf at Town Landing, and the ecological balance of the Chesapeake Bay became recurring themes both in his battles with the town and in his later writing—those notes, comments, letters to the editor, and essays that combine the traditions of Mark Twain (one of Bill's heroes), H. L. Mencken, and E. B. White.

Bill and I passed many evenings in his ground-floor dining room. In winter it was kept warm by a wood stove; and in thinking back on these dinners, I am reminded of Boswell's dinners with Dr. Johnson in dank London taverns. Bill often talked about his Depression childhood, the early death of his father, how he and his sisters were scattered among relatives. As he wrote in one essay:

> My brother, getting skimpy meals when possible at public soup kitchens, went off, as did thousands of crews, to live and work in the forest for $1 a day and a bunk bed, restoring forests that became national parks. I had a job in a department store in Johnstown, Pa., at 15 cents an hour. I worked 11 hours a day and on Saturdays 14 hours with a bonus: a sandwich and soup supper.

Bill's ticket out of the Depression and the surrounding coalfields of western Pennsylvania was a quick mind, an ability to think and write quickly, and a reporter's job with the Johnstown Democrat, where during off-hours he researched his first book about the 1888 flood.

One story I heard often from Bill was his meeting with President Franklin Roosevelt aboard a campaign train—a scene he later recalled in print:

> In the autumn before the historic re-election of Franklin D. Roosevelt to a third term as president in 1940, I was a fledgling newspaper and radio news reporter in the Bethlehem Steel Company town of Johnstown,

Pennsylvania. In the dual role of political observer and author—having published a dreadful book about the Johnstown flood three years earlier—I was cleared along with a gaggle of office seekers and City Hall familiars to board and ride the Presidential train for the day and shake hands with FDR as he sat, imperial and overpowering in his great Navy cape, out on the observation car. The special train was then, and became later for Harry Truman, a kind of heraldic crusade artifact for whistle stop campaigning.

During World War II, Bill joined the merchant marine. For several years, during the worst years of the U-boat campaigns, he served as a purser on Liberty ships that made the perilous run between the East Coast of the United States and such distant ports—ports that forever stirred his imagination—as the Gulf of Archangel in northern Russia or Basra in the Persian Gulf.

On one voyage, while serving a night watch on a convoy decimated by U-boats, he discovered a light near the bow—this on a ship that had been blacked out. Next to the light was a nervous sailor. As if he were a character in a novel by Joseph Conrad, Bill confronted the light and the sailor. But he could not decide, listening to the sailor, if the light was a beacon for salvation or destruction. In that cruel sea, he decided the light meant redemption, and his ship was the only Liberty, in that section of the convoy, to greet the dawn.

After the war, Bill worked on PM (the liberal New York daily), the Philadelphia Inquirer, and then as a specialist rewrite man for the Herald Tribune. He later wrote for national magazines, including Harper's and The Nation. I do not think journalism—in his lifetime—ever lived up to the standards that those early newspapers set. Bill was always taking journalists to task for sloppy prose—misuse of the word hopefully was his bête noire—or lazy ambition. Later he wrote this about Watergate:

Six summers ago when Richard Nixon was setting up Senator George McGovern for electoral slaughter, I was working with a colleague on a small foundation grant trying to uncover corruption in the Nixon administration. Our goal was to prevent the re-election and retention in power of people we were positive should be, if not in prison, out of office.

The institution least interested in, although pretty well informed about, the conduct of Mr. Nixon and his legions—and one must remember that the events, even the Watergate break-in, had long since occurred—was the press or, as it had become fashionable to say, the media. McGovern himself tried forcefully a time or two in televised speeches to warn Americans that the country was awash in corruption and—he used the word—criminality. He was inundated in a sea of vituperation and assaulted unmercifully for his callused smearing of "The Presidency" and for demeaning our nation. The issue of corruption became quiescent and then invisible.

Bill practiced democracy as it was best imagined by the Founding Fathers. His style was direct, confrontational, literate, open, eloquent, witty, and often foreboding. He came to his views, as the phrase has it, without fear or favor, based on what he read, saw, or heard with the part of his only good ear. For this he was sometimes labeled an outsider, iconoclast, gadfly, or crank. But he delighted in engaging any of his critics in open debate:

> I acknowledge the futility of entering a colloquy with your Queen Anne correspondent of January 25 who says I live in a cage and can't put two thoughts together. But I do wish to enlighten those Star-Democrat readers who were misinformed by him on the matter of lunatics voting for Ronald Reagan. The truth is I have only marginal data about whom the lunatics voted for in the Reagan election. Half the time I can't tell who's loony and who's just moving

up. Some people think Reagan himself imagines Communists want to kill all Americans and that he has odd visions. I think he's a bubble or two out of plumb but not much out of line for a Republican president.

Your guest commentator says I categorized Reagan voters as lunatics. I did not. And even if I did, I support faithfully and patriotically our system of government under which one doesn't have to be sane, moral, heterosexual, Caucasian, fertile, literate, solvent, sugar-free, toilet-trained, or rational to vote. Lunatics are free to vote for Napoleon if they like and so is anyone else. I suspect they just spread their votes around the Liberals and other losers.

Bill met and later married Eugenie Zorn about the time that I met and later married Constance Fogler. In fact, Connie and I got engaged in Savannah on the weekend that Bill and Genie married in Charleston. The four of us spent many weekends together, enjoying meals, talking about books, reviewing each other's gardens. And it was Bill who once took me aside, as only he could, and said: "Hey, Buddy," as he liked to call me. "She's the best thing in your life."

Connie and I named our first daughter, Helen Rodgers Stevenson, and her first trip, at six weeks, was to his arms in Centreville—not unlike my sister Nanette's first visit to Bill a generation earlier. Shortly after that first visit, Bill wrote Helen a letter:

> I had not thought any pair of parents had ever pro-
> duced, or ever could produce, a small human being capable
> in 35 days of such a wondrous gobble. If there is a lesson
> here it is simply that, about such living newcomers as you,
> I, who know so much and have forgotten more, have been
> ignorant up to now of the magic and power in a little,
> freshly delivered human being.
>
> I hope to be seeing you soon—and at intervals there-
> after until the memory I now find so new is shared between

us as we share a name. The embodiment of a magic, marvelous new time and world has been revealed to me in meeting you these past few days and in holding you to my heart while learning much I had not known from any other experience. Thus you have already performed without effort or intent a great service. What possibilities may be opened to you when your consciousness unites with your will and your mind and your memory to define your destiny!

During Bill's last, difficult years, he divorced Genie, we moved to Switzerland, and his memory failed. He lost the ability to write. But we kept in touch by phone, through Michele Francis, and on my trips to America when I would land at Dulles and drive up the Eastern Shore, just as today, to visit him.

We ate lunch in restaurants, and I found that with Alzheimer's it was possible to prime the pump of memory by telling Bill about his life.

"Remember, Bill," I would almost shout over crab cake sandwiches, "you wrote many books," and after a while he could pick up the theme. I knew Bill was failing, but these were happy visits. He always greeted me like Odysseus coming home from Troy, with his arms outstretched and the familiar voice: "How ya' been, Buddy?"

Bill was sad to be so far from Connie and the children, not to have them, especially Helen, in his life. He was always badgering me for gift ideas that might please her. On one trip, at the Corsica bookshop, we found a tape of E. B. White reading Charlotte's Web, which became—although neither knew it—a bridge between the space and time that separated an eighty-year-old man in America and a five-year-old girl growing up in the vineyards outside Geneva, Switzerland.

Night after night I heard Helen listening to E. B. White's resonant New York voice tell the story of Wilbur, Charlotte, and Templeton in the barn. But the sense of language, the words spun in the web, like radiant or terrific, were words that Bill might have used himself with Helen, and White's epithet for Charlotte is mine for Bill. He was "a good writer and a good friend," and we will miss him.

Delivered in Centreville, Maryland, May 17, 1997

'96 Election Course Guide

MG 364 ADVANCED ACCOUNTING.

Professor Balwant Singh analyzes the use of futures markets, derivatives, options, and various hedging techniques in the pricing of political favors. Hillary Clinton's commodities strategies are explained. The markets in congressional votes are also discussed. Case studies include the voting records of Senator Alphonse D'Amato and former Speaker of the House Jim Wright.

GG 198 DIPLOMATIC GEOGRAPHY.

Professor Richard Peterec explores the uses of geographic abstraction in the modern presidential campaign. There are no prerequisites, but students must be able to locate on a map Quemoy and Matsu, the gulfs of Tonkin and Fonseca, Bihac, and the harbors of Haiphong and Mariel.

AR 305 THE ICONOGRAPHY OF THE NUDE.

Using computer enhancements, Professor Gerald Eager recreates the images of Marilyn Monroe, Donna Rice, and

Gennifer Flowers as if painted by Botticelli, Titian, and Ingres. Correggio's *Playboy* interview is recalled. Those taking the course for credit are asked to compare and contrast the presidencies of John Kennedy and Bill Clinton with Edouard Manet's *Le Dejeuner sur l'Herbe*.

PY 356 ABNORMAL PSYCHOLOGY.

Professor Ernest Keen introduces the student to politico-pathology. The course provides an overview of physiological, psychological, and sociocultural effects in mental disorders and surveys major diagnostic categories, including Billy Beer, the novels of Patti Davis, the collected sales receipts of Jacqueline Kennedy Onassis, and the closets of Nancy Reagan.

MU 211 MUSICOLOGY.

The domestic agenda of recent American presidents is revealed through an analysis of the musicians who appeared at their inaugural balls. Professor Lois Svard examines the rhythmic connection and harmonic chords between Frank Sinatra and Iran-Contra and traces the failures of the Carter administration to the president's fondness for the songs of Loretta Lynn and Willie Nelson. The economic policies of George H. W. Bush are set to the music of Lawrence Welk.

CE 110 CIVIL ENGINEERING.

In this popular introduction to contemporary politics, Professor Robert Brungraber explains the political romance with public works. The Panama Canal, the interstate highway system, Star Wars, and Washington, D.C.'s, imperial designs are discussed. Those taking the course for credit are asked to submit designs for a prefabricated presidential library.

RE 412 RELIGION AND POLITICS.

In God we trust? Professor Douglas Sturm explores the political uses of religion in the American presidency. Among the subjects covered are Billy Graham's prayer breakfasts, talk-show Christianity, the demonization of Islam, and the $10 billion in loan guarantees given to Israel.

PL 105 INFORMAL LOGIC.

"Where's the beef?" . . . *"You're no Jack Kennedy"* . . . *"I have lusted in my heart"* . . . *"Peace with honor"* . . . *"I didn't inhale."* Professor Joseph Fell introduces this study of inductive inference and the nature of argument through an analysis of modern political language. The theory of the sound bite is explored. Guest lecturer: Professor Willie Horton.

EN 201 THE GREAT AMERICAN NOVEL.

F. Scott Fitzgerald said that there are no second acts in American lives, but Professor John Wheatcroft outlines the literary origins of the modern presidents. Lineage is traced between Ronald Reagan and Jay Gatsby, Bill Clinton and Huck Finn, Richard Nixon and Captain Ahab, George H. W. Bush and Tom Swift, Lyndon Johnson and Willie Stark, Gerald Ford and George Babbitt, John Kennedy and Jake Barnes, Jimmy Carter and Elmer Gantry.

EC 497 MACROECONOMICS.

Money and politics are the theme of this senior seminar given by Professor Peter Kresl. Among the questions posed: Why is a Senate seat worth $20 million? Who is paying the bills of Paula Jones's lawyers? On the balance sheet of political action committees (PACs), are contributions to politicians assets or liabilities?

MG 275 INVESTMENT STRATEGIES.

Fund management, equity valuation, diversifications, fundamental and technical analysis, and asset allocation are the subjects of Professor George Kester's survey of investment strategies. Model portfolios include Lady Bird Johnson's broadcasting empire, peanut subsidies paid to Jimmy Carter, Gerald Ford's greens fees, Ronald Reagan's $2 million in appearance money from the Japanese, and Elizabeth Dole's corporate directorships.

PS 245 PARTY POLITICS.

What is the future of the two-party system? Is a functioning democracy compatible with a television culture? Are Hollywood endorsements more important than Iowa caucuses? Professor Charles Longley argues that television and sensational journalism have long been part of the political process. Examples include Thomas Jefferson's interview on *Geraldo* ("Presidents Who Slept with Their Slaves") and Abraham Lincoln's appearance on *Live with Regis and Kathie Lee.*

[1996]

The Fall of the
Kansas City Hyatt

I have just come from spending the night in the lobby of the Kansas City Hyatt Regency Hotel. I left at dawn, leaving behind the two large cranes that helped rescuers fish for the dead and also a scene that could only have been more vivid had it been created by Dante and not the imperfections of a civil engineer.

For more than ten hours, from a little perch on the fourth floor, I looked down on firemen and policemen as they—with the skill and care of archaeologists—uncovered what seemed like a generation trapped beneath the two collapsed walkways.

I was there by accident, not design. I had begun the evening with no greater hopes than a walk through the Crown Center and a visit to its newest jewel, the Hyatt Regency, but ended up stumbling across what turned out to be similar to a war zone.

Shortly after 7:00 P.M., I found myself near the Hyatt, wondering about the sirens and flashing lights near its front door. The number of emergency vehicles grew quickly in number until the entire area in front of the hotel resembled the television clips of police rescue shows.

A woman was led out the front door of the hotel; she then collapsed on the green lawn. Ambulances and police cars arrived from all directions. Another woman appeared, numb with shock—her eyes languished in her sockets—and her mother cradled her like a child. A man on a stretcher writhed in pain as medics held packets of blood over his left arm.

Soon a medical helicopter, with "Life Flight" painted on the side, landed on a tiny parking lot. It scooped the injured like Charon on the River Styx and ferried them to uncertain destinations.

Nobody knew just what had happened. I talked with one woman who in a matter-of-fact way described being inside the hotel as the walkways collapsed to the floor. She said a man she can't remember saved her life by forcing her out a door into the side parking lot. She smiled as if it were all a drama made for television. Although I am not a doctor, I guessed that she was suffering some form of shock.

As the helicopter and the ambulances were dragging away the dead and dying, the spectators wandered like some lost herd. Rumors were abundant. One woman said no one had been killed. A young black man, who boasted of having been inside the hotel, said he saw tables piled high with mangled bodies.

I found a telephone and called home. No, my family had not heard of the accident. We chatted politely. "Yes, well, I'm glad you called," was the drift of the conversation, as though I had phoned to chat. But from the phone booth, I could see firemen using axes to break open the large glass front of the hotel. I had the feeling that I am sure many soldiers felt when they called home from Vietnam and heard about Little League scores.

After putting down the phone, I walked around to the north side of the hotel, which was patrolled by one policeman. He was watching a fire escape that led to the second floor. I showed him a card bearing the name of a magazine I worked for, and he let me pass, with the proviso that my climb would be in vain. Nobody, and that included the press, was to go inside. At the foot of the iron staircase up the side of a building, a man claiming to be an orthopedic surgeon rushed through the crowd of onlookers and disappeared inside.

I, too, went up the stairs and, as expected, was told the hotel was off limits. The policeman on guard stood in a hallway that had led to one of the walkways that now lay in ruin. He directed me to the stairs and instructed me to descend. Instead, I went up, left the stairwell on the fourth floor, and stumbled upon the ledge that was the remains of the upper walkway, the one that had first collapsed, causing the disaster.

My knees literally buckled as I crept, clinging to the wall, down the short hallway to the great open space. Where once there had been a walkway that reached one hundred feet in the air across the lobby, there was now only a void. I could see the other side; policemen were standing near the cordon that had been hastily rigged. In between, there were only the panic cries of the injured and, I assumed, the dying. To peer down at the floor was to look into an abyss.

What had happened was this: The hotel had held, according to schedule, its Friday afternoon "tea dance," as it was called on the banner that hung, almost majestically, among the ruins. Two thousand people had showed up to dance, to drink in one of several lobby bars, or simply to mingle. So enthusiastic were the dancers that many climbed up to the second, third, and fourth floors to dance on the walkways that cross the lobby high above the dance floor. The dance floor itself was already full.

From the dance floor, the undersides of the catwalks look like sleeping cars. They are stainless steel, about 170 feet long and 10 feet wide. The walk on the third floor stands alone. The second and fourth are aligned, separated by 60 feet, but joined by steel cables—modern versions of those that hold up the Brooklyn Bridge.

About fifty people were dancing on the fourth-floor walk when it collapsed. Two hundred, roughly, were on the second floor. Who knows how many hundreds were on the dance floor itself. The walk dropped as might have a Pullman. There were no interruptions. It simply engulfed the second floor walkway and, with an explosion one man described as like that of a plane crash, drove them into the brick-tile ground floor. The band, Steve Miller and the Hyatt Regency Orchestra, stopped playing. And it is not melodramatic to say that death was loose on the floor.

When I first looked down on the tangle of cables and shattered concrete, I felt that I had entered a time warp and come out at Antietam in the Civil War. Legs and arms sprawled from lifeless bodies neatly cut in two by the falling walks. A man in his thirties, wearing pants and shoes much like my own, lay face down as though a giant had treated him like a fly. Firemen and medics were everywhere, hacking at bits of steel, hauling away stuffed body bags. The two walkways were as neatly stacked as books left on a table, and rescue workers were trying to do everything they could to pry open the pages.

The lobby of the Hyatt, whose two end walls were made up entirely of glass, looked like a creation of Escher. Staircases appeared out of nowhere. Lights shone down from the modernistic ceiling. But in the confusion of the moment, surrealism was the only guide.

To illuminate the room, rescue workers used lights like those that front a Hollywood production. Some spectators sat in chairs in the second-floor terrace bar and looked down on the rescue as though from box seats. And to lift the nine-ton slabs of concrete off the victims, the rescue units used dinosaur-like derricks whose noses punched through the glass to get in position.

It is impossible to exaggerate the courage and professionalism of the rescue workers. I watched them work nonstop for ten hours, taking breaks only long enough to drink water passed out by Red Cross and Salvation Army volunteers. After they cleared the floor of the untrapped injured and dead, they set about to lift the two huge walkways off the remaining victims. To make it easier to imagine, an equivalent task would be to put a derailed train back on the track without spilling anything in the dining car.

From time to time rescue workers could hear the faint cries of those under the rubble; a burly fireman would rush to his knees and yell, "Can you hear me? Can you hear me?" If he heard a reply, all the workers would drop what they were doing and drill through the mangled concrete and steel lining as if the victim were a miner trapped below. Indeed, outside on the sidewalk, where the anxious families and friends were gathered, the atmosphere resembled that of a coal-mine disaster in West Virginia.

The statistics will never be known, but my guess is that about ten persons survived the crushing weight of the walkways. Most of those survivors were trapped for at least seven hours, sometimes longer, under the fallen slabs. How they survived no one knows. One boy raised his fists to signal victory when rescuers finally dug him out with jackhammers. Another man asked, "How the hell did I get here?" To reach them the rescue workers would jackhammer the concrete, spoon the dust frantically with their hands and hard hats, and clip the steel ribbing of the walkway cables with large cutters.

But most were unlucky. They were in the wrong place. Period. It was over in an instant. I watched the rescue workers drag out mangled bodies one by one in near horrifying slow motion that seemed captured in time—as if the workers themselves had been struck by lightning. A woman in white high heels held her hand, now fixed by rigor mortis, to a rescuer's cheek as though flirting with a dance partner. An elderly black man in a sports shirt had the look of someone on his way to dinner; his body was dug out near the front door.

There were whole clusters of people who obviously had been chatting amiably during the dance when the Damoclean block fell, and they all died in place, like those French soldiers at Verdun who were buried alive with only their bayonets sticking out of the ground.

There was a dull rhythm to the rescue operation. For more than ten hours—in what to me seemed ten years—I stood at the railing that overlooked the entire lobby, like a passenger on a cruise ship that was circling a wreck. I held my palm to my chin as the workers lowered the derricks, picked up the pieces of the walkway, and then fished underneath for the bodies. No one near me made conversation, except to grunt yes when offered water by the Red Cross. I stood for hours next to a policeman on my right and a man with a tool belt on my left. This was a time when even the survivors chose not to celebrate their good fortune.

By three in the morning, the dance floor had taken on aspects of a slaughterhouse floor. A red pool marked the position of the front door, which had long ago been demolished by the rescue vehicle. The workers spoke in shorthand, using hand signals instead of the shouts that earlier had sufficed. One by one, the slabs of the walkways were being hoisted off the slain and then dragged outside. A Parthenon of sorts was coming apart under the wrecker's crane.

When there was conversation, it was entirely about the body count—seventy-six, by early morning. A Salvation Army worker, conspicuously out of place in his dapper blue suit that he wore while pulling bodies out from under debris, predicted twenty more would be found by morning. With near complacence, he told a Joseph Conrad-like story of a head whose eyes stared out from under a piece of steel. Only at the last were they able to reach the body. One of the doctors on hand, a medical student, in fact, talked about the numerous concussions and fractures he had treated of the lucky ones who had somehow been thrown clear when the Leviathan dropped.

As the crane was lifting the last slabs of the walkway off the dance floor, I walked away. I went down the familiar fire escape, past the Life Flight helicopter whose pilot had earlier been so magnificent, and into the street where the lights were still flashing red and white after all these hours. I bumped into a camera crew for NBC News who told me that any reporter who went inside would be arrested and put in jail. I thanked them for the advice, but I no longer wanted to be inside. What I wanted was breakfast and a place to cry. I found neither. Instead, with rain bleeding the ink of my notes, I could hear nothing but the sound of smashing glass and see nothing but the balloons inscribed "Tea Dance at the Hyatt Regency," wafting over the abyss.

[July 18, 1981]

World War II
in Modern Memory

In *Saving Private Ryan*, after Steven Spielberg clears Omaha Beach of Germans, Captain Tom Hanks is given the assignment to wander through Normandy until he finds Mrs. Ryan's surviving son. Along the way, he encounters death and destruction, wipes out a few enemy machine-gun nests, and eventually stops a panzer counterattack at a river crossing with a squad of stragglers. In the last encounter, Captain Hanks dies on the bridge, defending both Private Ryan and the Allied cause. A few American fighters strafe the lines, causing the panzers to flee in panic, as if they were conscripts in the impressed legions of either Slobodan Milosevic or Saddam Hussein. Private Ryan is sent home to his mother, the army has an open road to Berlin, and faith is confirmed in the American experience.

Although *Private Ryan* did not win for Spielberg the Academy Awards against which he had apparently written options, reviewers praised the opening sequence at Omaha for letting the real war get into the movies. Even though the footage is largely a colorized version of *The Longest Day*, the assault battalions of the 16th and 116th regiments are shown cut to pieces in a thin red line between the landing boats and Omaha's protected seawall. Eventually uncommon valor and supreme sacrifice clear the berms leading to the top, and Spielberg can get on with the search for Private Ryan, a story less complicated than the Allied confusion in the Ardennes or the miscalculation of Russian war aims.

"It's a war movie by a guy who has seen a lot of war movies," was the assessment of my father, who commanded a Marine Corps company in World War II amphibious assaults. But *Saving Private Ryan*'s release coincided not just with the nominations for the Academy Awards but also with a continuing wave of nostalgia for World War II. Recently, movies, books, History Channel specials, and medals of freedom have hit these beaches of remembrance. That leading day trader of American values, Tom Brokaw, celebrated "the greatest generation"—those who survived the depression and won World War II—with the kind of praise he might normally lavish on an NBC hierarch or a newly elected president.

Even the political arts have imitated the movies. In Haiti, Somalia, Bosnia, and Iraq, the United States tried, without much success, to reassemble the grand coalition. Against Serbia, Secretary of State Madeleine Albright rereleased some great Munich footage as a trailer for the NATO mini-series in Kosovo. In his foreign policy decisions, President Clinton longs for the national purpose of Normandy, much the way Ralph Lauren recycles olive-drab fatigues and bomber jackets in the shop windows of Madison Avenue. But would any of them have been comfortable with Dwight D. Eisenhower, who after some meetings in Washington confided to his journal: "Not one man in twenty in the government realizes what a grisly, dirty, tough business we are in. They think we can buy victory."

Because I have lived in Europe for the past nine years, I am distant from the front lines of nostalgia but constantly reminded of the war. The Swiss village where we live overlooks a corner of occupied France where the likes of Klaus Barbie rounded up Jews for the concentration terminals. Our children go to school in a village that both allowed passages to freedom and held the gates closed. At work in a Swiss bank, I am asked to pay war reparations. On weekend excursions in the French Alps, we stumble across last stands of the Resistance.

After business meetings in various parts of Europe, I often find myself looking for what were once the front lines. In London, the underground British war-cabinet rooms, in the neighborhood of Westminster, evoke a struggle against odds, a few against many, defiance in the face of rockets and bombs. In the Ardennes, Bastogne has a small marker in the town square, recalling General McAuliffe's response to the German request for the surrender of the 101st Airborne: "Nuts." Berlin has the skeleton of a bombed cathedral, much like the remains of the town hall in Hiroshima, both being their countries' muted claim to victimhood. The Warsaw ghetto is now as faceless as the housing project that was built over the ruins. In St. Petersburg or parts of Alsace, as on many Pacific islands, the fighting remains as difficult to fathom as an encounter at sea.

While evocative and haunting, the American cemeteries in Europe, from Nettuno to Normandy, speak of tragedy without narrative. The battlefields themselves, from such a mobile front, are lost in urban settings or developed landscapes. Only at the movies does World War II remain immediate, and usually then it is a stage set on which the virtues of American innocence are wrapped up in such metaphors as Private Ryan or the bridge at Remagen.

The monuments and museums don't bring the war to mind as effectively as Paul Fussell does in his social history,

Wartime: "Now, fifty years later, there has been so much talk about 'The Good War,' the Justified War, the Necessary War, and the like, that the young and the innocent could get the impression that it was really not such a bad thing after all. It's thus necessary to observe that it was a war and nothing else, and thus stupid and sadistic."

After World War I, commemoration became a rite of atonement. As Jay Winter writes in *Sites of Memory, Sites of Mourning*, the war "brought the search for an appropriate language of loss to the centre of cultural and political life." At Vimy Ridge, along the River Somme, and in the symbolic trenches at Verdun, it is possible to contemplate the loss of four million in the mud of the Western Front. But on a recent drive from Antwerp to Amsterdam, where the Allies confronted Hitler after their breakout from Normandy, I found it difficult to imagine the fighting in anything other than the close quarters of Hollywood-at-arms.

To be sure, there are the tablets of freedom at bridge crossings and walled cemeteries with their phalanxes of headstones. But only a dedicated historian, driving along the corridor from Nijmegen to Arnhem, can understand why Operation Market Garden stalled at the bridge "too far" or what the strategic differences were between Eisenhower and Montgomery.

For all its big-screen revivals, much of World War II today remains a silent theater, where, even for those showing up at Normandy, Bastogne, and Anzio, it is difficult to hear the voice of battle. Often, when I stop in a rented car at Aachen or in the Po Valley, I feel as lost as President Reagan at Bitburg, unsure about the differences between our allies and enemies. On many of these trips I carry campaign histories or battle memoirs. But until recently I had never found in one volume a readable history of the European campaigns so that I could make a connection between the fight for the Falaise pocket and the Heurtegen Forest.

In my search for a World War II guidebook, I recalled *The Struggle for Europe* by Chester Wilmot, published in 1951 and only recently returned to print and Internet accessibility. I first came across it in John Keegan's annotated World War II bibliography, *The Battle for History*, in which he singles out Wilmot's book as one of the finest histories to come from the war:

> *The Struggle for Europe* remains, in my estimation, a revolutionary book in which are combined, as I believe had not been done before, not only strategic commentary and historical narrative, but penetrating economic and operation analysis, character portraiture, and, above all, riveting tactical description.

My copy, published by the Wordsworth Military Library, came from the bookstall in Churchill's war cabinet bunker and sold at remaindered prices. In the foreword Professor Michael Howard compares it favorably to General Sir William Napier's *History of the War in the Peninsula*, "both as an eyewitness account and as an authoritative survey of a large and complex campaign."

An Australian, Wilmot covered the North African and European campaigns for, among others, the BBC. He was a contemporary of such war correspondents as Alan Moorehead and Drew Middleton. He landed in Normandy on D-Day in a glider and covered the battles of Western Europe, mostly in the company of General Montgomery and his staff. After the war, he had early access to the papers of the German high command, not to mention his Allied pedigree, to probe such questions as:

> How and why the Western Allies, while gaining military victory, suffered political defeat; how and why, in the process of crushing Nazi Germany and liberating Western

Europe, they allowed the Soviet Union to gain control of
Eastern Europe and to prevent the application there of the
Atlantic Charter for which they had fought.

Fresh from the immediacy of the battles, his friend, Alan
Moorehead, thought the book "too dry," at least for his tastes,
more a strategic history than a memoir of the fighting. But his
praise for Wilmot as a friend is what still today defines the
writing: "What struck me about Chester was his complete
freshness, when we were all feeling pretty tired, his generosity and his very clear brain."

The Struggle for Europe was to be Wilmot's only book. In
1954, having survived five years of war near the front lines, he
was killed in a commercial plane crash over the Mediterranean, flying from Australia to London on an early Comet
airliner.

Not many writers have ever been able to see war and then
detach themselves from their histories. Even the campaign
narratives of Xenophon and Caesar are largely their personal
accounts, and by the time we get to Vietnam, reporters' memoirs are far more important than the fighting. But in his 717
pages, Wilmot only mentions himself once, and then in a
footnote understated even by British standards. As such he is
able to describe World War II in Europe as a military victory
and a political failure—a war that was not about Private
Ryan's homecoming but about the control of Europe, in
which the Allies had only limited success.

On my first visit to the Normandy beaches, I drove west
along the seafront, which reminded me of the New Jersey
shore. During the landings, British and Canadian troops
secured the left flank of the beach, beginning with the glider
attack at Pegasus Bridge, and then came ashore near Caen, at
the beaches code-named Sword, Juno, Gold. At Juno, the
Canadians took heavy casualties, breaching a defense that

turned the summer bungalows into a Maginot Line. On Gold, before British forces cleared the German obstructions to encounter the blind alleys of the Norman *bocage*, a Royal Marine remarked during a torrent of fire: "Perhaps we're intruding. This seems to be a private beach."

Even in summer, the Normandy shore is cold and monochromatic, where a gray sea meets nondistinct seaside attractions—the front lines as Asbury Park. Wherever the fighting was heaviest, Hitler's Atlantic Wall has been replaced with Allied monuments. A few towns, like Arromanches, have dioramas and museums, crowded with old jeeps, faded uniforms, and black-and-white newsreels of the landings. But the setting of summer innocence fits well with Eisenhower's remark to Walter Cronkite, during an interview overlooking the same stretch of water. The Americans, he said, landed "not to conquer any territory, nor for any ambitions of our own. But to make sure that Hitler could not destroy freedom in the world."

Hollywood invested Normandy with the same sense of goodness when it filmed *The Longest Day*, an operatic treatment of June 6, 1944, in which the American Century hits the beaches with a reinforced division of clichés. Scenes are drawn around the fickle weather in the Channel, decadent Germans draining the wine cellars of French châteaux, nervous paratroops scattered over the Normandy countryside, rangers scaling the cliffs at Pointe du Hoc, daft Englishmen coming ashore with bagpipes and teapots, and the deadly logjam on Omaha beach. The battle hangs in the balance, despite Sophia Loren's heroic resistance, until Hollywood puts John Wayne and Henry Fonda ashore at Utah to turn the deadly tide.

If the British and Canadian beaches take their reference from the Jersey shore, then Omaha, where the Americans landed, seems more like a windswept corner of Cape Cod. High bluffs look down on clusters of sand dunes, and the beach, forlorn even in July, is a broad expanse of dry granular sand, difficult for either children's castles or the boots of the infantry. On the cliffs above Omaha are the white crosses and hallowed symmetry of the American graveyard, through which the elder Private Ryan searches for his savior. A few mosaic maps with arrows show where Omar Bradley's troops drifted off course to their rendezvous with destiny. But the setting has become a metaphor for American sacrifice, like Cemetery Ridge at Gettysburg, where the actual battle is lost in the echo of presidential speeches or marching bands.

In *Why the Allies Won*, published in 1995, and which I read as an addendum to Wilmot's book, Richard Overy writes: "For all the attention lavished by historians on the land battle in Normandy, Overlord was a classic example of Admiral Mahan's famous dictum that the sea rules the land." Or, in this case, the air. By June 1944, the Luftwaffe had all but vanished from the Channel skies. The British and American air forces had 5,000 fighters operational from Britain, while over the Channel the Luftwaffe could count on 169, of which, according to Wilmot, "119 [were] fit to fight." In addition to the fighters, the Allies could send up 3,467 heavy bombers and 1,645 medium bombers, almost matching the 5,333 craft in the landing armada, numbers that might have given pause to Sir Francis Drake.

Even though they knew it was well fortified from high ground, the Allies had no choice but to land on that stretch of the coast. Otherwise a German wedge stretching fifty miles from Sword to Utah would have divided the invasion forces. Wilmot explains the German defensive strategy: "The invasion must be defeated on the beaches if it is to be defeated at all."

Although on D Day he was out of position—presenting his wife those famous shoes for her birthday—Field Marshal Erwin Rommel previously had said: "It is more important to have one panzer division in the assaulted sector on D Day, than to have three there by D plus 3." Had Rommel had his way, Eisenhower might have found a use for his famous words of contrition: "Our landings . . . have failed. . . . If any blame or fault attaches to the attempt it is mine alone"—words to have been released in the event of defeat, and celebrated by Fussell and others, for the sense it conveys of Eisenhower's humility.

Only for several hours at Omaha, and then only at certain zones, did Rommel's strategy succeed. Because Hitler thought the Normandy invasion was a feint, and also because the scattered American airborne divisions created the illusion of Allied troops everywhere, the Germans failed to counterattack the beaches. In many Normandy sectors the landings were, with only some exaggeration, a day at the beach. On D Day, the Allies suffered 4,000 casualties—dead, wounded, and missing—while putting 175,000 soldiers ashore. Although it is an invidious comparison, almost as many marines were killed and wounded in the forgotten assault at Peleliu as there were casualties at Omaha, despite Spielberg's special effects. But in both cases the losses could have been mitigated.

No one can walk the beach at Omaha, looking up at the cliffs still laced with German bunkers, and not feel the sense of courage and sacrifice that it took to go forward. The historian Cornelius Ryan has written: "For this great seaborne assault which the free world had toiled so hard to mount, only about three thousand men were leading the attack." One in two never lived past the beaches. But only from books like Wilmot's is it possible to gauge the extent to which the disaster had origins in the planning. The air attacks against Omaha were a failure. To maintain the element of surprise, Allied heavy guns only registered on the beach fortifications for an hour. Nor did Bradley and Eisenhower, according to Wilmot, heed British advice to land sufficient armor ahead of the infantry. He writes: "It took 3,000 casualties on Omaha to persuade the Americans that gallantry is not enough."

Because he writes often from the British perspective, if not from Montgomery's headquarters, Wilmot offers a balanced assessment of the Eisenhower legend. After Eisenhower's presidency, he was remembered less for his World War II command than for his often inarticulate political leadership. But a number of recent histories, especially several best-sellers by Stephen E. Ambrose, have recast Eisenhower into his wartime context, in which, as Wilmot writes, "he may not have been one of the great captains, but he was a man to whom the great captains of his day gladly paid allegiance."

"The war was not so much led as administered," is one of Overy's conclusions, and toward that end Eisenhower was the chief operating officer. His finest hour, during the Normandy landings, was, on the one hand, to juggle the strong-willed war aims of his political chiefs—Franklin Roosevelt and Winston Churchill—and, on the other, in the field, to let headstrong generals of different temperament—Patton and Bradley come to mind—have their lead in battle. Most of all he found ways to work with his British counterpart, Field Marshal Viscount Montgomery, who could not always resist the temptation of telling off his American superior. At one meeting, after Montgomery lost his temper, Eisenhower calmed his subordinate: "Steady, Monty! You can't speak to me like that. I'm your boss."

Wilmot describes Montgomery, whom he knew well, as "not a man of snap judgments, but once he had made up his mind, he gave the impression of supreme confidence, in the rightness of his decision, and was frequently dogmatic in expounding his views because he had no time for cant, humbug or pomposity." In North Africa, he gave one of the war's better quotes: "This man Rommel is a nuisance." On numerous occasions he made it clear that "you can't run a military operation with a committee of staff officers in command. It will be nonsense." But he reported to one of the great staff officers in history: Dwight Eisenhower.

If the two had a broad philosophical difference in their approach to crushing the Germans, it was that Montgomery—perhaps fearing a Great War stalemate—preferred to mass his troops for "a single annihilating stroke," while Eisenhower and American doctrine preferred an "all-out coordinated attack by the entire Allied line, which would at least put our forces in decisive motion." When Montgomery suggested reining in Patton's advances, to concentrate their troops for a thrust to the Ruhr, Eisenhower replied: "The American public would never stand for it; and public opinion wins war." To which Montgomery replied, "Victories win wars. Give people victory and they won't care who won it."

The Americans sometimes thought of Montgomery as Lincoln had described General McClellan—as someone with "the slows." In their minds he was usually preparing for battle, rarely in one. In turn, the British believed that Eisenhower lost a chance to end the war in 1944 when in August he landed troops in southern France, and thus had to push toward the German heartland with a front stretching from Switzerland to the Channel, as cumbersome as most offensives in World War I.

As a former quartermaster, Eisenhower won the battle of supply against the German army. In the first six weeks, the Germans suffered 116,000 casualties but found only 10,000 replacements to move up in the lines. During 1944, Eisenhower landed 1.5 million soldiers on the continent and only overstretched his lines in the Ardennes, where, in December, Hitler counterattacked into the Bulge, judging that the Allies "exclusively lived in the thought of their own offensive."

By then Hitler was fighting the kind of multifront war he had earlier vowed to avoid. In the West, he could only deploy 76 divisions while he needed 24 in Italy and 133 against the Russians. Another 40 were wasted in Scandinavia and Yugoslavia and on the fringes of the dwindling Reich. Like

Grant before Richmond, Eisenhower knew that the German army could not sustain the attrition of a three-front war.

Both Eisenhower and Montgomery were lucky that when they squared off against Hitler in 1944, the German commander, as Wilmot writes, "was living in a world of fantasy, sustained by optimism, ignorance and his unrivaled capacity for self-delusion." Early in the war, he had avoided fighting on several fronts, and, by the summer of 1942, "four hundred million people lay under the yoke of German rule." Less than three years later, the collapsed German empire extended only to the frontiers of its leader's delusions.

In painting a portrait of Hitler as commander, Wilmot draws heavily on Hitler's correspondence with his generals, who after 1944 appear trapped in an indecisive no-man's-land between going forward into the Allied lines or retreating into one of the Führer's firing squads. Before the war, according to Wilmot, Hitler, "the one-time corporal," had "outmaneuvered the strongest general staff and gained absolute control of the most formidable military machine that the world had ever seen. In this there lay the seeds of Germany's ultimate defeat."

By the time Eisenhower and his generals came ashore in Normandy, Hitler had gone underground, having survived no fewer than forty-two attempts on his life. Not only did these attempts fail, they had the paradoxical effect of discouraging any formal military opposition to his leadership. German generals recoiled from the least dissent, less they be tarred with conspiracy. When Field Marshal von Kluge knew that he was suspected of plotting against Hitler, he chose suicide. With his death and the isolation of other senior commanders, the German army was paralyzed with indecision because of Hitler's delusions, and it was encircled repeatedly on many fronts. For example, without any appreciation for the facts on the ground, Hitler ordered a last stand on the Cotentin

Peninsula. As Wilmot writes: "With this enraged sweep of the hand, Hitler ensured Cherbourg's swift fall."

Hitler's staff was there "to keep from him any facts which might undermine his faith in himself and his mission. Their object was, says Speer, to maintain Hilter's *nachtwandlerische Sicherheit*, his 'sleepwalker's sense of security.'" Hitler, one of his generals said, "had a special picture of the world, and every fact had to fit into that fancied picture. As he believed, so the world must be; but, in fact, it was a picture of another world." Intruding into this reality in 1940, the Russian foreign secretary, V. M. Molotov, asked his German counterpart, J. V. Ribbentrop: "If England is in fact defeated and powerless, why have we been conducting this discussion in your air-raid shelter?"

Among Hitler's fantasies was the notion that he had mobilized Germany for total war against the Western Allies and Russia. Film clips of the illuminated columns at Nuremberg and other triumphs of will boast of a nation on a total war footing. But a major reason Germany lost was that it failed to match the West in industrial production. "Factory for factory," Overy writes, "the Allies made better use of the their industry than their enemy."

Into 1943, Germany had no central planning for the economy, and in the output of aircraft, trucks, and tanks, it seriously lagged behind the United States, which in 1944 was producing a new bomber "every 63 minutes." Overy states: "During 1942 another 400,000 horses were brought to Russia from German-dominated Europe; the same year German industry turned out just 59,000 trucks for an army of three million men. . . . By 1944 American and British forces were fully motorised, but the Germans were still using one and a quarter million horses."

The war was prolonged, in Wilmot's opinion, because of the Allied demand of Unconditional Surrender. That principle, plus postwar proposals to plow under Germany's industrial base, gave the German soldiers a reason to fight long after they had abandoned the Führer. As Goebbels wrote in his diary: "The more the English prophesy a disgraceful peace for Germany, the easier it is for me to toughen and harden German resistance." For the Allies, Wilmot believes, the necessity of having to lay waste to Berlin allowed the Russians to secure the East: "Unconditional Surrender upon Germany would leave the USSR the dominant power in Eastern Europe."

To America's matinee imagination, there is no question who won the war and why. Did not Spielberg show the Germans in flight? Was not John Wayne ashore on D Day? But Wilmot concludes that some of the Allied victories were Pyrrhic, and he ends with the thesis that "the two most serious miscalculations of the Second World War both concerned the Soviet Union: Hitler's miscalculation of Russia's military strength, and Roosevelt's miscalculation of Russia's political ambition." The last line in the book is a pessimistic quote from Tom Paine: "Tyranny, like hell, is not easily conquered."

For a traveler in Europe, no theater is more difficult to understand than the long battle lines of the Russian front. In the last ten years, I have spent time in Moscow and St. Petersburg, the Baltic States, Kiev, Hungary, and Yugoslavia. But in each place I have learned little of the fighting that literally stretched thousands of miles during the four years of combat. The battle for Moscow, which claimed a million lives, is remembered in museum photographs and traffic-circle statues. But the siege lines that starved Leningrad for six hundred days are as difficult to trace as the trams I rode fruitlessly in search of where the Russians had held.

In many standard histories, Russia is the West's determined ally that bloodied the German Reich on its long retreat from Stalingrad to Berlin, thus enabling the Allies to open a second front in Normandy. The success of the Red

Army in 1944–45 is thought to have compensated for Stalin's atrocity against Polish officers in the Katyn woods or his 1939 pact with Hitler. But Wilmot does not hold the Russians blameless in the origins of the war, quoting at length from Churchill:

> They [the Russians] certainly have no right to reproach us. They brought their own fate upon themselves when, by their pact with Ribbentrop, they let Hitler loose on Poland and so started the war. They cut themselves off from a second front when they let the French army be destroyed. If prior to June 22nd they had consulted with us beforehand, many arrangements could have been made to bring earlier the great help we are now sending them in munitions.

If the book has a weakness, it is the simplistic hard line that Wilmot takes at the causes of the Cold War, which he sees to be a result of the West's failure to push into the Balkans in 1944–45 and the expansionist policies of the Soviet Union. According to Wilmot, the Americans believed that "to pursue a political aim is to practice Imperialism." Eisenhower chose the shortest route to Berlin, as opposed to a detour through the Balkans, which would have cut off the Russian advance. He argues that to Stalin "Vienna was more important than Berlin," but he never weighs how, through the mountains of Yugoslavia, the Allies might have opened a serious Balkan front.

By Wilmot's interpretation, the Soviet Union fought the Germans not just to roll them back from the Russian interior, but to secure a sphere of influence in Eastern Europe— fortunes of war the British opposed but which Roosevelt appeased. "In his eyes Britain was an Imperial Power, bearing the 'colonial stigma'; Russia was not." Hence Roosevelt made concessions in Europe, to win Stalin's cooperation against the Japanese. As FDR remarked to his son Elliott: "I see no reason for putting the lives of American soldiers in jeopardy in order to protect real or fancied British interest on the European continent."

At Yalta, Roosevelt was tired and in bad health, although confident that he could cajole Stalin into postwar accommodation. He said afterward: "I am sure that—under the agreement reached at Yalta—there will be a more stable political Europe than ever before." With six years of hindsight, Wilmot was more cynical, observing that "the Russians regard international conferences as opportunities for the recognition of situations which have already been created by the exercise of power."

Wilmot believed that "Western democracies, for all their sacrifices, had succeeded in rolling back the tide of totalitarianism only from the Rhine to the Elbe." Overy seconds this opinion: "Victory proved a poisoned chalice. The Soviet people did not win freedom or prosperity, but their sacrifices have made it possible for all other warring states to enjoy them both. . . . If anything," he concludes, avoiding a Hollywood ending, "the war made the world safe for communism, which was as embattled as democracy in the 1930s and close to eclipse by 1942."

On a trip through the Vosges Mountains, I carried a copy of Fussell's memoirs, *Doing Battle*, thinking I might better understand how General Patton's Third Army pushed through such a Wagnerian landscape of steep ravines and brooding mountain peaks.

Fussell was an infantry officer with the 103rd division, on the extended right flank of the Allied push. But like the World War I poets whose work he admired in earlier writing, Fussell describes more vividly the Neverland of battle than he does its strategic initiatives: "The Second World War has so rapidly joined the deep past that it's not easy now to convey a vivid sense of the futility and waste of training and retraining and finding some work to do for the expendables awaiting their moment to be expended."

In Fussell's narratives, troops are sent into action without complete orders, without sufficient cover, or sometimes in the wrong direction. "As we went on," he wrote of the fighting in Alsace and Lorraine, "we became always more aware that the idea of war is synonymous with the idea of mortal blunders." Not only was he terrified of killing his own men or being shot by friendly fire, he was aware that his fate always turned on a wheel of misfortune: "And as I became more familiar with war up front I perceived that in addition to being a theater of terror and mortality, war is an exemplary theater of the absurd."

Doing Battle begins with Fussell being badly wounded in March 1945, during an artillery barrage in which the two men near him are killed. He recovers, but his fighting ends, as does any sense that he had been part of a "Good War." He suffers torment recalling the men killed by his side, and to one he later dedicates *The Great War and Modern Memory*, an account of World War I literature, in which he describes war as "a major source of modern myth."

When working as a magazine editor in the early 1980s, I had the pleasure of editing several of his articles, including "My War," which forms the core of *Doing Battle*. Editing Fussell meant little more than sending him a check on acceptance. But we spoke several times in my office, and from the tone of his voice, which he once described as that of a "pissed-off infantryman," I recognized the skepticism that my father acquired in his Pacific battles.

After the war, Fussell became a writer and an academic, and I can imagine him dismissing Wilmot as a "generals' reporter," one of Monty's boys, churning out publicity to keep the home fires from smoldering. In my experience veterans are skeptical of any campaign history unless it is written about their unit, and then the author cannot have moved above the rank of corporal.

As a historian, however, Fussell might find in Wilmot one of the few who saw the war up close, read the documents, and had the narrative ability to preserve a history that otherwise has become as implausible as Jurassic Park. Many, including Fussell, agree with Walt Whitman that the real war will never get into the books. Yet it is only in the literature—books like Wilmot's or other faces of those battles—that the war has a chance to survive Hollywood's uses of the past.

What appealed to me then and now about Fussell's writing was his observation that "America has not yet understood what the Second World War was like," a thesis that matches one of Wilmot's conclusions: "The most striking moral paradox of the war years was the willingness of ostensibly liberal states to engage in the deliberate killing of hundreds of thousands of enemy civilians from the air." Fussell writes that "the Great War brought forth the stark, depressing *Journey's End;* the Second, as John Ellis notes, the tuneful *South Pacific*," or—he could have added—the parable of *Saving Private Ryan*.

Prominent in Spielberg's Normandy search for American innocence and virtue is the solemn reading of President Lincoln's letter to Mrs. Linda Bixby, "the mother of five sons who have died grievously on the field of battle." No less a personage than the General of the Army, George Marshall, reads the letter aloud, connecting Lincoln to Mrs. Ryan with the words: "the solemn pride that must be yours to have laid so costly a sacrifice upon the altar of freedom."

Although it does not detract from Lincoln's eloquence, both war departments had it wrong. General Marshall had more pressing demands on his time than to anguish for Private Ryan, and when Mrs. Bixby received Lincoln's letter, she had lost only two sons, not five, in the fighting. "War," my father likes to quote William Tecumseh Sherman, "is about dying in battle and then getting your name misspelled in the newspapers."

[1999]

Communist Poland
on a Bicycle

Friday evening, John F. Kennedy International Airport: A driving rain blanketed the car as it edged through traffic to the terminal. I was beginning to agree with friends who, on hearing our plans, would ask incredulously: "Why Poland?" or "Why on a bicycle?" My doubts were the obvious ones: Would the bikes make it to Warsaw? Would my wife—a bit dubious about the undertaking—divorce me before we reached Gdansk, the Baltic coast city that, I assured her, would have ample hot running water? What about the Poles? How would they react to two Americans on ten-speed bikes, wearing space-age stretch clothes? Would we stray off course and be arrested as spies or, worse—at least to us—face angry drivers on lonely country roads?

Saturday afternoon, Warsaw: The bikes survived the flights from New York and Frankfurt. For the trip we had removed the pedals, turned the handlebars, and packed the frames into large cardboard boxes. Our gear was loaded into panniers, specially made bicycle saddlebags. For emergencies we had spare tires, inner tubes, nuts and bolts, wire, tools, and a copy of *Anyone's Bike Book*, a manual for roadside repair. The packs were also laden with maps, phrase books (neither of us knew Polish), and the guidebooks of Nagel and Fodor. We took only a few changes of clothing. Formal dinners would have to be avoided.

The airport's arrival hall was a maelstrom. Everyone seemed to have excess luggage, laced together with string. To be visible on the road, we were wearing helmets and reflective vests. The other passengers stared as if we had come not just from abroad but from another galaxy. The bikes, however, made no impression on the customs officials. They only wanted to know if we had video equipment. We had none, but everyone else in line had VCRs and shopping bags full of tapes. The man in front of us paid two months' worth of Polish wages to import Walt Disney classics and *Rambo*.

All my anxieties disappeared on the ride from the airport to the hotel. It was a brisk afternoon. The changing color of the leaves and the patchy sky made me think of fall weekends in New England. Because it was Saturday, we had the streets to ourselves. Warsaw has broad, tree-lined boulevards and an endless succession of parks. Although virtually all of the city is new since the war, palaces along a royal route, now embassy row, give it the feeling of Europe at the turn of the century. The exception was the American embassy. Holiday Inn modern, it had a video playing at the front gate and pictures displayed of Bruce Springsteen and Madonna.

Saturday evening, the Grand Hotel: Over a dinner of turkey, wild rice, and cranberry sauce—our Thanksgiving for having arrived in one piece—we went over the itinerary. We planned to spend several days in Warsaw, the capital, and then take the bikes several hundred miles north to the Masurian Lakes—Poland's Vermont. Next would come Gdansk, the Baltic city of hot running water. We would end up in Cracow, the city of medieval splendor.

For the long hauls between cities, we would take trains. Nights would be spent in hotels or, if convenient, with friends of friends. Tell people you're going to Poland and immediately you'll be given names and phone numbers and encouraged to call.

Early Sunday morning, Warsaw: We went exploring in the Old Town. Walking the bikes over treacherous cobblestones, we visited churches, spent time in the coffeehouses, and sat in the sun on the promenade that overlooks the Vistula River. The fighting during the war destroyed the Old Town. But when it ended, Polish architects and builders, using prints and photographs, reconstructed it around the Market Square, so that today it is as sweeping as anything in Brussels or Antwerpt.

We had lunch back at the hotel with a family related to Joseph Conrad, the English author (*Lord Jim, Heart of Darkness*), who grew up in Poland. Speaking to them in English and French, we learned how travelers, even those on bicycles, lead charmed lives in Poland. The food and beer we were having for lunch, they said, were only available in the hotels. Other staples—coffee, sugar, meat, chocolate—were also hard for Poles to find. It was a trade-off: Poles enjoyed a degree of political freedom, but the economy suffered.

Sunday afternoon, Warsaw: What we loved most about the city were the parks and gardens. I never expected to find so many so well tended.

Lazienki Park, not far from the hotel, is one of the world's great city parks. The grounds are immaculate, the paths are groomed in gravel, and the benches are freshly painted. At one time it was the gardens of Lazienki Palace, which was built as a bridge across a lake. The first time you see it from a distance, it appears to be floating.

Six miles from Warsaw, past blocks of high-rise buildings that are typical of the new city, we found Wilanow, a palace drawn along the lines of Versailles. Jimmy Carter stayed there on his 1977 visit to Poland, made memorable by the translator who said the president "lusted in his heart" for the Polish people, when all he meant to convey was admiration.

Monday morning, the Jewish Quarter: Of the millions of Jews who lived in pre-war Poland, four hundred thousand were in Warsaw. Most were killed in camps such as Treblinka or Auschwitz. Others died in a heroic but futile uprising in 1943. More perished in 1944 when the Germans razed Warsaw. Less than ten thousand Jews live in Poland today.

Almost nothing remains of the Jewish ghetto that the photographer Roman Vishniac recorded in the late 1930s. On a day of brilliant sunshine, we rode around large high-rise buildings where once there were twisting narrow lanes. Sandwiched between several tall buildings was a Jewish synagogue, and off Zamenhoff Street was the monument to those who died in the uprising. Otherwise the Jewish quarter resembles an American housing project.

At the Jewish cemetery it was still possible to glimpse the civilization that vanished. We found it off an industrial highway, behind high concrete walls. We leaned the bikes against a fence and wandered for more than an hour among headstones with names familiar to any American: Stern, Cohen, Shapiro, Levy, Garfunkel, Stein. Many of the markers dated back several centuries and were covered with layers of growth, even trees. But these twisted, fallen stones form one of the few links between Poland today and the world remembered in the stories of I. B. Singer.

Near the cemetery we found the churchyard where Jerzy Popieluszko, a Catholic priest, is buried. This cleric preached mass to striking Solidarity workers in 1980 and was killed by Polish policemen in 1984. His murder shocked the nation and transformed him into a martyr; in death he continues the work of his life. Popieluszko's headstone, an enormous slab of granite in the shape of a cross, has become a rallying point for many in the Polish opposition.

Shortly after we arrived, the churchyard filled with people from all walks of life. I mostly remember the older women who wore shawls covering their heads. They were there for the funeral of a woman who was well known because her son, a member of Solidarity, had also been killed by the police. The service lasted an hour, and when the casket was carried from the church, the crowd of perhaps a thousand all held their hands aloft in the Churchillian V-for-victory sign, which is the rallying gesture of Solidarity. The demographics of the mourners demonstrated that the opposition is now the middle class.

That evening, our last in Warsaw, was like many we spent in Poland. Friends introduced us to some of their friends, and we ended up sitting around a dining room table, drinking tea, talking about books or politics or why anyone would bring their bikes to Eastern Europe. When it was time to walk to the hotel, many of the street lights were off, and the air was heavy with the smell of burning coal. The way to get home was to follow the lights of the streetcars.

Tuesday, Warsaw to Olsztyn: We had wanted to take a train to the Lake District, but the schedule was impossible: the morning train took six hours to go 170 kilometers. So after long negotiations with several drivers, we hired a car to take us to Grunwald, several hours north of Warsaw, where the Polish King Jagiello defeated the Teutonic Knights in 1410. Price of the ride: $20.

The car dropped us off in what appeared to be the middle of nowhere. Actually, it was the parking lot of the monument that commemorates the battle of Grunwald—Poland's Bunker Hill. In summer this is a popular spot with schoolchildren and tourists. But at noon on an autumn Tuesday, the battlefield was forgotten. The weather was also cold and windy. We had a look at the monument, packed our gear, and departed. Olsztyn lay forty-five miles to the northeast, if one was traveling, as we were, on back roads of the Lake District.

We ate apples, cheese, and chocolate at Stebark, a town just up the road that was the site of another historic battle—Tannenberg, in World War I—and the setting of Alexandr Solzhenitsyn's novel *August 1914*. Bicycling could not have been easier on the road leading from Stebark. The countryside was gentle rolling farmland. Trees lined the route in imperial fashion. Occasionally a truck would pass, or we would come upon a horse-drawn cart. Otherwise we had the road—and at times, the sun—to ourselves.

After Olsztyn, the hills grew steeper, and the scenery was like little I have ever seen. Birch forests edged each side of the road. Tall pines surrounded many of the lakes. On a barn roof we saw a nesting stork. It was a landscape worthy of the Dutch masters.

Towns were nothing more than clusters of several farmhouses. In Kurki, we visited a small chapel just off the road, fortified ourselves with Rachel's brownies—which I had brought from New York for sagging moments—and came to the conclusion that we would not make Olsztyn in daylight. It also began to rain.

Dressed in rain gear, we pedaled through the late afternoon. This countryside was the Europe that Tolstoy described in *War and Peace*. Once it grew dark, we had no choice but to continue—there was no place to stop. In a thick forest near Butryny, we came upon a car with a broken axle. No one could have been more surprised to see us than the driver, who explained his problem in German. There was nothing we could do except wish him well. Finally, around 7:00 P.M. we saw the lights of Olsztyn. A desert oasis could not have looked better.

In the city we still had to find the Novotel, part of a chain of Polish motels. While following signs to the town center, we were stopped by a policeman. He was angry that we didn't have headlights. In truth, I had left them in New York to save on weight. We had never expected to ride at night. The phrase book, however, did not convey this logic. I'm sure he wanted to take us to the station house or at least to give us a ticket, but it was dark and rainy, and we were clearly mad foreigners, so he waved us on in disgust.

Wednesday, Olsztyn to Gdansk: A soggy morning. We biked around Olsztyn looking for the train station. The architecture was more German than Polish, since this was once a provincial capital of Prussia. At the station we confronted the mystery of taking the bikes on a train. Did we need extra tickets? Would they go in the baggage car? The phrase books helped us to secure two first-class tickets to Gdansk, and we simply carried the bikes into our compartment. We didn't know what else to do.

Shortly before the train was to depart, a man in his twenties, dressed casually, entered our compartment. He wanted something, but we didn't know what. I thought for a moment that he might be secret police. We apologized about the bikes, but that didn't make him happy. He went away, but returned with a note. From the dictionary in the phrase book, we figured out that he needed money to take the train to Warsaw. My understanding of the translation was that he wanted to visit his girlfriend. We gave him several American dollars, which was enough for the ticket, and, after a round of handshakes and pledges of eternal friendship, he went away.

Thursday, Gdansk: We stayed the night with the wife of an acquaintance in New York. She was awaiting permission to join her husband who had already emigrated. It was wonderful to be in someone's home, to talk about what we had seen, to speak freely in English. Few people are as generous or hospitable as Poles.

The day was spent riding around the city and out the long, windy sandspit to Westerplatte, where the first shot in World War II was fired from a German warship at a Polish battery. Gdansk is a city of cobblestone streets, Baltic architecture, and long piers that give it the feel of Stockholm or Helsinki. Looking at one of the ships in port, we fell into conversation with a retired sailor, reminiscent of characters in Conrad's works. He spoke fluently of New York and Hong Kong, of books published in Boston and Cape Town; but now he was home, apparently for good, although it was clear that he longed for the sea and the worlds he had seen on its shores.

Promptly at 2:00 P.M. we rode to the gates of the Lenin Shipyard. Two concrete masts, entwined with anchors at their tops, commemorate the lives lost in the shipyard strikes of 1970. Nearby is the gate that Lech Walesa climbed in 1980 to christen, in a symbolic way, the birth of Solidarity. We had been told that if we waited there, we would see the Nobel Prize winner, who usually got off work with the morning shift. But we waited in vain. The workers leaving the yard looked like many you would see in Pittsburgh or Detroit— men with lunch pails on their way home for supper. But Walesa was not among them. We learned later that it had been his day off, which he devoted to his many children and to a Solidarity press conference.

Thursday evening, the night train to Cracow: Even though the visit in Gdansk lasted little more than one day, we felt a special warmth for our new friend. While we were out cycling, she lined up at the station and bought our tickets. She also cooked us a lavish supper, told us what to visit in Cracow, helped with phone calls, and even dragged out an old radio so that I could search the Voice of America for World Series scores.

Just before 8:00 P.M., she walked us to the train. The lofty train shed at Gdansk is worthy of the French impressionists.

Our friend pestered the conductors to find out how the bikes would be handled and, finally, waved us into the night as though we had all been together a year, not just a day.

Friday, Cracow: The night before leaving New York, I had met a man at a party who told me that his parents live in Cracow. He encouraged me to give them a call. I did telephone from Gdansk to say we would be coming South, but I never expected that his father would meet the train, especially as it arrived at 5:30 in the morning. (Now when I am asked what Poland is like, I reply that it is about strangers who will meet your train at 5:30 A.M.)

Unable to give us a ride in his car because of the bikes, he drove slowly and we followed, as if in training for the Olympics. The spires and medieval towers of the old city appeared as silhouettes in the half-light of dawn. If more tourists were to visit Poland, Cracow would have the same reputation for grace and beauty as Salzburg or Florence.

Because the father was leaving town for the weekend, we were passed on to one of his son's friends, Edward, with whom we had breakfast at that early hour. He became our host, unofficially, for the weekend. We agreed to meet the following morning for a day in the country.

In the meantime we biked back into the city—getting hopelessly lost on the way—and spent the rest of day at Wavel, the royal castle and cathedral that for many years was home to Pope John Paul II. From the castle windows, the skyline of Cracow was an etching of church spires, cupolas, and hills in the distance.

Saturday, Cracow: For those inspired to take a European bike trip (I would go again in a minute), keep in mind that there will be days when you will not even want to look at your bicycle. On this day we locked ours to the chair in the hotel room, met Edward at 10:00 A.M., and drove northwest of the city in his car. How easy the hills seemed from the front seat of his Fiat.

At Ojcow, a national forest, we hiked along the waters of the Pradnik River, which over the centuries has cut a towering gorge through the surrounding limestone. At Pieskowa Skala, a nearby castle, we met the only Americans we were to see in Poland. Apparently they hadn't met many countrymen either, because, after a brief exchange, they invited us to visit them at their home in Springfield, Missouri.

"Martin," the man called as he left. "We're in the book."

Lunch was in the small farming village of Rudawa, where Edward had grown up. To our delight, wedding cake was left over from a reception the night before, and it matched any of the great pastries from Germany or Austria. In the late afternoon, we drove farther west to Oswiecim, which in Polish is the town of Auschwitz. When we were planning the trip to Poland, a friend had remarked that every civilized person should visit there, and he was right.

The original camp, which today is a museum, is a series of red brick industrial buildings, like those in nineteenth-century mill towns. The simplicity of the exhibits is what makes them horrifying. One display is nothing but thousands of eye glasses. Others have shoes, dentures, hair, luggage, and articles of clothing. Together they call the roll of millions.

The extermination camp was at Birkenau, several miles away. Hundreds of wooden barracks spread across an open plain. Inside what has become known as the Gate of Death are the tracks where the trains were unloaded. Most prisoners were killed shortly after their arrival. Some were selected for slave labor. Prisoners slept floor-to-ceiling in wooden racks more suitable for stables. At the camp's far end were the crematoria—brick buildings destroyed to their foundations as the Nazis retreated. Beyond them is a small lake where the ashes of the victims are still visible.

The museum at Auschwitz was crowded with tour buses from all over the Eastern bloc. East Germans who visit Poland are required to visit Auschwitz. Birkenau, however, was desolate. While we were walking back to the main gate, the sun set among the rows of barracks. The bleakness of this landscape recalled the words of Primo Levi, Elie Wiesel, or other diarists of the Holocaust. In darkness, and in silence, we drove back to the city.

The last day, Cracow: We were up early with the brilliant sunshine to walk through the renaissance courtyards at Jagiellonian University and to bike up to the Kosciuszko Monument in the Wolski Woods that overlook the city. Afterward we met a magazine publisher—yet another friend of a friend—for pastries and coffee, and we talked about the many small businesses springing up in Poland. He speculated about the possibility of Poland adopting China as an economic model, which might allow a degree of freedom within the existing communist structure.

Our last excursion of the trip was to the Wiekiczka salt mine, which dates to the thirteenth century but is still operable today. All the guidebooks speak reverentially of the United Nations' declaration that lists it as a site of worldwide historical interest. One or perhaps several salt chambers would have satisfied our curiosity, but visitors are not free to wander on their own. Not speaking Polish we ended up with a Bulgarian tour group that studied each salt sculpture in agonizing detail. Only after several hours did we break away.

Before loading the bikes one last time and heading for the station, we returned to the Hotel Francuski, which has one of the better dining rooms in Cracow, and treated ourselves to a farewell meal: mushroom soup, wild duck with applesauce, sauerkraut, and salad, all washed down by a delightful Zywiec beer. We lingered over coffee, remembering the parks in

Warsaw, the night ride through the Lake District, the departure from Gdansk, and the charms of Cracow. Already we were forgetting the cold, knife-like wind that whipped off the Baltic or our near misses with cars. But most vivid were our new friends, who with so little notice did so much and who with few comforts of their own were so generous.

[1986]

Electoral College Bowl

Article II of the Constitution provides for the indirect election of the president, although it is doubtful that the founding fathers wanted to delegate this decision to the Iowa State Fair or the editorial board of the Manchester Union Leader, let alone the board of elections in Broward County, Florida.

Searching for alternatives to the electoral college, it should be possible to adopt a system that not only allows each vote to count, but also enables Americans to cast ballots from the comfort of their living rooms, perhaps by the television remote control.

In amending the original intent of the Constitution, a ratings' sweep could be used to determine the winner of the presidential election. The Nielson organization could certify the outcome, and that would eliminate either the need for recounts or the possibility of a disagreement as to who the winner is, because no group has a more accurate measure of the American electorate.

Every four years, each citizen would have the solemn responsibility to watch as much television as possible—thus insuring a large voter turnout. Those running for the highest public office would be required to star in a popular series; third-party candidates would have to launch a pilot. The new president would come from the show with the highest ratings, which would be announced on the first Tuesday in November at a black-tie dinner hosted by Billy Crystal.

Strong nominees from the past would include:

MY THREE SONS: George Bush, Sr., shares a large Kennebunkport house with his three amiable, if distracted, sons, who have taken after-school jobs as governors of various states. Uncle Charlie gets angry when one of the sons is caught running for president.

DALLAS: J.R. decides to seek the nomination of the Reform Party.

ER: A Red Cross executive rushes to the hospital with her husband, a former Senate majority leader, who complains that everything in his vision appears blue. Parental discretion advised.

HOME SHOPPING: Viewers place bids for oil-depletion allowances, tax incentives, and Superfund contracts.

REAL TALES OF THE HIGHWAY PATROL: Troopers pull a prominent congressman from the Tidal Basin in Washington and seek help for an unsolved arms deal in Iran.

LET'S MAKE A DEAL: Flush with federal-match funding, host Al Gore joins the fun with a live studio audience.

PROFESSIONAL WRESTLING: Jesse "the Body" Ventura discusses the flat tax, Kosovo, acid rain, and vouchers for private schools.

BAYWATCH: Gary Hart's yacht founders off Bimini. Guest star Donna Rice can't save him.

MARCUS WELBY, MD: Dr. Welby examines all the major candidates and finds them in excellent health.

CHARLIE'S ANGELS: Out on his morning jog, the governor of a southwestern state solicits Jill (Farrah Fawcett), who is staking out a McDonald's.

THE X-FILES: Agents Mulder and Scully travel to rural Georgia where a killer rabbit is stalking a family from the plains.

LOU GRANT: Mary tells Lou that the new cub reporter, Steve Forbes, has twice run for president, so Grant decides to check his expense account.

THE SKINS' GAME: Gerald Ford, Bill Clinton, and George Bush play for the biggest prize of all: the defense budget.

COMBAT: The sergeant orders Cage and Little John to find a candidate (Michael Dukakis) who is missing in one of their tanks.

THE BEVERLY HILLBILLIES: Granny wants to get even when Jed's neighbor (Warren Beatty) decides to run for president and Ellie May is rumored to have been one of his girlfriends.

FRIENDS: Monica breaks up with her boyfriend.

ESPN Classic Sports: Marv Albert discusses defense issues with former Knicks Dick Barnett and Earl "the Pearl" Monroe.

I LOVE LUCY: Ricky is furious when his old friend Ronald Reagan drops by and Lucy doesn't believe he's president. (Rerun)

BONANZA: Ben gets an offer from Ted Turner to take over the Ponderosa.

NYPD BLUE: A big shot suburban lawyer is elected to the U.S. Senate, which has just tried her estranged husband for adultery.

ARCHIE BUNKER: Archie finds a Ferraro bumper sticker in Edith's purse.

LATE NIGHT WITH DAVID LETTERMAN: Hulk Hogan talks about his qualifications for the Supreme Court.

CHEERS: Sam gets jealous when Diane consoles a handsome Atlantic City casino owner who buys everyone a drink and announces he would be a great president.

HAWAII FIVE-O: McGarrett decides to investigate why the vice president's limousine is parked in front of a Buddhist temple.

LEAVE IT TO BEAVER: Beaver can't figure out how Eddie Haskell raised $55 million to run for class president until Ward explains the democratic process.

THIS OLD HOUSE: Host, Jimmy Carter.

GET SMART: The chief assigns Max and Agent 99 to eliminate the Cuban president.

SEINFELD: Kramer has to take Hillary Clinton to the stadium, and Jerry decides to double date.

[Spring 2000]

The Dead Presidents' Society

Consider me old-fashioned, but I see nothing wrong either with Albert Gore, Jr., trying to scale the fence at the White House on the back of class-action lawsuits or, for that matter, with George W. Bush telling his loyalists that the radio station is theirs. Fixing elections is a cornerstone of the American political tradition.

Most newspapers have issued sirens on the "constitutional crisis," as if *The Federalist Papers* contained a chapter on the inalienable rights of anchormen to certify elections. But in deciding the presidency on the basis of which party can cut better deals in Florida courthouses, American democracy is getting back to the original intent of the Constitution: that of letting the best political machine win.

A few commentators have recalled that Mayor Richard Daley of Chicago, the father of the Gore campaign chief, William Daley, delivered to Senator John F. Kennedy key graveyard precincts, perhaps because the deceased had trouble understanding the ballots. But less on display in the virtuous civics lesson that passes for American political debate is the record of stuffed ballot boxes, horse-traded votes in the electoral college, and back-room deals that have decided many presidential elections.

Leaving aside the fact that America's first president and the father of the country, George Washington, was elected unanimously—voting irregularities that only a Soviet politician might understand—let's recount the election of 1800, which swept into office the American icon and slave romancer, Thomas Jefferson.

The Federalist Party of President John Adams (who was called "His Rotundity" during the campaign) had hoped to protect the White House from the "jacobin" Jefferson and his running mate, Aaron Burr, the first candidate for the vice presidency who was well versed in stock options.

During the campaign Alexander Hamilton wrote to New York Governor John Jay, hoping to tilt the election by reconvening the old (Federalist) state legislature rather than to let the newly elected (Republican) legislature send electors for Jefferson and Burr. "In times like these in which we live," wrote Hamilton—a Founding Father but known as the "amorous general" to his detractors—"it will not do to be over scrupulous."

The Republicans prevailed, although both Jefferson and Burr each received seventy-three electoral college votes for president—the confusing ballot having lacked punch holes for the vice presidency. The election went to the House of Representatives where Burr's transition team kept the ballots deadlocked until the same Hamilton, who despised Burr, shifted votes to Jefferson. Three years later, Burr—who once said, "Great souls care little for small morals"—killed Hamilton in a duel, an early example of "going negative."

Such was American participatory democracy that no one bothered to count the popular vote in presidential elections until 1824. In that year John Quincy Adams, the son of President John Adams, received 30 percent of the vote against

43 percent for the frontier general, Andrew Jackson. Both men, however, were members of the same Republican Party, as was the third candidate, Henry Clay, who received 13 percent. With no one receiving a majority of electors in the college, the race went again to the House of Representatives, of which Clay was speaker. After throwing the election to Adams—never known as "Q" during his long career—Clay became Secretary of State.

A few other early elections may not have been technically fixed, but they do show the winds of change that often followed the quadrennial "gust of folly." In 1860, Everyone's Greatest President, Abraham Lincoln, drew only 39.8 percent of the popular vote. He owed his term in office to a third-party candidate, John C. Breckinridge, who the press today would describe as a "consumer slave advocate" and who cost the election for Stephen Douglas.

The winner of the popular vote in 1876 was a New York governor, Samuel Tilden, who, like Gore today, found himself short in the electoral college. An election commission, however, voted strictly along party lines, backhanding the election to Rutherford B. Hayes, who during his four years in office was known as "His Fraudulence" or, more informally, "Rutherfraud."

Gusts in smoke-filled rooms may also have decided the election in 1880, when Representative James A. Garfield beat a General Hancock by only ten thousand popular votes but swept to victory with New York's thirty-five electors. New York ballot boxes were then the domain of Senator Roscoe Conkling who, in what was called the Treaty of Fifth Avenue, delivered the state to Garfield in exchange for the spoils of patronage. As father Daley observed: "Don't take a nickel, just hand them your business card."

New York again decided the election in 1888, when President Grover Cleveland won the popular vote but lost in the electoral college. As governor of New York, Cleveland had ruffled the fur of Tammany Hall, which returned the favor by delivering the state and the presidency to his opponent, Benjamin Harrison.

Not that any of these elections would have surprised the Founding Fathers. Of the United States Constitution, Benjamin Franklin lamented: "It cannot be sufficiently deplored that the federal constitution should be so inexplicit as to lead to such a variety of modes of choosing Electors as have been adopted throughout the Union."

Nor has electoral reform been high on anyone's bipartisan agenda in the last two hundred years. The last improvement of the electoral college came in 1804, reform in the guise of the Twelfth Amendment to the Constitution. Under the amendment, if no candidate wins a majority of electors or later a majority in the House, on March 4 of following year, the vice president becomes president, and the candidate with the next highest vote is vice president.

If applied to the current situation, it will make the results of the 1800 election look like a Ronald Reagan or a Lyndon Johnson landslide. Under the Twelfth Amendment, if the deadlock in Florida spreads to the college and then into the House and no candidate wins a majority, come spring 2001, Al Gore will be president, George W. Bush vice president, none of the campaign's four billion dollars will be lost, and a bedrock of the republic—the right to the finest democracy that money can buy—will be preserved.

[November 2000]

Drifting Down to Croatia

Even during the NATO blitz over Yugoslavia, I kept alive my daydream that for our family summer vacation we might drift in the soft currents off the Dalmatian coastline. If the lightning warfare achieved neither the demise of Slobodan Milosevic nor peace in Kosovo, it prompted in me a memory of summers past when I walked the ramparts of Dubrovnik and wandered among the Roman ruins outside Split. But every time I slipped these recollections into holiday discussions with my wife—usually when she sat down for dinner with expensive-looking Greek brochures in hand—her raised eyebrows questioned whether I had switched travel agencies to the one that had once convinced Charles Bronson of New York's *Death Wish* pleasures.

In *Cook's Continental Timetable*, I discovered Dalmatian and Istrian Travel and its proprietor, Boris Marelic, at a far-flung London address. After our telephone conversations, I would begin many dinner-table reports with the phrase "according to Boris" and follow with a bulletin about how

Sarajevo had "opened up" or how the bus from Trieste to Dubrovnik "took only thirteen hours."

After the bombing subsided, through Boris's good offices I reserved four nights on Brijuni, once Tito's summer resort (the Italian name is Brioni), and four nights on the small island of Lopud, near Dubrovnik. The rest of the time, as I explained to our four children, we would be "tramping," save for a night on the coastal ferry that sailed south from Rijeka, which, according to Boris, would be something of a "mini-cruise."

On a hot July evening, in the company of other back-packers, we boarded the midnight Geneva–Trieste express and scrambled to our compartment, so that long into the night the children could bicker about who was most deserving of the upper bunks. We were headed to Brijuni, off the west coast of Istria, a peninsula of Tuscan-like hill towns and medieval seafaring villages.

Not even Boris had known the schedules south from Trieste. On arrival, I confirmed my suspicion that a hydrofoil to Brijuni had departed an hour before our train reached Trieste, and it became clear that no other ferries called along the coast. The next bus departed midafternoon. Seated in the back seat of a cab, my wife took this news stoically, as if trapped in *The English Patient*'s sandstorm. Conceding defeat, I opened negotiations with an Italian cabdriver to take us two hours south. He agreed, for an amount equal to the gross national products of Slovenia and Croatia, whose borders and soft rolling hills we would traverse. Thus our tramping began in the contour seats of a white Mercedes.

Brijuni is a cluster of low, pine-covered islands, about three miles from the mainland, across a windy—at least that day—strait. It served as Tito's summer capital—the people's Hyannis Port. In the small harbor where the ferry docks, the Marshal had greeted a procession of foreign dignitaries coming to pay their respects to the doctrine of nonalignment. We had reservations at the Hotel Neptune, three stars of pleasant socialist realism on a harbor that otherwise evoked the imperial tranquillity of a Habsburg backwater, which it had been until Istria's largely Italian population was awarded to Italy after World War I.

Our adjoining rooms, both with a view, were fit for a commissar. Unpacking in a room that could have been a Kremlin lounge, the children staked claims to various spheres of influence—like Stalin at Yalta—and then we set off to find the beach on a paved path leading away from the harbor through a pine forest. After a ten-minute walk, we found both a quiet cove and a restaurant that had grilled fish and white tablecloths. Like socialist youth, the children launched themselves off a 1950s-era cast-iron slide, while from the restaurant deck chairs we bay-watched.

Over espresso, we congratulated ourselves on finding such a paradise far from madding Greek crowds. But that night, while we ate like noblemen in the hotel dining room, a gale swept the island, and we remained under that ill wind for the next four days. Beyond the breakers, the sea churned with whitecaps, as though Poseidon were taking revenge against Odysseus. In the following days we had to retreat from our enchanted cove, first on rented bicycles and then, more to the kids' taste, on the electric golf carts on which Tito had chauffeured the likes of Patrice Lumumba and Kwame Nkrumah.

Brijuni has Roman ruins and the foundations of a Byzantine outpost, little of which interested the children, who used their strictly allotted five minutes at the wheel stalking deer or trawling for peacock feathers. On our first joyride we toured what one leaflet described as Europe's finest championship golf course—one made more challenging by the deer tending the fairways and the greens rolled hard with white clay and stones, as if the Marshal had switched to bocce for his short game.

Tito's several summer houses, now sublet to the Croatian government, are hidden behind guarded fences. But the rest of the island—apart from the summer ministries—has rolling meadows and pine forests, through which herds of deer and other animals wander. Every time a head of state presented him with an elk or a llama, Tito would add it to the island's safari park; peacocks and deer he turned loose. Only a select few were mounted in the museum.

After a brief war with the Yugoslav National Army in 1991, Croatia became an independent republic. But prior to the break with Belgrade, the Croatian parliament, in an early effort at nation building, had declared Brijuni a national park. Ironically, although born in Croatia, Tito was coolly distant to its nationalist aspirations, preferring the fraternal collaboration of socialist republics. In Belgrade, after the partition, a Tito museum was consigned to the dustbin of history. In Croatia, President Tudjman, who had been one of the Marshal's generals, rehabilitated at least his Croatian origins, much the way American candidates run for office in various presidential graveyards.

We spent several afternoons, when rain mixed with gale winds, in the Tito museum. The first floor has dioramas of the African plain and frozen tundra; the corresponding text favorably compares Tito's ecological foresight with John Muir's. On the second floor are the Marshal's family albums, a chronicle of the Brijuni years, displayed on long gallery walls. During his time in office, 1945 to 1980, nearly all the world's leaders came to Brijuni, either to cull the deer population or to enjoy a barbecue. In most of the photographs, Tito looks like a movie-studio executive—in an open shirt, enjoying his yacht or decanting his wine. But not all his visitors appear to be taking time off.

Leonid Brezhnev, in a black suit and necktie, looks stiff and unforgiving, as if there to collect a past-due receivable, as

I suppose he was. The Chinese agricultural delegation looks equally ill at ease, perhaps wondering how they will break the news to Mao that Tito has a golf course. Workers' collectives seem far from Tito's mind whenever he is entertaining such stars as Elizabeth Taylor or Sophia Loren, the latter appearing in a number of photographs. Both actresses seem delighted with the Marshal and the Istrian air—at least more so than Ho Chi Minh, who, seated awkwardly beside Tito in a speedboat, does not give the impression that he is there to drop the second ski.

The English historian A. J. P. Taylor called Tito the "last of the Habsburgs," and like the emperor Franz Josef, the Marshal spent six months a year running an ethnically diverse empire from his summer quarters. The image of Tito as an Austrian prince conflicts with the reputation of Josip Broz, mountain revolutionary and Comintern agent. But in searching for the reasons of Yugoslavia's collapse, too little attention has been focused on the federation's economic principles, in which Tito—with all the detachment of a noble landlord—funded the theories of Marx and Engels with the budget deficits of Habsburg largesse.

Tito's early five-year plans followed the Soviet model. He allocated heavy industry around the Yugoslav federation with the same political consideration with which congressmen dole out defense plants. Undeveloped regions such as Bosnia and Kosovo were burdened with the smokestacks of self-sufficiency, and Yugoslavia's competitive advantages in trade and agricultural production were sacrificed for the Stalinist means of production—few of which ever made money.

By the 1970s, nonalignment meant playing both sides of the Cold War for easy money, which funded the country's worker socialism and held the national debt to a level of five billion dollars. Although the Yugoslav dinar was hailed in the West as a convertible currency, behind it were mirrors that deflected attention from both increasing budget deficits and the country's dependence on foreign aid.

Yugoslavia collapsed after the Russians and the Americans lost interest in paying for the swing votes in the Cold War. In 1991, when Yugoslavia went into liquidation, Tito's heirs owed foreign creditors twenty billion dollars, one reason few of the constituent republics decided to wait around for Belgrade to add up the bill. As the fighting began, columnists pontificated—whether accurately or not—on what they called "age-old" antagonisms between Serbs and Croats, but missed the fact that one in four Yugoslav families was living along the poverty fault lines of Austro-Hungarian peasantry.

As part of my pre-vacation due diligence, I had gone as far as accepting an invitation to have dinner in May with the U.S. ambassador to Croatia. We had graduated from the same American university, which now arranged the meeting. It was a chance for me to see Zagreb and to glean from informed State Department sources whether it would be safe to visit Dubrovnik, a hundred miles from the bombs then falling on Montenegro.

Ambassador William Montgomery is a professional diplomat who speaks Russian and a number of Balkan languages, having been posted for more than twenty-five years in several of the region's capitals. That morning we met in his office, overlooking Zagreb's central park, and chatted briefly. He then went to a series of meetings, and since our dinner was not until evening, I was free to wander the city. Zagreb reflects five centuries of Habsburg rule. At first glance, it could be Graz or Salzburg, and the divide between Zagreb's Austrian, Catholic spires and Belgrade's Slavic, Orthodox domes speaks volumes about the eventual Yugoslav dissolution.

Nurtured by Pan-Slavism in the nineteenth century, Yugoslavia emerged in the twentieth, not because both Croatia and Serbia shared a dream of central government, but because each feared an imperial restoration by either the Habsburgs or the Ottomans. However, in 1918, after the Kingdom of Serbs, Croats, and Slovenes emerged from the wreckage of the Austro-Hungarian Empire, an American envoy wrote: "The city of Zagreb itself has a predominant autonomist sentiment, because the people would like to see Zagreb the most important city in Yugoslavia and do not welcome the idea of being second to Belgrade."

Walking under the linden trees of a Zagreb spring, I found it hard to reconcile the city's graceful symmetry with its history of political disequilibrium. As early as 1921, it had lost its parliament, the Sabor, which had been tolerated by the dual monarchy. Through the 1920s, the city's hopes of self-government—in a fractured federal system—were displaced by the desperate measures of the king and Belgrade to assert their waning central authority.

During the 1930s, as in modern times, Yugoslavia's disintegration mirrored the earlier collapses of the Habsburg and Ottoman empires, from which the inhabitants of Yugoslavia had sought refuge in collective numbers. As Professor John R. Lampe writes in *Yugoslavia as History*, "The idea [of central government] itself could not . . . create political consensus."

In the afternoon, I inspected many of the city squares, aware that, in rewriting history, the government of Franjo Tudjman had committed the city's bronze horsemen to the service of forgetting the past. Gone with the busts of solidarity were reminders that Croatia had willingly suppressed the democratic revolutions of 1848 and that the country in its modern form had sprung from the ribs of fascism, in whose legions the Ustashi ruthlessly served their German and Italian masters.

In the 1990s, Croatia became a nation without a memory, defined only by its perceived opposition to Serbian aggression. Even President Tudjman, who died a few months after my visit, had climbed to power by rewriting the past, arguing that the alleged holocaust against Serbs and Jews in fascist Croatia was exaggerated—and had thus reinvented himself as a nationalist statesman, not simply another former Yugoslav general skilled in the choreography of agitprop.

During my visit to Zagreb, I heard the story of Croatia's economic evolution from Tito's workers' paradise to what sounded like Russian capitalism mixed with a little Indonesian insider trading. Instead of returning the Yugoslav state assets to the workers, whose councils presumably held title, the Tudjman government had treated itself to a management buy-out, using the leverage of political office to cash in the stock options. So-called manager credits had been redeemed for controlling stakes in the large public enterprises, which now had the same choke hold on the economy that Belgrade's ministries had previously held.

In the rush toward a market economy, Croatia had spawned at least sixty new banks, many of which were little more than the teller windows of industrial combines, some with links to the presidential party. Under this crony capitalism, banks recycled deposits into their shareholders' pockets, and more than a few people I met whispered that the Tudjman circle had undeclared dividends exceeding one billion dollars.

That evening at dinner, I came to admire Ambassador Montgomery, a man of accomplishment and courage who had won a Bronze Star in Vietnam and now had his career on the line in the Balkans' cauldron. As a young diplomat in Belgrade, he had dealt with a rising apparatchik, Slobodan Milosevic. But when war with Serbia over Kosovo loomed, the State Department had not sought his advice on how to deal with the Serbian leader. Now he was committed to implementing the Dayton Accords, with its *laissez-passer* for all refugees, and to integrating Croatia's dynastic economy into the trade belts of western Europe.

As we ate, we recalled the Dalmatian coast as though it were a familiar poem, and I left the evening with the confidence to journey south in the summer. Ambassador Montgomery's wife had assisted in Dubrovnik's reconstruction, and they loved the Istrian medieval villages. Even during the NATO attacks, the Montgomerys had enjoyed Dalmatian weekends, but it haunted me to hear them describe Dubrovnik as a ghost town, as if it had turned into Edgar Allan Poe's "kingdom by the sea."

Because I surrendered to another taxi ride, from Brijuni to Rijeka—it was still pouring rain—we were early for the coastal ferry, which departs for Dubrovnik at 6:00 P.M. I proposed lunch in Opatija, the Austrian resort where James Joyce rewrote chapters of Ulysses. We found his Hotel Imperial. But rather than drinking coffee on its terrace or imagining walks across Dublin, we went farther down the tawdry seafront, ordered pizza, and spent the bleak afternoon at a concession with trampolines and battery-powered Formula One cars—as Joyce said in another context, "a nightmare from which I am trying to awake."

The *Liburnija*, our "cruise" ship, was built in 1963 and is much like a tramp steamer: in the hold were trucks, cars, and the trailers of summer; our cabin was permeated with engine fumes; the decor throughout was linoleum, as in a mobile home; and a huddled mass of backpackers was on the deck. We tried a meal in the ship's dining room, which served Chicken Kiev and Iron Curtain Cole Slaw—after which the children subsisted on ice cream and soda from a snack bar.

Dalmatia is a vast archipelago of pine-covered islands, like Brijuni, and others parched hard by what could equally well be the Greek summer sun. Before the Yugoslav wars, more than three million tourists clogged the coastline, but this year it had an out-of-season feel, even in July. The ferry calls along the coast and among the islands, discharging tourists, camper vans, and wind surfers, and sometimes taking on crates filled with local fruit, much of it delivered to the pier by wraiths dressed in dark shawls and woolen stockings.

Venice ruled Dalmatia from 1409 until the end of the Napoleonic wars, after which it became—depending on the wars raging across Europe—Austrian, Italian, German, or Yugoslav. Although it is now part of Croatia, only in 1939, during the waning moments of the first Yugoslavia, was it linked to Slavonia, the other side of the Croatian horseshoe. Dalmatian accents remain Venetian, and most small harbors have a bell tower, a chapel, and a promenade. Korcula, Bill Montgomery's isle of fancy, may have been the birthplace of Marco Polo.

During lunch, such as it was, the ferry called at Vis. During World War II, before Yugoslavia was liberated, Vis was captured by the British and served as a forward base of operations. In their wartime memoirs, both Fitzroy Maclean and Milovan Djilas tell of traveling here to make the case for Tito's partisans, rather than for aid to the Chetniks of royalist general Drazha Mihajlovic. Winston Churchill had wanted a more active front in the Balkans to deny the Russians future influence in eastern Europe. The Americans preferred the soft underbelly of southern France. But even tepid British support for Tito's partisans helped to leave postwar Yugoslavia in the galaxy of red stars.

In my mind, and according to Boris, we were to spend our day at sea mini-cruising down the Adriatic, soaking up history and perhaps a few German beers. In reality, despite the splendors of Korcula and Vis, I found it impossible to rouse the family from our cabin, where, for most of the day, my wife read aloud from the collected works of J. K. Rowling. To the children, Venetian beaux arts were no match for Harry Potter, Ron Weasley, and Albus Dumbledore. I prowled the deck with my map, guide, and Yugoslav histories, in some ways feeling like Mister Roberts.

Lopud had come with several recommendations. Friends had sung its praises because it exists without cars and is close to Dubrovnik. Bill Montgomery had entertained a congressional delegation there, giving it the junket seal of approval. Boris, equally enthusiastic, had booked us into the Hotel

Lafodia, although he hinted that it bordered both the sea and the architectural backwaters of the Central Committee.

Urchins pulled a wagon with our luggage along the medieval waterfront, and shortly after sunset I presented our vouchers to an indolent circle of desk clerks. I had taken vouchers to give Boris a piece of the action, but in looking around the Lafodia, I realized that I had traded into a non-convertible currency. We had two rooms, on upper floors reached by an elevator without doors, as in a low-budget housing project. We unpacked and headed to dinner, which was served in a ballroom of empty tables, large enough to accommodate five hundred members of the Croatian-Bulgarian Friendship Society.

Dinner featured a "French salad," and as my wife slowly picked frozen peas and carrots from the mayonnaise, I could tell she was silently dissecting the vacation as well. We had had four rainy and windy days on Brijuni, afternoon idylls at the Tito museum, and the mini-cruise on the Liburnija, inhaling diesel fumes and cream soda. Now at the Lafodia we were footnotes in a five-year plan. I imagined a divorce lawyer pleasing the court with a brochure of the Greek islands.

The next morning, after a breakfast of hot dogs, I went in search of a hotel that might redeem the vacation. A guest house I tried was full, and the Hotel Grand, a specimen of 1960s cubism, was boarded up. I tried to reserve a table for dinner at an attractive restaurant, but the waitress explained that this seaside terrace, shaded by an arbor and dappled with impressionist sunlight, was available only for guests with a meal plan. (*His vacation in doubt, Ivan Denisovich decided to face his wife back at the Lafodia . . .*)

Before trudging home to my fate, I asked the waitress a few more questions and discovered that I was standing outside the Hotel Lopud—by some twist of fate, a subsidiary of the Lafodia. Only those with Lafodia vouchers could be guests at the Lopud. I felt like someone with food stamps being told that he was accepted at the Oak Room. I traded our Lafodia tenements for rooms with a view, booked the terrace for dinner, and went off to fetch the luggage. My wife responded as if she had been fitted with Cinderella's glass slipper.

During the following days we never tired of swimming in the island's crystalline waters or eating lunch at the beach under an awning of thatch. Each night after dinner we strolled along the harbor promenade, where my wife could dream of restoring Venetian villas and the children could demand souvenirs from a seafront kiosk. And on all our walks we passed the restaurant where the U.S. congressional delegation had been wined and dined.

A hundred years ago, that imperial mission would have been Austrian, celebrating Vienna's conquest of Bosnia in the 1878 Treaty of Berlin or, after the 1912–13 Balkan wars, the establishment of its puppet government in Albania. Each was designed to deny Serbia access to the Adriatic's warm water. In both cases the Austrians dealt blows to Slavic expansionist dreams—much as the Clinton administration, with its policies of Balkan occupation, cut Russia out of Europe.

Something about a congressional delegation fact-finding on Lopud reinforced my sense that the Clinton administration had taken up the Habsburgs' burden. Whatever was stated in official communiqués, the Dayton Accords left Bosnia an American protectorate, much as the nineteenth-century peace conference in Berlin had awarded it to Austria. In Kosovo, American and NATO hussars quelled a disturbance on a distant frontier—to teach the Serbs a lesson and to keep Russian proxies from meddling in the empire's realm.

Time and again, Washington's war footing against the Serbs reminded me of a Viennese imperial masquerade. Secretary of State Madeleine Albright beat the familiar war drums of Count von Berchtold, the emperor's foreign minister, and ultimatums were delivered to Belgrade before cruise missiles, latter-day dragoons, were dispatched across the Sava

River. President Clinton's miscalculation—that Milosevic would not cleanse Kosovo in response to the NATO bombing—recalled Austria's bungled 1914 invasion of Serbia, which fell only after more than a year of war.

Accounts of the Kosovo fighting brought to mind the extravagance of Vienna's imperial war games. NATO launched twenty-three thousand missiles and bombs against the Serbs, but failed to dent the entrenched Yugoslav armor. The bombing cost four billion dollars, and the aid and peacekeeping that followed cost another fourteen billion dollars. But all this brought little peace to Kosovo. After the smoke and the press conferences had cleared, the black hand of Slobodan Milosevic remained on the controls in Belgrade. Despite the Western press allegations of a holocaust by Serbs during the fighting, fewer than four thousand Albanian bodies were uncovered in Kosovo—not many more than the Serbs killed by NATO's lancers.

For the Blair and Clinton administrations, however, Kosovo was a splendid little war, a chance for everyone to trot out regimental colors or share the pain of the Albanian refugees. As Frederic Morton wrote of Vienna in 1914: "Nothing but style underpinned the Empire—style and an army with the world's smartest uniforms." But a month after the war's end, as we approached Dubrovnik in twilight, the battle for Kosovo was as forgotten as last spring's light opera. To judge by the copy of the *International Herald Tribune* that I read as we sailed from Lopud, Washington had turned its attention to the waltz of the president and the young woman on his dance card.

I had first seen Dubrovnik and the Hotel Argentina on a family vacation in 1970, when one evening, by miscommunication with a desk clerk, my parents had taken their three children to a striptease club. It was to the Argentina, if not to my childhood memories, that we now returned.

In 1970, the hotel had represented a great leap forward

for Yugoslav tourism. The marble stairs echoed the ambiance of a Party Congress. During the fighting between Serbs and Croats in 1991, the Argentina had been shelled and partially burned, and now the gloss of its lobby and the elegance of the cliffside dining suggested that the hotel had inherited one of the fortunes of war. International tourists were still absent, but there was a contingent of off-duty diplomats, aid workers, soldiers, and journalists. They had driven down from the nearby peace lines in Bosnia and had, perhaps, a bit of the five billion dollars for Bosnian reconstruction on their expense accounts.

Dubrovnik was always a free city—it wasn't Turkish, Italian, Serbian, Austrian, or Croatian. In the early Renaissance era, when it was known as Ragusa, the city-state never fell to Venice, though it adopted many of Venice's mercantile and democratic ideals. Beyond the boundaries of the Ottoman Empire, it served as an entrepôt and brought prosperity to the Balkans by exporting local goods and produce. In a book about Yugoslav literature, my grandfather, then a Columbia University professor, sang Dubrovnik's praises as "a little republic, whose population did not surpass a few dozen thousands of inhabitants, [that] produced from the end of the fifteenth century a relatively prodigious number of writers and savants, and a great majority of them of superior merit."

In 1991, when Croatia seceded from Yugoslavia and took Dubrovnik with it, the Yugoslav army decided that the only way to save the city was to destroy it. Shells fired from the surrounding hills spread terror and burned a number of buildings, including the Argentina. "It was the revenge of the poor boys from the mountains," the journalists Laura Silber and Allan Little have written, "on one of the richest, most westward-leaning parts of the former Yugoslavia. It culminated, in November [1991], in the systematic destruction, by wire-guided missile, of every last yacht in the harbor of the old town."

The architects of greater Serbia had hoped to isolate the city, perhaps to retain its tourism profits for the shortchanged Yugoslavia. Dalmatia, they claimed, had few historical ties with the Croatian heartland in Slavonia. But in the battle for hearts and minds ("public opinion wins war," as General Eisenhower said in 1944), sympathy for Serbia became a lost cause when Milosevic or some regional Montenegrin commander ordered the first shots fired in anger against Dubrovnik's red-tiled roofs.

Until that moment, the arguments in the Balkans were as difficult to comprehend as the fourteenth-century poetry of Kosovo treachery and salvation. Who knew, then as now, the history of the Krajina Serbs, the significance of the Sporazum, or why King Alexander was murdered in 1934? But every Western tourist knew Dubrovnik's magnificence— its Renaissance charms amidst Balkan deceit, its Italianate grace on the edge of Tito's brave new world. The good ship *Liburnija* was pressed into the service of the city's relief, lifting the siege with cargoes of food and medicine, and even a PEN, presumably there to give the Serbs a whiff of the adjective.

On walks through the town, I bought several books that celebrated Dubrovnik's martyrdom, each replete with photographs of Serb atrocities. The pictures evoked Beirut, much as the headlines recalled the plight of Dresden. Friends who lived through the shelling, however, speak of its symbolism rather than its casualties. Eight years later, it is hard to recognize the war damage. The replacement red tiles do not match the deeper colors of the old roofs, and many buildings have been pockmarked by shells—although to the untrained eye it is difficult to tell during which dark age the shells were fired.

Omitted from the published accounts of wailing walls, however, are the cynical reasons why the Serbs raised the siege. In 1992, the war had begun in Bosnia; Serbs and Croats shared the sentiments of President Tudjman that "Bosnia was a creation of the Ottoman invasion of Europe." Dubrovnik was left alone so that Serbs and Croats could press their campaigns against the Bosnian Muslims. Once again Ragusa was free of foreign entanglements.

It was only at the end of our stay in Dubrovnik that I addressed the question of how we would get home to Switzerland. At a few dinners, I mentioned circumspectly that we still had tickets for a ferry to Bari, the Italian port, and train reservations to Geneva. Had I shoved aside Harry Potter to read aloud from Rebecca West's 1,181-page *Black Lamb and Grey Falcon*, which lay untouched in my wife's luggage, I couldn't have found a less receptive audience.

On our afternoon excursions—great souvenir treks—I collected airline schedules. But few Western carriers fly into Dubrovnik's treacherous airport. From a local travel agent I learned that we could take a bus to Sarajevo and there connect with a Swissair flight. I knew Boris would approve. He might even call it a "mini-tour." But my wife tempered her enthusiasm.

We finally departed on an early Croatia Airlines flight to Zagreb. Backpacks, topped with Brijuni peacock feathers, were in the Argentina lobby at 5:30 A.M., and not even our three-year-old complained during the pre-dawn ride along the coast road's hairpin turns. With a handful of travelers, we cleared security and waited near the tarmac to board the jet.

Looking up at the jagged, forlorn peaks that had claimed the lives of Secretary of Commerce Ron Brown and his colleagues, I mused on how little tramping we had done in the previous two weeks. We had traveled Istria by taxi, fled the Lafodia to the Hotel Lopud, lounged in the Argentina's deck chairs, and now we were flying home on an Airbus.

As the plane climbed to altitude above the mountainous Croatian littoral, I retrieved from my backpack the *London Times* review of my grandfather's book, printed in 1922, in which he praised Dubrovnik. He was born a Serb, four years after the Treaty of Berlin, but fled Belgrade in 1908, a victim of the political repression that still maintains its grip on that sad country. He lived sixty-five years after coming to America, and he never returned to Serbia or to the successive Yugoslavias— fearful that either its kings or its new class might remember how he had treated them in print.

The *Times* called him "erudite without being pedantic." His dream for Yugoslavia was that it would emulate the pluralism of Switzerland, where we now live. Dubrovnik was his ideal for economic and artistic development. But German recognition of Croatia and Bosnia in 1991–1992 (which pushed a bankrupt Yugoslavia into the abyss of civil war), the 1995 American occupation of Bosnia, and the NATO onslaught for Kosovo's autonomy would have filled him with a dread of imperial restoration, of which he wanted no part. Nor would it have come to him as a surprise that the Viennese waltz was all the rage in Washington and London.

I knew my grandfather only when I was a boy—at the same ages as the children now around me, with their backpacks and peacock feathers. But I have always sensed his kindred spirit. Even at this early hour of the day, his words amused me. His description of Renaissance Yugoslav authors applied equally well to modern political commentators: "They go on writing after their inspiration is exhausted, and as a rule inspiration comes to them only in short passages." As we headed home, it pleased me to think of Dubrovnik linking my grandfather with my children across the lonely chasm of the generations.

[1999]

Diplomatic Immunity

As an American raising children in a Swiss village near Geneva, I often worry about their sentimental education. They go to Swiss schools, speak French, but grow hazy when the conversation turns to Paul Revere or Benjamin Franklin. So with alacrity I accepted an invitation to take my oldest daughter, Helen, age nine, to a Fourth of July celebration at the residence of the American ambassador. Bern, the Swiss capital, is two hours by train from Geneva, and I used the time to review Helen's curtsey until a call home to my wife linked such obeisance to court practice that, I was told bluntly, had departed with Cardinal Richelieu.

The receiving line to meet Ambassador Madeline Kunin stretched past the main gates of the residence. We waited our turn with an Internet executive ("you can start with twenty free hours . . .") and wondered which important guests had been allowed to park their cars all over the ambassador's front lawn. Closer inspection revealed the parked cars to be Chevys, so my first July Fourth lesson for Helen was to explain that because both John Adams and Thomas Jefferson were citizen statesmen, each kept a car dealership on the side.

An accomplished writer and political theorist, Ambassador

Kunin, a Democrat, was governor of Vermont during part of the time that Bill Clinton was governor of Arkansas. A photograph in the embassy residence shows the two of them traveling on Air Force One. As if a still life of Leslie Nielson, the president is positioned behind a mile-high desk while, seated opposite, the Ambassador has the tentative posture of a job applicant.

When it came time to introduce us to Ambassador Kunin, who lived until age eight in Switzerland and emigrated during the war, the aide-de-camp got it all wrong. "Where are you from?" the aide asked me. "Laconnex," I replied. In Switzerland, the village is all. But then to clarify, I added: "Geneva." "No," she said, getting flustered. "Where are you *from*?" "Oh," I said, confused, figuring she wanted a U.S. zip code, like a mail-order house. "We moved to Switzerland from New York in 1991." "No," said the aide-in-panic. "Don't you work for a corporation or something?"

Presently we were upon the ambassador. "Ambassador, may I present the Stevens," was how we were finally passed along. Politically correct, Helen shook hands, and I followed. Then flanking the ambassador, we turned for the ceremonial picture, the kind they take with the captain on the QE2. As the camera whirred, I delivered my diplomatic credentials: "Both Helen's grandmother and aunt graduated from the University of Vermont," I said, near bended knee but avoiding the regal curtsey. "And both have described your eloquence as a speaker." The grounds of the residence had the look of a Vermont trade show. But Ambassador Kunin has little of the small talk of her once fellow governor from Arkansas. Without a reply, Helen and I passed into a large tent, which even on foreign soil wonderfully evoked a village green on the Fourth of July. Men dressed as Paul Revere, if not Samuel Adams, passed out bottles of beer, hamburgers, hot dogs, and potato salad, and Helen learned the important lesson, from Ben & Jerry, that not all ice cream is created equal.

Half of those under the tent were diplomatic types. But there were also overseas Americans, there, in small part, as Henry James wrote, "fighting the superstitious valuation of Europe." Marine guards marched in the colors and the ambassador, who read a Hillary-and-I letter from the president. She followed with remarks that started eloquently—"I want to quote from the actual Declaration"—but ended by hectoring the Swiss on the subject of Nazi gold and the need to settle dormant accounts, including, as it turned out, one with the ambassador, whose mother (not a Holocaust victim) left behind a nest egg when the family emigrated. That America temporized with Hitler between 1939 and 1941, traded with the enemy, restricted news of a Holocaust, sold the Swiss twice as much gold as did the Nazis, and after the war swept up the savings of death-camp victims into state treasuries was not a theme that mixed with either the Boy Scouts on hand or the pitch the ambassador made for the Chevys. In American foreign policy, it's the small countries that absorb the sticker shock.

The ceremony ended with the singing of the national anthem. The diplomats scurried for the main gates, and the Americans returned to the tent for more hamburgers and coleslaw. Helen was elbow deep in her first ear of corn in two years when the ambassador approached our little group. Winding down, as was the party, she teased my daughter about the size of her corn and then drifted to the Pizza Hut stand. There were no fireworks, but Helen and I, having briefly touched American soil and clutching our samples of maple syrup, walked to the station as if in their reflected glow. I delivered a short discourse on the American experiment, which I ended by saying: "Listen, kid. If you want snow tires, go to the German embassy."

[1997]

Riding the Blind

To many older Americans, my father, Nikolai Stevenson, is known for his work for the Association of Macular Diseases, in whose cause he travels two hundred thousand miles a year. Legally blind, but, with the kindness of strangers, easily finding airport gates, he travels the American heartland to give seminars on managing life with limited eyesight—much as in his business life he rode the crack express trains in search of the sugar trade.

His work for the "maculars" is more than full-time, and so for vacations, one would think he and my mother would stay close to home or grandchildren. Yet this year—for both their eighty-third—they are spending the summer on a Black Sea cruise.

My parents have not spent all their life traveling, but a lot of it, given that they met in 1930, when they were both in the seventh grade in Montclair, New Jersey. That acquaintance didn't blossom into a romance until after World War II. In the interlude, while at Columbia College, my father and his life-long friend Robert Lubar (later managing editor of *Fortune* magazine) traveled America by what was called "riding the blind"—a hidden spot between a coal tender and the baggage car on the railroads of the 1930s.

After college, my father spent the six years on the front lines of the Pacific war. But the one thing that mitigated the face of those terrible battles was that the U.S. government gave him free trips to such remote islands as Guadalcanal, Peleliu, and, during the occupation, Japan itself.

For my parents' honeymoon in 1951—did the courtship really last twenty-one years?—they traveled the Caribbean in search of love and, I suspect, a little sugar. In the 1950s, despite children, cats, and responsibilities, travel remained a pleasure, even if it meant taking toddlers to Virginia Beach or strolling the boardwalk of Atlantic City with a carriage.

I am sure we are one of the few American families that never traveled the United States in a station wagon. We had one, with fake wood paneling and a Buick ornament. But for family trips we departed by train from New York City's Pennsylvania Station and took long loops through western states, such as Arizona or Wyoming. Nights were spent in upper berths or commercial hotels, and it was not unusual for a trip to include a sugar convention, a Marine Corps reunion, or a national park.

In the early 1970s, my father's business started taking him overseas. The entire family or sometimes just my mother or a few children often went with him. We first crossed the Atlantic on Icelandic Airlines, an eighteen-hour odyssey that included a refueling stop in Keflavík, Iceland. On the subsequent grand tour, we missed London, Paris, and Madrid, but rode an overnight sleeper to Belgrade and visited the forgotten Great War trenches at Verdun.

In 1974–75, I spent my college junior year abroad, first in London and then in Vienna. My father visited twice. The first time, we met in Brussels and spent the day exploring

Brugge and Waterloo. On the second trip, in March 1975, he brought my younger sister, Julie, and took us to Bucharest and Constanza, both in Romania, which in those days was locked behind Stalin's iron curtain of dreariness. For two American kids, however, it felt as if we had sailed over the horizon.

To this day, our family dinners sound like the chatter of travel agents. We endlessly compare airfares, cheap hotels, and international political questions. (*Was you there, Charlie?* is the rhetorical question, if anyone ventures an opinion without having visited the country in question.) At a recent family reunion, to celebrate my parents' fifty years of marriage, I complained that my wife was indifferent to a planned family vacation in Macedonia—the kind of teasing that only a Stevenson would understand. In turn, my father reported proudly that their Black Seas cruise would include two stops in Bulgaria.

The best-selling author Paul Theroux wrote in an early book that sometimes it is "better to go first class than to arrive." But only on a handful of occasions have my parents treated themselves to luxury. If I could summarize their motto, it would be: "Better to go, and then the memories will be first-class."

To be sure, sometimes we have taken the wrong fork in the road. I missed it, but according to family legend (I wasn't on this trip), my father passed up a wonderful restaurant in Morocco, and then, to save time, gave everyone a picnic of stale breakfast rolls near a roadside bush in the sweltering desert. I remember a train in Mexico that, for a moment, I thought had departed without my father (who was buying a chicken for dinner, there being no diner on that evening train to Oaxaca).

Now the family is spread between Anchorage, Alaska, in the west, and Geneva, Switzerland, to the east. Many parents might find it difficult to connect the dots of their children's lives, but my parents, despite the usual infirmities of age, still take the night flights to Europe, travel Italy with a rail pass, and swim in the breakers of the Atlantic Ocean, as undaunted as Phileas Fogg in their shared lifetime of circumnavigation.

[2001]

The TBR 500

It is hardly a secret, even outside the walls of the publishing industry, that the best way to settle a lingering grudge is via the well-placed book review. Unlike the gangland rubout, with its attendant necessities of clubs, chains, and abandoned warehouses, the review requires only a few quotations from Homer or a spot in the *New York Review of Books* for the "hit" to be mistaken for a work of critical importance. Done well, it is almost impossible for the untrained eye to perceive the wound, let alone determine the cause of death.

I find little that is offensive about this system of criticism, which is almost exclusively a product of the invisible hand; over the years it has produced a number of vivid essays and is about as close as the literary world can come to a system of checks and balances. And, naturally, it works both ways. For every review intended to correct some salon snub there is another by the author's college roommate that makes suitable comparisons between the book and passages from Plutarch.

As long as people were reading books, such philippics and well-constructed advertisements could be measured against what was actually in the books. But these days, in most conversations that drift around the subject of publishing, it is rare ever to encounter anyone who has in fact read any of the books under discussion. Instead, as opinions are needed to enliven a discourse, it is reviews that are trotted forth as paleographic evidence that the writer either possesses aspects of Milton or is worse than Charles Colson on the subject of his days with Jesus.

But beyond the literary world (which, in the only extant charts, resembles a kind of Polish corridor running through the center of Manhattan), the true intentions of reviewers are difficult to decipher. And when reputations are established, bookstores' orders are placed, and readers are herded along like sheep, it seems that it is leaving too much in the industry to chance if editors are allowed to go on assigning books for review in much the same whimsical fashion as Tom Landry, coach of the Dallas Cowboys, is allowed to send plays in from the bench.

Under the present system, when it becomes known that an established author—William Styron, say—is publishing a new book, hostile reviewers immediately start skirmishing in the hills like followers of Pancho Villa, each hoping he will be selected to ride down on Mr. Styron's wagon train and pull the gold from his teeth. Likewise, those who live by the proceeds of Mr. Styron's typewriter—his publisher, his agent, the various book clubs—send out a few marshals to quell the insurgents and ensure that he arrives safely at the B. Dalton stores on the other side of the pass. No wonder the industry is having hard times—laying off employees and searching for protection from those waiting in ambush.

Although even publishers acknowledge that notices, good or bad, generally sell books, a new system, as befits any regulated industry, would adopt standards to eliminate "unwanted competition." Once it was announced that Mr. Styron had completed his book, his agent would then hold an auction—much like those now conducted for the sale of paperback rights—to lease the rights to review the latest work. The leasing arrangement would be similar to that required by drillers before they can start looking for oil in the lower forty.

An exchange, resembling the Chicago Board of Options, would be set up to handle the volume of trade. On it would be listed the industrial giants, such as Roth, Mailer, Cheever, Vonnegut, Updike, and Solzhenitsyn. Lesser-known properties, as well as monographs put out by the major universities, could be traded over the counter. As under the present system, the *New York Times Book Review* (*TBR*) would be the market's newsletter and analyze the various offerings, as well as list the week's trades. And the terms of all sales would naturally have to be filed with the Securities and Exchange Commission.

No more, then, would it be possible for some enemy of Mr. Styron's to seize the pages of the *New Republic* to speculate on the possibility of a lobotomy. Nor could some professor of English literature take issue with Mr. Styron's use of the subjunctive merely to expand his own curriculum vitae, since all critics would first be compelled to bid on a lease before sinking their drills into Mr. Styron's property.

Naturally, the publishers, like the large oil companies, would buy up most of the leases (in much the same way they do now when they place their advertising dollars), and wildcat reviewers—the type that might want to harm the industry—would be driven from the prairie forever.

[1980]

Michael Huberman

1940-2001

Like everyone here today, I wish I were not hearing those words from King Lear—"The weight of this sad time we must obey." But Michael—friend, father, husband, colleague—as was said of another thoughtful American, now belongs to the ages. On occasions such as these, we want to lift the weight of recent shock and sadness, to see Michael as we all knew him to be—kind, insightful, with laughter that moved through his eyes and his spirit.

Michael was born on Christmas Day 1940, in Cambridge, Massachusetts. Without knowing for sure, I suspect that from his mother Michael got his taste for literature, his sense of others, his love of teaching; and from his father he got the drive to accomplish and the optimism that was America at mid-century.

For college he chose Princeton. The writer F. Scott Fitzgerald wrote in *This Side of Paradise*, as if about Michael:

From the first he loved Princeton—its lazy beauty, its half-grasped significance, the wild moonlight revel of the rushes, the handsome, prosperous big-game crowds, and under it all the struggle that pervaded his class.

Michael succeeded in his struggle and went on to Harvard University, where he received his doctorate in 1967. He moved abroad in 1970, to Paris, UNESCO, and later to Geneva and the life he made with Laurie. But it was to his roots in Cambridge and the world of Harvard that he often returned—connecting the best of American thought and letters to the villages of Switzerland that had become his home.

My wife, Connie, and I rented the Huberman house in Laconnex when they moved from Switzerland to the United States in 1991. For everyone here, I would like to recall that day on which we met, because it fixes Michael in a setting that he loved.

It was a Laconnex morning of an early spring that offered the full promise of summer. Past the garden were waves of grain, one part the American heartland, the other an impressionist painting—with vineyards in the foreground and the Alps shimmering in the distant sunlight.

I can't remember exactly what Michael and I talked about, sitting in that garden of Eden. I suspect we touched on Swiss schools, American history, French wine, the meaning of the first grade, the failings of the L bus, the novels of Balzac, the best places to ski in the Alps, the villages of Provence. Everyone here had those delightful conversations with Michael—a white Burgundy of friendship.

Also in that still life were sons Ben, David, and Anthony—ranging in ages between twelve and fifteen. We took a break from our coffee to play baseball with the boys. Fathers playing catch with sons, to me as an American, speaks of the bonds that Michael had with his boys. It wasn't a ball that passed between our gloves, but the pendulum of the generations. I know, too, that Michael, the educator, took great pride in his sons' accomplishments, their friendship with each other, but most of all their ability to live as native sons in both Switzerland and the United States—perhaps a dream he also had for his many students.

In speaking today, I wanted to find a poem that would capture the devotion that Laurie showed to Michael, as she said in her wedding vows, "for better or for worse, in sickness and in health." She never gave up, and she never gave up hope.

I chose a translation of Homer's *Odyssey* by Robert Fagles, a classicist and poet, who may have known Michael at Princeton or at some point in their inspirational careers.

Odysseus, like Michael, spent many years abroad. On his journey home, he enters the underworld, seeing his lost companions of battle—the Great Ajax, Agamemnon, Patroclus, and Achilles. Of his long wanderings Odysseus tells his friends:

Never yet have I neared Achaea, never once
Set foot on native ground . . .
My life is endless trouble.

In the land of shades, Odysseus also sees his mother, whom he can hear but not approach. He tells her:

I first set sail with King Agamemnon bound for Troy,
The stallion-land, to fight the Trojans there.
But tell me about yourself and spare me nothing . . .

Tell me of father, tell of the son I left behind:
Do my royal rights still lie in their safekeeping?

Please, tell me about my wife, her turn of mind,
Her thoughts . . . still standing fast beside our son,
Still guarding our great estates, secure as ever now?

In the many senses of the word, Michael was a classicist. He was patient, literary, funny, insightful, generous, a political man—in the Greek sense of the word—well-read, and, most of all, a good listener. We all owe a lot to Michael. I can thank him for the presence of my children in Swiss schools, and Laurie and Michael for our Laconnex lives.

He was a hero to everyone, except, more recently, to himself. I can only hope that, like Odysseus—on the journeys that take us through life and sometimes the underworld—Michael finds his way home.

Delivered in Cartigny, Switzerland, January 10, 2001

Dead Puppets' Dance in Albania

Albania is one of the riddles of the Eastern Question. It seems incredible that a fine country, with at least two harbors possible of development, and, within a few hours' steam of Italy, should be the most uncivilized land in the Balkan peninsula, and that for centuries no European power should have made any serious attempt to acquire it as a colony. Thus what might be one of the finest countries in Europe, is left in a condition such as nowadays disgraces few Central African tribes.

—1905 travelogue

At the turn of the millennium, on the assumption that it lay beyond the computer horizon, I spent a week in Albania—my first look at the country for which, in Kosovo, the Holy NATO Empire fought its savage war of peace. On my invitation it was noted that I was there to fish from the pool of state assets stocked for privatization. But even if I was reluctant to bid for a stake in the Karl Marx hydroelectric plant, I did want to fulfill a lifetime dream to see what remains of Enver Hoxha's brave old world.

A subsidiary of Swissair flies daily from Zurich to Tirana,

the Albanian capital. On this clear January afternoon, the Jumbolino crossed the spine of the Italian Alps and flew down the Dalmatian coast. Tirana lies thirty-five miles inland, at the head of a broad valley. Behind the capital is a long, white line of snow-capped peaks, over which NATO fighters flew their missions into nearby Kosovo and Yugoslavia. But before clearing for our final approach, we circled above the Adriatic, and I caught a glimpse of the Karaburun Peninsula, whose unknown chapter in the Cold War I was reading on the flight.

In *Betrayed*, Lord Nicholas Bethell, my friend and an English historian, describes the hapless missions launched by Britain and the U.S. in the late 1940s to overthrow the Hoxha government. The idea was to land covert operatives in Albania who would then lead the call to arms. The North Atlantic allies had sought to detach Tirana from the Soviet orbit, which with little opposition had established satellites in Poland and Czechoslovakia. But the British liaison officer in Washington was Harold "Kim" Philby, and he betrayed the missions. At Karaburun and elsewhere, the operatives found it was the secret police who were waiting, not the rebel cry of freedom. Hoxha followed up the incursions with executions and show trials to strengthen his power and, later, as a pretext to seal Albania from imperialist designs.

At Rinas Airport arriving passengers walk from the plane to the terminal along a palm-fringed promenade, a pleasant respite from accordion jetways, although inside, the arrival hall has the feel of a Balkan bus station. I paid forty-five dollars for a visa, but the man behind me paid fifty-five dollars. Baggage claim meant chasing down a free-lance handler who had a prior lien on the luggage trolleys. Because I was met by a scheduled car and driver, I was spared jostling for a taxi among the huddled masses yearning to breathe dollars.

Until it merges with an industrial suburb, the road into the city snakes across dust-bowl farmland, notable for its absence of tilled soil and for its crops of architectural folly.

Fields may lie fallow, the sad harvest of central planning and, now, a capital shortage. But on many hectares there is the work-in-progress of stillborn villas: incomplete three- and four-story houses that await either a family conference, the return of a construction team, or the next remittance from Milan.

Elsewhere in the countryside are the concrete igloos of Hoxha's civil-defense plan. After the Soviet Union invaded Czechoslovakia in 1968, when Albania's only patrons were in China, Hoxha ordered four hundred thousand bunkers to be built around the country. On the shore, in fields, on hillsides, almost everywhere you come across these crumbling pillboxes—the People's Maginot Line—now as difficult to comprehend as the mathematical equations that show up in Iowa cornfields.

TIRANA: *A Sleepy Balkan Village*

Until the 1920s, Tirana was a sleepy Balkan village. But Ahmedi Zogu's royal pretensions—he proclaimed himself King Zog I in 1928—and the work of Italian architects transformed it into a regional capital. "Much of the domestic state budget went on public buildings during Zog's reign," British historian Miranda Vickers writes in *The Albanians*. "In fact, of the 11 million Albanian gold francs budgeted between 1928 and 1938, 75 percent went on the construction of public and other residential edifices in the capital, which then had a population of around 25,000."

For a while Tirana was the Brasília or Canberra of the Balkans. As well, like many U.S. state capitals, it was a geographical compromise. Even today a tribal fault line divides Albania between Ghegs in the north and Tosks in the south, and—in a country where guns are everywhere—it was estimated recently that sixty thousand people still had a stake in a blood feud.

Between checking into an Austrian-run hotel and my first meetings, I had both a car and a driver and time to explore the city. A city of open sewers, sidewalk bazaars, and idle throngs, Tirana has the forlorn look of a city in Soviet Central Asia, a hub of dust and socialist realism. Near downtown, the university looks like a warehouse district, and most apartment buildings, in several ways, appear held together with clothesline. But such are the city's borrowed metaphors that a 1930s travelogue, *Dead Puppet's Dance*, could describe the Parliament as looking "like a Methodist Chapel transplanted from a London suburb."

At the city's center is Skanderbeg Square, which mixes Stalinist urban planning with a few Maoist sensibilities. Around a space about the size of Red Square is the Palace of Culture, the central bank, and a national museum, including a fresco of Albanian peasants on a long march toward the new world order. In the fifteenth century, Skanderbeg led an uprising against the Turks, and his mounted bronze reincarnation bestrides a corner of the plaza, although his Viking helmet makes him look like a Norse god on Pegasus.

Elsewhere what defines the city is trash, as if garbage men were swept away in a purge as revisionists. At one time there was a popular Kosovar expression: "The streets of Tirana are so clean because the Albanians have nothing to throw away." But times have changed, and today, if rubbish were an economic indicator, Albania would find itself in the growth tables of Singapore. Vacant lots, roadsides, parking lots, and even windowsills at important ministries bear witness that Albanians have joined the ranks of the disposable society.

In some corners of Tirana, minarets are the only things distinctive on the monochromatic skyline. Nominally Albania is a Moslem country. But most of the mosques look as forlorn as the shop windows. Hoxha suppressed religion, fearing Catholic encroachments or Orthodox hegemony. One of the ironies of Kosovo is that Moslem Albanians often took better care of the Serbian Orthodox churches than did their parishioners. More recently the Pope has described Albania as an emerging market, perhaps in keeping with a local expression: "Where the sword is, there lies religion."

FRIEND ENVER

As a winter fog encased the city, I stood before the gates of the former Hoxha residence, a sprawling complex that anywhere in Eastern Europe could be a People's Hall of Friendship. Until Communism fell in 1992, Albanians were barred from the neighborhood, lest they glimpse the leadership—a bit like Boo Radley—living in their gated mansions. Today several guards, with the air of forlorn retainers, patrol the grounds. Otherwise the house is dark, save for the security lamps, which glow in the mist, as if it were still darkness at noon.

Even though, during Hoxha's time in power, a leading Albanian export was his collected works, not many can recall particular details about the Communist dictator. He got his start as a Party functionary, but only reached power as the agent of the Yugoslav general secretary, Marshal Tito. During the war Hoxha was just one of many Partisan officers who fought both the Axis occupation and their domestic foes, real or imagined. On the battlefield he is noteworthy for campaigning with his catamite. Only after the war did he consolidate his reign of terror with Yugoslav backing.

When his master, Tito, broke with the Soviets, Hoxha supported Moscow. But the suggestions of Krushchev, among others, that Albania's future lay as a Soviet banana republic pushed Hoxha into the arms of the Chinese, who littered the countryside with now-decaying industrial works. He dated his fear of imperialism to the betrayed 1949 covert actions.

Such was Hoxha's paranoia that his food taster worked overtime, as apparently did others in his retinue. He led an opulent lifestyle but went by the epithet Shokut or Friend. It was natural causes that dispatched him to his tomb, an enormous marble wigwam in downtown Tirana, which, after the Communist liquidation, some wanted to convert to a disco.

In the damp chill of the national museum, I was the only visitor. The attendants and guards never stirred from their corner space heaters, so I walked alone among the marble busts of Albania's Greek, Roman, and Byzantine past. Albanians cling to their Illyrian origins, in part to distance themselves from neighboring Slavs, but also to stake the earliest possible claim to Kosovo.

During Hoxha's curatorship, the museum celebrated the heroic people's struggle. But after 1992—to the country's credit—the directors posted a roll call of those killed during "the Communist occupation" from 1949–1992. The names are listed, just as they are at the Vietnam Memorial, on stark tablets, and maps show where each fell, including those whose blood remains on Philby's hands. The exhibit also re-creates a prison cell of the secret police—further testament to the Albanian obsession with concrete bunkers.

ALBANIAN BANKS: *Where the money isn't*

My first business meeting was up a dark flight of stairs at the Ministry of Public Economy and Privatization in an office the temperature of a meat locker. I made the mistake of taking off my overcoat, and during the presentation my mind wandered from the case the minister made for an Albanian investment to the desire for warmth and dinner.

Most of the men running the Albanian economy are in their thirties and forties, as if the government were an Internet company. I liked the people I met, and I admired their optimism. Many were trained abroad and used phrases like "foreign investment" and "joint venture" as easily as those earlier, perhaps in this same meeting room, had quoted the theorems of Marx and Engels.

With our breath misting over the conference table, we reviewed the privatization as though we were discussing a five-year plan. Albania needs a natural-gas pipeline, an airline, a road system, increased oil production, a tourism infrastructure, and investment in the financial system. But few beyond the Clinton administration have banked on Albania's future, and even then Washington has put little into the country aside from its displays at the air show over Kosovo.

So far investments have been limited to Greek and Italian companies, many run by Albanian expatriates. International oil corporations have not tried to colonize the offshore oil acreage, despite whispers of reserves exceeding a billion barrels. What sends most transactions to the dustbin of deals are the terms. When I interrupted one meeting to ask what investors would get if they invested sixty million dollars in a certain project, everyone fell silent, as if in warming my hands I had, by accident, given the Zogist salute.

As best as I could tell, Albania is one of the few countries outside Africa that missed the economic revolutions of the twentieth century. Prior to 1939, when he fled the Italian invasion to the Ritz Hotel in London, King Zog had franchised the economy's few assets to Rome's interests, and his ministers took the rest, giving rise to a popular expression, "True, there are no brigands in Albania, because all of them have gone to Tirana, where they rob with authority from behind their desks."

After the war, Friend Enver sublet the economy to Mao's theories of industrial self-sufficiency. In remote valleys he used the country's limited foreign aid to build Chinese oil refineries and power stations. Petroleum production reached two million tons a year, far below the country's requirements, so he banned the private ownership of cars and rationed the balance to Party stalwarts, who proved as demanding as the king's courtiers. In short, Albania spent most of the twentieth century devouring its own—resources or otherwise.

In the transition from Communism to capitalism, governments became impossible to distinguish from hedge funds or crime syndicates, where a perk of office is to leverage influence in cornered markets. In the mid-1990s, for example, the ruling Democrat Party did brisk business in fuel oil, girls, cigarettes, drugs, and weapons, not to mention running one of the many Ponzi schemes whose collapse in 1997 brought down the government of Dr. Sali Berisha—adding Albania to the footnotes of *Extraordinary Popular Delusions and the Madness of Crowds.*

LOOKING FOR WORK IN A BMW

The premise behind Albania's pyramid schemes differed little from the asset and liability management of an Arkansas savings and loan. Alluring deposit rates blinded customers to the reality that their investments were worth little more than Dutch tulips, and before long the shareholders had skipped town, leaving clients to ponder a future without either toasters or deposit insurance.

Despite the economic three-card Monty, the central bank has recently maintained the *lek* as one of eastern Europe's more stable currencies, even if most foreign exchange dealers crowd the sidewalks outside the bank rather than the desks of its trading rooms. Albania has few commodities to export, and it lives on the remittances of overseas workers, who send in about one million dollars a day. The country has thirteen banks and about three hundred million dollars in foreign reserves. Like Washington, Tirana covers the trade deficit with easy money from abroad.

After some meetings, we would drive into the countryside as part of the due diligence. Albanian roads, which have seen little improvement since the Italian occupation in the 1930s, are rivers of potholes. Car rides feel like descents into white water. One morning, for example, it took us four hours to drive seventy miles south, and thus we had to abandon our hope to inspect either the tourist potential of Vlorë or a refinery at Ballsh, both of which were another twenty miles down the road.

Since the ban on the private ownership of automobiles was lifted in 1991, Albanians have made up for lost time by building up a fleet, of which—as even ministers acknowledge—60 percent of the cars are stolen, most from Western Europe. The average Albanian wage is between one hundred and two hundred dollars a month, and judging by the throngs of idle men in most town squares or those selling roadside soda, unemployment is the highest in Europe. But pitching among the potholes are the latest Mercedes and BMWs, part of what a World Bank report might call invisible imports.*

THE PYRAMID COLLAPSES ON KOSOVO

The Albanian economy as the province of pyramid schemes and stolen cars would have no more consequence than Hoxha's paranoia, except that it was the country's domestic anarchy that set in motion the events that led to war in Kosovo.

A consequence of the pyramid-scheme collapse in 1997 was the government's fall, during which the stores of the Albanian army were looted. More than a million guns and rounds of ammunition were hauled off. When arms sales and barter put this weaponry in the hands of the Kosovo Liberation Army (KLA), the dream of rebellion became a reality.

In searching for the causes of war, the NATO alliance found reasons only in Belgrade: Milosevic had revoked Kosovo's 1974 autonomy and flouted the diktats of Rambouillet; Serbia ruled the province by oppression and fiat;

* My friend Michael Heslop has suggested the following slogan to promote tourism: "Visit Albania. Your car's already there."

without intervention, the Serbian predilection for ethnic cleansing would bring another Holocaust to the region. But it was by Allied design that Kosovo was Serbian for most of the twentieth century.

Turkish for five hundred years, Kosovo was a spoil of the First World War, awarded to Serbia after it lost a fifth of its population while fighting the Central Powers. Following the Italian and German occupations of World War II, when an Albanian division fought ruthlessly for the Nazis, Tito made it an autonomous region within Serbia, both to weaken Serbian influence in Yugoslavia and to placate Albanian separatist sentiments. But when Tito's dream of a Communist Balkan federation incorporating Bulgaria and Albania faltered, Kosovo became yet another minority stepchild, caught between Serb nationalism and Hoxha's bunker mentality.

Similarly, Kosovo has never been an easy issue for Albanian governments. When I raised it in conversation, I generally got a standard answer that Albania has few problems with nearby countries, save for Serbia. But since its creation in 1912, Albania has been at odds with its neighbors. The Greeks have a long simmering claim to southern Albania, which has a largely Greek population. In turn, with its large Albanian minority, Macedonia fears a rerun of Kosovo.

Kosovars have often dismissed the Albanians across the border as poor relations and feared unification much the way many in Northern Ireland want nothing to do with the Republic. Nor did they welcome those Albanians who fled into Kosovo seeking the prize of a Yugoslav passport, on which they could flee Hoxha's regime. Although both Zog and Hoxha avoided irredentism to cultivate better relations with Belgrade, the postpyramid governments had to support insurrection in Kosovo, lest they find themselves the target of the looted guns that were eventually aimed at the Serbs.

Throughout the 1990s the United States thought it could impose peace in the Balkans by drawing Wilsonian borders around the feuding nationalities, even though an ethnic map of the region looks like a Jackson Pollock painting. In 1908, after traveling through Albania, the English writer Edith Durham described the futility of setting policy by Balkan borders: "The frontiers drawn by the Treaty of Berlin were so impossible that in many places they could not be defined, much less enforced. As the borderers themselves described it . . . [t]he frontier floated on blood."

THE AUDIT OF WAR

Waiting for the flight home at Rinas Airport, where much American weaponry was staged for the attacks on Serbia, I recalled the after-action reports, few of which justify the press notices of the Clinton administration that Kosovo was a splendid little war.

According to the BBC's *Audit of War*, it cost NATO four billion dollars to drop twenty-three thousand bombs on the remnants of Yugoslavia. Some ten thousand bombs, scattered across Yugoslavia, never exploded, to create future havoc for farmers or curious children—the same group at risk to run across the depleted uranium dropped to revive the Prizren League. The seventy-eight-day air campaign killed about six hundred Yugoslav soldiers and, depending on whose figures you believe, disabled either thirteen or ninety-three enemy tanks—which for General George Patton would have been an afternoon's work.

In its lavish ways, the U.S. Army alone paid $480 million to move its Apache helicopters to Albania, where they never fired a missile in anger. Just to position the squadron at Rinas Airport, according to the *Washington Post*, required an escort of M1 Abrams tanks, 6,200 soldiers, 42 support vehicles, and another 37 Chinook and Black Hawk helicopters. But after two Apaches crashed during training missions, the armada returned home to base, save for the equipment that later turned up in Albania's used-car market.

At war's end many of the 800,000 Kosovar refugees (who fled NATO's blitz just as they had Milosevic's goons) returned home. But the Allies turned a cynical eye to the cleansing of 150,000 Serbs from Kosovo—much as in 1914 they went to war to defend violated Belgian neutrality, but nine months later promised to partition Albania to entice Italy to the Allied side.

The Clinton administration couldn't prove its Holocaust charges against the Serbian government. Toward the end of 1999, 2,108 Kosovar war dead had been found, not many more than the numbers of Yugoslav civilians who were killed by the NATO air campaign. Charles Simic's assessment in the *New York Review of Books* was this: "As for the much-praised 'humanitarian intervention,' no matter what Ms. Albright says, the NATO bombing was a form of collective punishment in which innocent Serbs were made to pay the full price for the sins of their leaders who, of course remained well protected in their shelters."

The Yugoslav army and its leader, Milosevic, survived the war unscathed. The closest NATO came to deposing the Party stalwart was blowing up his empty house. But the air campaign over Serbia, which took out 44 percent of Yugoslavia's industrial capacity, consolidated Milosevic's power better than any Communist purge. The cost to rebuild Yugoslavia is estimated at thirty billion dollars—that for a country now the poorest in Europe, still embargoed in the West, and without foreign reserves—thus insuring regional instability for the next generation.

Even by Hollywood standards, so dear to the Clinton administration, the Kosovo production was a sequel to Waterworld. Never mind that the NATO stealth bombers could no more correct the injustices of the Balkans than they could locate Private Ryan on the outskirts of Pristina, or that our Albanian allies were in league with our enemies—the Islamic fundamentalists—who helped write checks to the

KLA. Perhaps one reason the Clinton administration was so eager for the studio rushes over Kosovo was that, if the missiles fell on either Serb militiamen or Moslem fundamentalists, the Pentagon could take credit for a direct hit.

While I was in Albania, the lack of an American presence was striking. During the war billions were pledged for Balkan reconstruction, especially for front-line states like Albania that contained Serb aggression. The president himself made a cameo appearance in Pristina to promise the Albanians that the world would not forget their suffering.

Unless the international community has hidden its aid in the trunks of stolen cars, most of the checks must still be in the mail. None of the ministers I met mentioned American largesse, and aid projects like the north-south highway are in the same state—idle disrepair—as Hoxha's bunkers, which in their own way sound notes of caution about foreign entanglements.

Waiting for the passengers to board, the pilot threw a stick for the dogs that linger on the tarmac. Before climbing the stairs, I tried to glimpse the heavy pods brought in to keep the Apaches from sinking into an airport pothole. But the army had left no trace of its encampment, and as I stood looking up at the snow-capped mountains, I thought of how the American alliance had paid four billion dollars to inherit the mantle of the Ottomans who came to measure the state of their empire by its ability to dictate events in the Balkans.

The Ottomans clung to power by violently dividing and conquering their subject nationalities, as in Kosovo, where in the seventeenth century the Turks treated the remaining Serbs just as later would NATO's Janissaries, the KLA. Vickers recalls one chapter: "In 1690, unwilling to convert and fearing a massacre if they remained [in Kosovo], the Orthodox Patriarch of Pec, Arsenije IV, led some thirty thousand Serbian families to migrate from Kosova to Hungary." It could easily be the modern story.

By driving the Serbs from Kosovo but leaving the province as part of Yugoslavia, the NATO forces—like some Turkish garrison—suppressed a nationalist uprising on a remote frontier. Just as quickly, a divide-and-rule occupation had resumed and, one suspected, the sultan had retreated to the pleasures of the harem—leaving only a legacy of violence, not the answer to a six-hundred-year-old problem. In the words of Robin Okey, who wrote about the Ottomans but might well have been describing the Clintonians: "The Porte made up in terror for what it lacked in efficiency."

[2000]

Extraordinary Flowering Delusions and the Madness of Crowds

In matters of commerce the fault of the Dutch
Is offering too little and asking too much.
                                        —George Canning

Between 1634 and 1637, the United Provinces of the Netherlands, of which Holland was the most important, traded tulip bulbs as if they were Internet public offerings. At a time when Dutch artisans lived on three hundred guilders a year, a single bulb could trade between five thousand to ten thousand guilders, and small baskets of prized tulips were worth more than mansions in Amsterdam or ships that worked the rich spice trades of the East. In the winter of 1637, as mysteriously as the speculation began, the bulb market collapsed, leaving the Dutch, by then a population of day traders, little more to do than cultivate their gardens.

I first read about tulip mania in Charles Mackay's *Extraordinary Popular Delusions and the Madness of Crowds*, published in 1841; later tulips were celebrated by such savvy investors as Bernard Baruch, for whom the tulip frenzy preached the mantra of contrarian investment. For Mackay, who called his book a "miscellany of delusions," the madness surrounding Dutch tulips recalled the follies of alchemy, the South Sea bubble, and other market applications of the philosopher's stone.

In *Tulipomania*, Mike Dash, a gifted writer and publisher who lives in London, recounts Mackay's grand delusion, the difference being that Dash tells the story of the tulip in history while Mackay limited himself to its epic in speculation. A wild flower that grew first on the slopes of Asian mountain ranges, the tulip was an ornament of the Byzantine court before it took root in western Europe.

In 1634 Dutch tulips served no economic purpose other than to relieve the cold wet spring with colorful petals that promised a change from the gray mist. At first those who traded bulbs were gardeners and connoisseurs searching for floral perfection. But as prices rose, rich and poor embraced the speculation: the rich to get richer, and the poor to spin their otherwise impoverished lives into gold.

Coming from the lawn mower side of gardening, I have never grown tulips, nor can I appreciate the subtleties of the more than six thousand varieties. On my last trip to Holland, I gave the greenhouses a miss to search near Arnhem for the "bridge too far." But I read Dash with interest and pleasure at a moment when the index of the National Association of Securities Dealers (NASDAQ) was in full bloom above 4000, and when it was reported that the Americans had paid four billion dollars for the splendid little war in Kosovo—where, incidentally, in 1389, the Turks had first carried banners embroidered with tulips into battle with the Serbs.

Not sure if it was the moment to go short with Microsoft

or the American empire, I found myself absorbed in Dash's history of the tulip: I learned more about runaway markets and the history of the Balkans than I do reading brokerage reports or editorials in the *New York Times*.

In telling the story of tulip mania, however, Dash avoids using it as a cautionary tale: "In the end it had been a craze of the poor and the ambitious that—contrary to popular belief—had virtually no impact on the Dutch economy." When the music stopped, the court orders that voided the tulip contracts also prevented the collapse from bringing down other markets of the Golden Age. Will the Internet Age be so lucky?

Just as the Ottoman Empire drifted West—Serbs in the Krajina, ironically, were in the front lines of the Christian defense—so did their prized tulips. Certain specimens may have reached Antwerp by 1560. According to Dash: "There were tulips in Vienna by 1572. They were in Frankfurt by 1593, and they reached the south of France by 1598 (possibly much earlier). Bulbs were sent into England as early as 1582, where they were soon grown in great quantity."

Tulips took root in the Netherlands partly because of the Dutch soil: "The bulbs," Dash writes, "flourished best in poor, sandy soils of the sort found in several parts of the republic and particularly in Holland, where a belt of dry, white earth ran parallel with the coast all the way from Leiden up to the city of Haarlem, just to the west of Amsterdam, and then on to Alkmaar, at the northern tip of the province."

Tulips also spread at a time when Dutch mercantile expansion abroad contrasted at home with some of the worst poverty in Europe. "To a Dutchman of the Golden Age," explains Dash, "the tulip was not a mundane and readily available flower. It was a brilliant newcomer, still bearing something of the allure of the exotic East and obtainable only in strictly limited quantities."

One reason tulips later lent themselves to frenzied

speculation was their limited supply. Most tulips will produce only two or three offsets in a year and can do so only for a few years before the mother tulip withers and dies. Dash calculates that "once a grower has identified, in a single flower of some new variety, great beauty or strength that he may be able to sell, he will have—even if all goes well—quite possibly only two bulbs the next year, four the year after that, eight in the next year, and sixteen in the fourth year of cultivation."

Perhaps the best known flower was the *Semper Augustus*—"the most celebrated, the scarcest and by common consent the most wonderful tulip grown anywhere in the United Provinces during the seventeenth century"—which in 1633 traded for fifty-five hundred guilders. At the height of the speculation, some of these bulbs fetched ten thousand guilders, more money than was needed to feed a Dutch family for a lifetime.

Because in the seventeenth century the United Provinces lived off its trade, the Amsterdam exchange made markets in more than 360 commodities. But even during the frenzy, tulip bulbs were not among them, nor were they the province of a guild. Like e-traders today, many of those dealing in bulbs were outside the organized exchanges. Trading often took place in saloons, inns that had names like "the Beelzebub, the Finch, the Lion, and the Devil on a Chain." "The trade," writes Dash, "was conducted for the most part in a haze of inebriation."

Even though many of the "specialists" in this trade were local farmers, with little commodity sophistication, they turned the bulb trade into a thriving futures market, in which most deals had a settlement date as distant as the following spring crop. The local expression for such futures business was "trading in the wind." The volume around these promises to buy or sell future tulips, during the four years of the mania, "was not less than 40 million guilders." By comparison, deposits in the Dutch banking system were 3.5 million guilders, and the

Dutch East India Company was capitalized at 6.5 million guilders. In his book on the art and culture of the Dutch Golden age, *The Embarrassment of Riches*, Simon Schama writes: "The bank was the church of Dutch capitalism; the bourse was its circus."

Tulip mania peaked between December 1636 and January 1637 when, according to Mackay, "people of all grades converted their property into cash, and invested it in flowers." But the flowers that drew the most attention, ironically, were infected with a virus, which—like most bull markets in dreams—gave them a last rare beauty before killing the bulb.

A lack of confidence, not a lack of money, brought down the market. Word spread through the tavern clearinghouses that prices were falling, and soon bulbs that had previously been quoted at six thousand guilders changed hands at six gilders. Mackay writes that "substantial merchants were reduced almost to beggary, and many a representative of a noble line saw the fortunes of his house ruined beyond redemption."

Dash views the collapse differently, suggesting that the fortunes wiped off the table were notional future prices and that the true losses were limited to fractional cash margins. In the months that followed, the Dutch courts, in order to limit the damage, refused to hear suits involving the nondelivery of tulip contracts and allowed buyers to pay 3.5 percent of their commitment and walk on the deal. The equivalent today would involve America Online forgiving the losses of day traders.

Among those unaffected by the crash was René Descartes, who lived in Holland because of his admiration for its political freedoms, and who completed his *Discours de la méthode* in the same year that the market peaked. Little wonder that he concluded: "The greatest minds, as they are capable of the highest excellencies, are open likewise to the greatest aberrations."

Had tulips only written the history of one speculation, they would never have aroused the so-called extraordinary passions. Even during the height of the mania, prized bulbs were confused for onions and eaten by unsuspecting sailors. But tulips also narrate a history of Ottoman rule, one that ironically explains why cruelty is one of the wild flowers of the Balkans.

Even the word *tulip* is entwined in Turkish sentiment. "The Turks," Dash writes, "called the tulip *lale*, and Busbecq [an ambassador] is generally believed to have described it as a *tulipan* because of the petals' resemblance to a folded turban."

In the inner sanctums of the sultans, the tulip reigned supreme: "In Süleman's time no fewer than five thousand servants toiled among the four courtyards. They ranged from humble watchmen to exotic specialists such as the chief turban folder and the chief attendant of the napkin, whose staff in turn included a full-time pickle-server." Mehmed IV was the first sultan to give himself over to the cultivation of tulips. (His father, Ibrahim the Mad, "once had all 280 women in his harem drowned simply so he could have the pleasure of selecting their replacements.")

Some of Dash's clearest writing describes the dichotomy of Turkish sultans—adorning the Sublime Porte with tulips but then ruling their far-flung empire, including the Balkans, with a barbarian's touch. "In the course of the fourteenth century, the Ottomans seem to have adopted this most holy of flowers to guard themselves against misfortune," Dash writes to explain that it was the Turkish standard at Kosovo, when the Serbs choose the "heavenly kingdom" of Martyrdom—a strategic option adopted by subsequent Serbian leaders.

Not all enemies were as easily defeated. Bayezid, the victor at Kosovo, and his talisman were subsequently beaten by Tamerlane, who was to show the "tulip king . . . no mercy." "The sultan he confined within an iron cage, which the Mongols took with them as they traveled. On state occasions Tamerlane had the once-proud Bayezid dragged before him so he could use him as a footstool."

At the Ottoman court, despite the soothing presence of

tulips, new sultans celebrated their ascension to power with ritual fratricide and a cleansing of pretenders to power. At the palace surrounding those who brought governance to the Balkans, Dash writes, "were a pair of white marble pillars on which were placed the severed heads of notables who had somehow offended the sultan, stuffed with cotton if they had once been viziers, or straw if they happened to have been lesser men. Reminders of the sporadic mass executions ordered by the sultan were occasionally piled by the entrance gate as an additional warning: severed noses, ears and tongues."

In 1607, the Ottomans replaced fratricide with the idea of the *kafes*, or cages—a place to lock unwanted brothers. "There, with eunuchs for company and sterile concubines for sexual consolation, unwanted princes lived lives that unpleasantly combined the immutable boredom of their daily routine with the nagging terror that execution might, after all, still be their lot." Among their few comforts were the rooms with a view of the inner courtyard, where they could admire their older brother's delicate taste in flowers. (All American vice presidents have to do is preside over the Senate.)

If, by its tilt toward the Muslims in Bosnia and Albania, the Clinton administration has taken up the Ottoman's burden in the Balkans, it has also presided over a rally in stock markets as exuberant as anything seen in Dutch taverns.

When I first began working on Wall Street in 1983, it was possible to assemble a high-quality stock portfolio by purchasing shares that traded either below book value or at a price-earnings ratio of less than ten. Banks, in particular, traded below their book or accounting value, and stocks that traded on a multiple above twenty times their earnings invariably attracted the word *high-flyer*. But today many who are clamoring to get into the markets put their money into companies with no earnings and valuations that make the *Semper Augustus* look like a Treasury bill.

Fundamentals such as book value or price-earnings ratio have become as dated as the high collars of the Dutch masters. Stock prices are quoted as a multiple of sales—with no indication of earnings or worth—and in the bubble that burst in March of this year (2000), certain biotech companies traded at two hundred times their revenues. In such an example, a start-up company with four million dollars in sales but no profit might, valued on the stock market, be worth eight hundred million dollars. Prices in this sector have approached seventy-five times the companies' book value, and 161 times cash flow—despite, in prospectus language, "no guarantee of future success."

In my experience, most investors spend less time reviewing the stocks in their portfolio than they do looking into their next vacation. At least with holidays, investors compare value and wonder where they want to go. By contrast, stocks are a package tour where everyone wants the same corner table at the same Internet cafe, even if the restaurant has yet to serve food and it costs two hundred dollars to check your coat.

Take, for example, the shares of Yahoo!, the Web portal that searches the Internet for "matches found." Along this stretch of the information superhighway, Yahoo! rents billboards to those hawking gas and motels. One hundred dollars invested in Yahoo! in 1996 was, at the end of 1999, worth $19,990, meaning that a $10,000 investment became $2 million—nice work for those who bought low and sold high. Those getting in more recently, however, would have found the bloom gone.

At the end of 1999, Yahoo! had equity of $1.2 billion and earnings of $61 million, but a market capitalization of $116 billion. Buyers of shares in Yahoo! were exchanging $2,000 of their wealth for $1 of Yahoo! earnings. By comparison, General Motors earned $6 billion last year on equity of $21 billion. At year's end its value was a third of Yahoo!'s or $45 billion. Since the millennium, Yahoo! shares have lost half

their value (to $62 billion), while GM has increased 15 per-
cent to $52 billion, a case where the onion produced the
prettier offset.

Around the cauldrons of our gilded age, it is the investment bankers who are wearing the conical hats. They bring to
market the new issues, often with little more to go on than a
reading of calf entrails or salamanders. Those buying the
credit of this full faith are asked to exchange present gold for
future lead. Mackay similarly described the sect of Rosicrucians,
who also believed in the secrets of transmutation: "Before
their time, alchemy was but a grovelling delusion; and theirs
is the merit of having spiritualised and refined it." Who would
subscribe for shares in an initial public offering if investment
bankers were required by the Securities and Exchange
Commission to disclose their debt to the dark arts?

Weighed against the Clinton era's conspicuous consumption,
Dutch tulips look like a harmless diversion—a trade in lottery
tickets. For example: Kenneth Starr received a sixty-million-
dollar advance for a pornographic novel that never actually
put the main characters in bed. Baseball team owners think
nothing of paying eight million dollars a season to pitchers
with losing records. The chief executives of the sixty largest
Internet or new economy corporations average twenty-seven
million dollars in salary, leaving aside the stock options buried
in the proxy statements. The Allies sowed twenty-three thousand explosives into Yugoslav gardens, to find that at war's end
Slobodan Milosevic had moved no further from power than
did Saddam Hussein after the Gulf War—thus denying Bill
Clinton the chance to use him as a footstool.

Dash observes that at the time of the tulip mania, there
was a striking dichotomy in Dutch life: "the urge to save and
the urge to gamble." But in American life today, prosperity
has only ridden a wave of debt. In the market itself, margin
debt totaled $50 billion in 1993; today it is $250 billion.

Net savings, as a measure of gross domestic product, used to average about 2.5 percent per year, or $2,500 for every $100,000 of economic activity. Today the net savings rate is negative, approximately minus 5 percent, confirming F. Scott Fitzgerald's observation that "nothing grows stale so soon as pleasure."

The Federal Reserve Bank, nominally a public institution, was afraid that the debt bubble might burst, and so it organized a $3.6 billion bailout of the partners of Long-Term Capital Management, which, when stripped to its essence, ran a pyramid scheme that bet the ranch on the theoretical difference between the interest spread on corporate and government debt. The Fed came to the rescue as though the hedge fund were an Asian nepotocracy.

Simon Schama believes that intervention by the Dutch government—fearing that it was paying the wages of sin—may have had a hand in breaking the tulip bubble. But he also makes the point that capitalism needed the twin impulses of thrift and speculation to conquer new markets at home and abroad. He writes: "If anxiety about the amorality of money loomed large in the mentality of the magistracy, they were not immune to a contradictory strain in the culture: admiration for heroic materialism." In that sense, a mania for tulips had to be absorbed if markets were to function in those commodities on which the Dutch republic survived. He concludes that "the pilloried speculators were close kin to the tolerated stockbrokers" but also that "speculation was Queen Money's revenge on her guardians."

In the late seventeenth century and through the eighteenth, the Dutch empire went into a slow decline. England, France, and the imperial houses of Europe divided and conquered aspects of its overseas trade. The Netherlands' support of the American Revolution, including its supply of guns and gunpowder, made the rebellion a more likely success. But an early American ambassador to the United Provinces sensed something in the Dutch character that suggested tulipomania was gone but not forgotten.

In the 1770s, our envoy, John Adams, of revolutionary fame, wrote about the Provinces: "This country is indeed in a melancholy situation; sunk in ease, devoted to the pursuits of gain, encumbered with a complicated and perplexed constitution, divided among themselves in interest and in sentiment, they seem afraid of every thing." Could he have predicted that those words might one day describe the republic he was founding?

[2000]

Coming in from the Cold War

A Journey from Ukraine to Poland

At a moment of Cold War revival, when the press and the State Department were writing off the former Soviet Union as if it were a bad loan, I made a trip from Kiev to Warsaw— the unhappy lands of the Pale between the rivers Dnieper and Vistula. On my visa, it said I was there to review investments, especially a new fund in Western Ukraine. In truth, I had grown weary of the new Cold War, in which Eastern Europe lies over a horizon of Russian gangsters, Serbian warlords, and Semex arms dealers. Along the way I might not make any deals in lands once claimed by the kingdoms of Poland, Lithuania, Ukraine, Russia, and Austria. But I would see for myself the borderlands that have often held the balance in Europe between war and peace.

Although I left my home in Switzerland on a day of early spring, I could see farmland edged with snow and ice as the plane descended into Kiev. Outside the Ukrainian capital, the oxbows of the Dnieper brushed against the still winter land-scape, while on the horizon the smokestacks of central plan-ning contributed to the great banks of fog above the airport. The frozen river and the squalls of snow flurries evoked January on the Mississippi at Rock Island, except that a grounded fleet from Aeroflot's past, now being stripped for parts, lined the runway down which the Swissair jet rolled toward its gate.

With fewer spies coming in from the cold, the border guards had the distracted air of motor-vehicle department staff. Asked to show proof of medical insurance, I mistakenly pulled from my wallet a Geneva library card. I was waved through nevertheless—remembering earlier journeys to the Iron Curtain that had ended prematurely for want of a photograph, a stamp, or an Intourist letter of transit.

In the arrivals hall, I found Raymond Asquith, my host for the week, who carries the imposing title of viscount, his great-grandfather having served Britain as prime minister during World War I. A tall man in his forties, with thick gray hair and an educated voice of reason, he divides his professional life between England and Kiev to launch a fund that would invest in promising Ukrainian companies. Previously he served twenty years in the British Foreign Office, both in Whitehall and as a diplomat in Russia and Ukraine. Although it was clear to Asquith that the smart money prefers to linger in Internet cafés, he remained tireless in his contrarian enthusiasm for Ukrainian investment—itself beyond the pale of random walks down Wall Street.

Is Kiev Mother Russia?

Our mud-encrusted taxi drove into Kiev on a highway lined with the brave old world of Soviet housing; the city that loomed above the Dnieper and spread along a hilltop forest, was more Rome than Arthur Koestler. In *Borderland*, a history of Ukraine that I had read on the plane, Anna Reid recalls a Russian proverb: "If Moscow is Russia's heart, and St. Petersburg its head, Kiev is its mother."

Even in fading winter, the contours of the old city had a soft mix of rolling hills, Orthodox domes, tree-lined promenades, and restored palaces. "Kiev," writes Reid, "stood for trams, electric light, the civilized and the familiar; Ukraine for low dark horizons, a strange language, fear of the unknown." As a center of Russian language and culture, it is older than Moscow. To those who first saw it after a lifetime on the barren steppe, it must have appeared through the mist like Oz's City of Emeralds. In the car, Asquith drew a distinction between Russia and Ukraine: "Russians are hunters. They stalk prey and then they move on. Ukrainians are settlers, farmers. It takes a lot to stir them."

During his years in Kiev, Asquith had helped to write and edit a guide to city walks. It was down one such trail that we spent the rest of the chilly Saturday afternoon. The walk began at Catherine the Great's Kiev palace, which the Bolsheviks had used as a stable. A more modern world was on display at the Kiev soccer stadium, under renovation to install sky boxes. Outside the national bank, restored to royal splendor, Asquith waxed eloquent on the government's successful defense of the local currency, the *hryvnya* (said grieve-na), when the Russian ruble collapsed in 1998. But he also acknowledged that, just as many government buildings have been restored to tsarist glory, so too have many of their tenants acquired the habits of imperial plunder.

Ukraine, which has a population of fifty-five million—about the size of France—broke away from the Soviet Union in 1991, when Mikhail Gorbachev was dispatched to the Sochi station. But its declaration of independence might well have been the prospectus for a management buy out, as Party minions, suddenly with their own franchises, treated themselves to stock options. A former prime minister, now under house arrest in California and awaiting extradition, cornered the gas market. Other officials leveraged their influence to open banks or divert tankers. Everyone else was told to make due with vouchers and inflated currency, each worth little more than Monopoly money, good for a few rooms on Baltic Avenue but worthless in the global economy.

Nor did Ukraine develop a culture of foreign investment to cover its shortfalls in goods and services. For a number of years, Asquith and I have worked with an English company that produces almost 5 percent of Ukraine's requirements for oil and gas, both of which are in short supply.

Rather than encourage additional production, the Ukrainian government tries every few months to seize the company's assets and dole them out as patronage to Party stalwarts. Gas sold to the government remains unpaid. During one negotiation in London to settle the past-due receivables, an energy minister pleaded government insolvency and then filled several limousines with bounty from Harrods.

Our walk ended at Asquith's office, where we drank dark Russian tea and he retold one hundred years of Ukraine's tragic history. Early in the twentieth century, it was a province divided between Poland and Russia, where little Ukrainian was spoken and nationalism was the dream of poets. Peasants on the farms had little time for the imperial cities of Warsaw, Moscow, or Vienna, although when World War I was declared, 3.5 million Ukrainians were conscripted into the tsar's armies. Another 250,000 fought for the Austrians, for whom Western Ukraine was Galicia, a Habsburg dominion.

At the Paris Peace conference, Asquith's great-grandfather, Herbert Asquith, according to Reid, "expressed polite interest in Ukrainian peasant customs, and asked which Ukrainian party corresponded to the British Liberal Party." Ukraine had the largest nationality in Europe not granted statehood at Versailles. Partitioned in 1919 between Russia and

Poland, Ukraine was absorbed by the Soviet Union in 1922.

During the Stalin terror famines of the 1920s and 1930s, along with the forced deportations, more than ten million Ukrainians perished—one reason the German armies were greeted as liberators in 1941. But enthusiasm for the occupation was short-lived. One in five Ukrainians was deported to serve as Nazi slave laborers. For four years, the country was a battleground, as both the German and Soviet armies took turns laying waste to the country and its population, including the thousands of Jews whose lives for centuries were restricted to the Pale of Settlement, which vanished in the vise of totalitarian anger.

During the postwar Soviet era, Ukraine was a socialist republic, with a quarter of its population Russian (many Ukrainians still speak Russian). In his polemical work *The Russian Question*, Aleksandr Solzhenitsyn argues that Ukraine is integral to the Russian motherland. In 1991 President George H. W. Bush made a similar case to keep Ukraine within the Soviet Union, fearing the instability of independent republics. But the Clinton administration promoted Ukrainian nationhood as a buffer state against a resurgent Russia— promising economic assistance for Ukraine's dismantled nuclear arsenal, including the glowing embers at Chernobyl. In the deal, the U.S. got a *cordon sanitaire*, Russia stripped fifty-five million dependents from its underfunded budget, and those running Ukraine were free to apply their invisible hands to state assets.

Night Flight to Lviv

It was snowing hard when our Lviv Airlines Antonov-24 landed in Lviv, the principal city of Western Ukraine. We checked into the Hotel Dniester. My room had twin beds and a table lamp, as if furnished by Tennessee Williams. At all hours the noise from the hallway was amusing, terrifying, or perplexing. In the Soviet Union, only the KGB pounded on your door at night; in capitalist Ukraine, the door-to-door salespeople are cut from cloth of easier virtue and work longer hours.

Not having meetings until the following afternoon, we spent the next morning walking around Lviv, which could be a poster city of twentieth-century tragedy. A hundred years ago it was Lemberg, the capital of Habsburg Galicia, where Josef Roth set *The Radetsky March*. From 1915–1918 the front lines of the Great War washed over the city. At the Paris Peace Conference in 1919, Lemberg became the Polish city of Lvov. When Hitler and Stalin partitioned Poland in 1939, Lvov became Russian, for the first time in its history. That rule lasted until June 1942, when the German *blitzkrieg* attacked the Soviet Union. The Germans ruthlessly occupied Lvov— deporting Jews, murdering the local population—until their retreat in 1944. After Yalta, Lvov was restored to Soviet suzerainty, which held until the union crumbled in 1991. After independence, Lvov was rechristened Lviv, its name in Ukrainian.

Approached from Paris or London, Lviv looks like a drab ex-Soviet city. But looming from the Ukrainian steppe, it is a city of wealth and culture, a metropolis of the great plains, like Chicago or St. Louis. Like Krakow to the east, Lviv retains its Habsburg accents. More than a few shops had portraits of Franz Josef, the last emperor, and the façades of the old town, such as the imposing university, recall similar walks through Vienna or Salzburg.

For much of the time in Lviv, we were with Anatoly Rosan, Asquith's local partner, who after independence put together a now-thriving investment company. On the flight from Kiev to Lviv, we had crossed the fault line between Slavic Orthodoxy and Roman Catholicism. Rosan, in his early forties, was of Polish origin, with the same light sandy hair and high cheekbones as many Poles. In 1992, starting with two hundred dollars, he invested in mundane local businesses: companies that made plastic tops or printed labels for chocolates. When I asked him how he was able to avoid the collapse that had brought down the Russian economy in 1998, he replied: "We know what a pyramid looks like."

Now Rosan was looking for seed capital to diversify into food processing and consumer products. Western Ukraine has a population of fifteen million, and when Poland joins the European Union, it will share a long border with the common market. It has an educated population (good secretaries can be hired for twelve thousand dollars a year) and some of the world's most fertile soil. Yet it lacks production in basic industry: fruit juices, wood processing, finance, beer, and meat—sectors for which Asquith would love to find front money in the capital markets. In Moscow, free enterprise has become synonymous with cornering the diamond market; in Lviv, Rosan is dreaming of slaughtering hogs or writing car insurance.

THE BLACK EARTH

Late on Sunday, we toured a World War II museum. In a house in the old city were displays of maps, machine guns, and orders of battle—clearly rearranged each time a new overlord marched into Lviv. Not often does the same war have so many different endings. Looking at a photograph of Ukrainian peasants in front of a farmhouse, I recalled that the family of an American friend in Switzerland, Laura Schmoll, was "from somewhere near Lviv." Calling her on a portable phone, I jotted down the name of the village, Zvenihorod, and three different spellings of the family named: *Poweleny, Pavelny, Povaleny*. If we could find any of the descendants of Anastasia Pavelny, who emigrated to America in 1923, Laura knew they would welcome us.

Not many business associates would rearrange a road

show to track down the relatives of a friend's friend. But Asquith never wavered; in fact, he saw it as a chance to assess potential investment in agricultural land. In a restaurant, detailed road maps were consulted. The next morning after breakfast, we drove forty minutes southeast of Lviv, through landscape described by Anna Reid: "Western Ukraine has ruined Renaissance palaces, walled towns, onion-domed churches. Villages dot its rolling valleys, in Conrad's words, 'like clusters of boats hidden in the hollows of a running sea.'" Many of the churches are works-in-progress, monoliths on the rolling plain, as if part of faith's Maginot Line.

In Zvenihorod, we headed to the office of the mayor, who, in trying to apologize for the disorder of the town, said things had not been the same since the Tatar invasion, which was at the end of the eleventh century. The mayor volunteered his secretary to lead us to the Pavelny household, and we set off down dirt roads, actually rivulets of potholes, until the car stopped before a village farmhouse.

Three men in suits are not what most Ukrainian villagers want to see striding toward their front door. The house belonged to Anastasia's niece, Mariya Stepanovich, now in her sixties, and, after a moment of doubt, she welcomed us as lost relatives, poured tea and offered brandy while her daughter-in-law retrieved a box of family photographs—including my friend Laura's wedding pictures—one of the lifelines that link towns like Zvenihorod to the lives that unfolded after Ellis Island.

The story of the village, with its population of four hundred, is also a history of Western Ukraine. Although nearby villages are Polish, Zvenihorod is Ukrainian and its church Uniate, a compromise between Catholicism and Orthodoxy. Communism has few roots in the soil, which is black, like tracts of the American Midwest. While rutted with spring mud, the main street was more prosperous than many I have seen in Eastern Europe. A village corporation, successor to the collective, holds title to the land, and families like the Pavelny pay royalties to the corporation to work the land. Anyone like Asquith or Rosan, however, who now wants to invest in the land will have to decipher titles and regulations more arcane than New York City's laws on rent stabilization.

Ukraine's Harvests of Sorrow

On many of our excursions, Asquith and I passed the idle moments discussing various books about Russia and Ukraine. He liked the history of Anna Reid, who was a friend from Kiev. The late British diplomat, Fitzroy MacLean, who witnessed Stalin's show trials and explored the Soviet Union by train, had also been a friend. We both appreciated Solzhenitsyn. Asquith thought the work of Orest Subtelny, who has written Ukraine's history in English, "dry," but several times he encouraged me to track down Robert Conquest's *The Harvest of Sorrow*, a history of Stalin's collectivization and terror famine that I had neglected when it was published in 1986. "Grim reading but necessary," was his terse assessment. It begins with a quote:

> *The black earth*
> *Was sown with bones*
> *And watered with blood*
> *For a harvest of sorrow*
> *On the land of Rus*

The villages of Western Ukraine—so many Zvenihorods—reaped many such harvests.

In the late 1920s, Stalin's "revolution from above" declared war on the peasantry: "Dekulakization is now an essential element in forming and developing the collective farms." As a first step, to feed the dictators of the proletariat, he confiscated the grain harvests after 1929. Then he purged the Soviet Union of *kulaks*, who in May 1929 were defined as those who "hired labor; or had a mill or buttermaking or similar establishment." Stalin evoked images of *kulaks*, many of whom were Ukrainian, as village usurers, but their average worth in 1930 was ninety dollars. Asquith said they were "anyone with a goose."

The new world order was completed when Stalin consolidated twenty million family farms into 240,000 collectives, which were to operate like rural factories. Conquest describes their exodus from such villages as Zvenihorod: "The *kulaks* were driven out on foot. . . . The women were sobbing—but were afraid to scream. The Party activists didn't give a damn about them. We drove them off like geese. . . . Not one of them was guilty of anything, but they belonged to a class that was guilty of everything." Six and a half million perished in the dekulakization. Another five million Ukrainians died in the subsequent famine, as fields lay fallow and Stalin confiscated the rest. As John Steinbeck wrote of a less fatal dust bowl: "The fields were fruitful, and starving men moved on the roads."

Conquest describes Ukraine at this time as a "vast Belsen." A quarter of all Ukrainian farmers perished in the famine. But not many western observers were able to describe how the future was working in Ukraine or the Soviet Union. An exception was Malcolm Muggeridge, who wrote of commissars: "Carrying out the instructions of the dictatorship of the proletariat . . . they had gone over the country like a swarm of locusts and taken away everything edible; they had shot or exiled thousands of peasants, sometimes whole villages; they had reduced some of the most fertile land in the world to a melancholy desert." Less prescient was Walter Duranty, the Russian correspondent of the *New York Times*, who, despite winning a Pulitzer Prize for his dispatches, concluded in August 1933: "Any report of a famine in Russia is today an exaggeration or malignant propaganda."

TOUR OF POLAND'S SOLIDARITY

After lunch in a restaurant that, to attract customers, had a caged bear near the front door, I flew LOT, the Polish airlines, from Lviv to Warsaw. I had last been to Poland in 1986, when my wife and I rode our bicycles across General Jaruzelski's martial state. In that era the airport felt like a dry-goods warehouse, and we rode our bicycles into a city that had more parks than cars. Fourteen years later, I rolled into the city in a white Mercedes taxi. Instead of staying at the Orbis Grand Hotel, I checked into the Bristol, recommended by a friend who obviously thought I was good for the three hundred dollars a night. In Lviv, the hotel had cost seventy dollars, and the hot dogs at breakfast were complimentary. But the prices at the Bristol confirmed my suspicion that Warsaw had become an expense-account city.

Meeting Henryk Wozniakowski—my friend and a leading Polish book publisher—in the lobby bar brought back memories from our 1986 odyssey. I had chosen Poland for our bike tour because the country was flat and a fulcrum of the Cold War; packed into our panniers were the addresses and phone numbers of leading Solidarity members. For several days in Warsaw, we rode to the apartments of the opposition—delivering tea, chocolates, and messages to men and women for whom Jaruzelski's oppression had taken a personal toll. I still remember the darkened city, lit by only a few street lamps and redolent with the odor of burning coal, making us think we were behind the lines of a wartime siege, as I suppose we were.

Leaving Warsaw to the north, we biked through the birch forests around the Masurian Lakes, using only the maps in the Solzhenitsyn novel *August 1914* as our guide. In Gdansk we rode to the main gates of the shipyard where we hoped to shake hands with Lech Walesa when his shift ended. At 4:00 P.M. we arrived at the entrance, only to discover that nearly all the men carrying lunch pails from the shipyard had Walesa's trademark walrus mustache and his same expression of fiery determination. In Gdynia, we saw the dockyards from which Joseph Conrad—born to those dark horizons outside Kiev, in lands no longer Polish—first went to sea, with advice from a family friend: "Remember, wherever you sail, you are sailing towards Poland."

By the time we reached the southern city of Cracow, my wife was ready to sell the bikes. Instead we locked them to a chair in the hotel room and tracked down Henryk Wozniakowski, who was working with his father in the publishing house, quietly nurturing the cause of rebellion. Like Lviv, Cracow is a city of Habsburg elegance. We responded to the cobblestones of Jagiellonian University, the old town, and Wawel Cathedral as if they were Beethoven concertos. On our last day, Henryk drove us the forty miles to Auschwitz. On a cold, blustery autumn afternoon we walked together down the tracks that led to the terminals of eternity, recalling words of Primo Levi that "hell must be like this."

Chance now, fourteen years later, put me in Warsaw on the same night that Wozniakowski was host to a writer's forum. A man in his forties, he was now free to publish both leading Polish authors and serious literature from abroad— with no thought of government recrimination. A man of courage and strong Catholic faith, he had sought to harmonize the anticommunism of the church with the reform elements of Solidarity, so that Poland could embrace articles of faith and an appreciation of dissent and the printed word. Poland's success—those of a pluralistic democracy and one of Eastern Europe's strongest economies—were the realization of the idealism that I had first heard him express in October 1986.

After tea in the hotel, we walked toward the rebuilt old city, where in a university lecture hall one of Wozniakowski's authors—the English writer, Timothy Garton Ash—delivered his remarks entirely in Polish—a counterpoint to Conrad, who was raised in Polish but wrote in English. After the panel discussion, I stood on the street next to a deputy minister of finance who regretted that Poland had just missed the requirements to join the European Union. But he was confident it would meet them shortly and take its place as a western European nation. We were standing opposite the illuminated façades of the old city, as grand as any street corner in Prague. Poland had made a long journey with those dilapidated trams that fourteen years ago had run on cobblestones and warped rails, apparently heading more toward Desire than anywhere else in the twentieth century.

FROM THE EASTERN TO THE WESTERN FRONT

Although I flew home from Warsaw's new air terminal, as modern as any in Germany, my journey did not end until a few months later when I spent a day outside Paris on the battlefields of the River Somme. In 1916, a generation of Allied soldiers, mostly British, bled to death there in a series of attacks that went over the top and into the sights of German machine guns. On July 1, in one hour, Britain lost forty thousand men—almost the number of casualties of America's seven years in Vietnam. In particular, I wanted to visit the grave site of Raymond Asquith—the grandfather and namesake of my friend—who died in an attack on the Guillemont Road, where he is now buried, outside the French town of Albert.

On a day of high summer, in wheat fields that could well be in Kansas, I found his headstone, on which is engraved: "Small time but in that small most greatly lived this star of

England." After he was killed, in September 1916, Winston Churchill wrote to his widow: "His was a character of singular charm and distinction—so gifted and yet so devoid of personal ambition, so critically detached from ordinary affairs yet capable of the utmost willing sacrifice." It was said that his father, Prime Minister Herbert Asquith, never got over the death of his son, as was true of many parents of the war dead. In less than a year, Herbert Asquith was out of office, although in 1919 he was present at the Paris Peace Conference, at which fourteen million Ukrainians failed to achieve statehood and the borders assigned to Poland were so artificial that it prompted John Maynard Keynes to remark that it was "an economic impossibility whose only industry is Jew-baiting."

Standing in the rolling farmland of Picardy, I thought of how the two Raymond Asquiths embodied so much of the hope and suffering of the twentieth century. The first was born into the Edwardian world of comfort, privilege, and responsibility that turned to mud and ashes in the trenches of he Western Front. After his death, Europe—especially the people of Ukraine and Poland—endured two world wars, numerous famines and pogroms, a holocaust, and totalitarian rage—opposition to which, in some distant way, had prompted him to go over the top. "Fate had elected him for a special deed," wrote Josef Roth in *The Radetsky March*, of similar heroism, "but then made sure that later times lost all memory of him."

A child of the Cold War, the second Raymond Asquith, my friend, had lived and worked more than twenty years behind the Iron Curtain. He had now posted himself to a backwater of capitalism, to make money, to be sure, but also to promote the cause of investment capital—as an alternative to the familiar barbarism of Eastern Europe. For the moment he might not attract many Western investors to the markets around Lviv, which remains as forgotten as was Cracow in 1986, when Henryk Wozniakowski longed for its new birth of freedom. But standing over the headstone of the first Raymond Asquith, I wondered if the twenty-first century would succeed in finding other ways to fight wars to end all war.

[2000]

Suicide Warriors

On the heights of the Gallipoli peninsula in 1915, a Turkish colonel, Mustafa Kemal, later known as Atatürk, rushed reinforcements to the front with the immortal words, "I am not ordering you to attack. I am ordering you to die." Colonial allied soldiers, known as ANZACS, had nearly broken through to the Dardanelles, which in turn would have led to the fall of Istanbul and the strategic Bosphorus Straits. The regiment of counterattacking Turkish soldiers died to a man, delaying the Allies' return to Constantinople. And even in the secular nationalistic world of Atatürk's modern Turkey, the lesson was learned that suicide warfare has its place in attack formations, perhaps abreast the scimitar and impalement.

Almost seventy years later a similar confrontation took place between the legions of Allah and American forces. In 1983, after the massacres in several Palestinian refugee camps, U.S. Marines were deployed to Beirut to maintain a fragile peace, although in the minds of local Arab militia, the leathernecks looked suspiciously like a crusader army in the Levant protecting captured walls of Jerusalem. In April of that year, the U.S. embassy was attacked. In October, a suicide truck bomber crashed into the marine barracks with a consignment of explosives, killing 260 Americans and 60 French soldiers. A marine sentry, who survived, recalled only the smile on the face of his assailant.

The suicide attack, however, succeeded in driving the Western alliance off the high ground in Lebanon. It allowed Syria and Iran to establish their cells of terror in Lebanon's anarchy, much as Osama bin Laden has his own free-trade zones inside Afghanistan. Hamas and Hezbollah, among a number of terror organizations, embraced the stealth qualities of suicide warfare, much as the Americans did in spending billions of dollars to develop the B-1 bomber. Those who killed themselves and others were given a hero's farewell, which played well on the recruiting posters around the Arab world: "Allah is looking for a few good men." Not only could the enemies of Israel strike within that country, but the front of the holy war could be extended past the shores of Tripoli, wherever anyone could be "ordered to die."

The Organization Men:
dying at "strategic crossroads"

Ariel Merari, a Tel Aviv professor, has studied suicide warfare in, among other places, Sri Lanka where they use Tamil Tigers, in Israel, and along the border with Lebanon. He testified to the U.S. Congress:

> In the whole series of Lebanese suicide terrorist attacks and Palestinian suicide attacks . . . there was no single case in which an individual on his own prepared this attack and carried it out. In all cases it was an organization that decided to use this tactic, found the person or persons to

carry it out, trained them, and then sent them on the mission at the time and place that the organization chose.

Nor does his research show that the suicide bombers strap on explosive backpacks in fits of divine revelation. He concluded that "the majority, almost two-thirds of the terrorist attack suicides, of terrorist attacks in Lebanon have been carried out by secular organizations. These are with nationalistic or territorial ambitions, much like those of Atatürk at Gallipoli.

Willing to die themselves and eager to drag civilians into their vortex of self-destruction, the new battalions of suicide soldiers are often described by their veils of fanaticism. Terrorists leave behind video suicide notes that describe their eagerness to enter Paradise wearing Allah's Victoria Cross, and other intercepted cable traffic, such that of bin Laden's "declaration of war," invokes a new samurai code on the salvation associated with self-annihilation at war. The Saudi prince of terror, for example, has often said, "The most honorable death is to be killed in the way of Allah."

Professor Merari emphasizes, however, that suicide bombers are made: they are neither born nor delivered to the battlefield in a convoy of angels. He writes that in carrying out suicide attacks, "an organization makes use of people who are willing to die to begin with." Hence the training camps of bin Laden in Afghanistan or those of Hezbollah in Lebanon can be seen as variations on the mission of Parris Island or Fort Bragg. Further he notes that "organizations involved resorted to this tactic when they thought that the time was critical, that they were at political strategic crossroads."

For example, the fires of self-destruction were carried to Tel Aviv when it was feared that peace might succeed between moderate Palestinians and Israel. In India, suicide assailants killed Indira and Rajiv Gandhi as a consequence of their policies in Amritsar and Sri Lanka.

THE THIN RED LINE BETWEEN SUICIDE AND PATRIOTISM

While rare in military history, suicide attackers are not unknown, although it is a fine line to distinguish troops ordered to death in battle and those that entered the conflict with the objective of killing themselves in battle. In 73 A.D. at Masada, located in the Judean desert, south of Jerusalem, Roman legionnaires besieged a Jewish garrison of Zealots, from whom we get the synonym for extremism. Rather than be captured, hundreds of Zealots hurled themselves from the fortress walls, denying the Roman tenth legion the spoils of war.

Along the River Somme on the morning of July 1, 1916, more than forty thousand British and colonial troops died trying to advance into wired German trenches that were laced with machine guns. A week-long artillery bombardment failed to cut the German wire, and the flower of what became a Lost Generation was ordered over the top to certain death. Siegfried Sassoon, who was among the survivors, entitled one of his World War I poems "Suicide in the Trenches":

> You smug-faced crowds with kindling eye
> Who cheer when soldier lads march by,
> Sneak home and pray you'll never know
> The hell where youth and laughter go.

A few British soldiers played bagpipes and kicked footballs on their short dashes to eternity, but not many expected to make the second line of German trenches. Research of many battles concludes that most soldiers, even those advancing to certain death, do so to maintain their bond with the others in their ranks. As Robert Graves writes in *Good-bye -to All That*: "Patriotism, in the trenches, was too remote a sentiment, and at once rejected as fit only for civilians, or prisoners."

In the early days of World War II, American forces encountered the terrifying onslaught of Japanese banzai charges, in which imperial Japanese soldiers hurled themselves sense-lessly into opposing lines. Entire companies and battalions rushed forward, in the name of the emperor, often to certain death in the sights of American machine guns.

The first American offensive of the war was on Guadalcanal, where my father fought with the U.S. Marines at the battle of the Tenaru River. His company C, of the First Marines, responded to a banzai attack with a bayonet charge of their own, wiping out the opposing Japanese forces. But it was the aftermath of that battle that so disturbed American marines, as one witness wrote of the battle's end:

> I have never heard or read of this kind of fight. These peo-ple refuse to surrender. The wounded would wait until men came up to examine them . . . and then blow themselves and the other fellow to pieces with a hand grenade.

Thanks to an alert corporal, Frank d'Enrico, my father survived one such suicide attack; but later in the war, the Japanese refined these tactics into a strategy that combined Masada's defiance with Beirut's indifference to death.

THE DIVINE WIND—OR KAMIKAZE:
"not victory but death"

By 1945, the American navy and air forces controlled nearly all the shipping lanes and airspace over the Japanese home islands. Conventional bombers and fighters had little chance against this U.S. dominance, except when they were converted into human-guided cruise missiles and launched against the invasion fleet. They proved both deadly and hard to stop, as with today's terrorism. One witness to an attack wrote: "A kamikaze screamed in under the guns of the picket ships, drove through wallowing transports like a ferret through a henyard, and exploded in a great orange flame against the side of a ship." With a few words changed, it could almost describe the attack on the World Trade Center.

Most of the 4,907 naval deaths in the campaign could be accounted for by the 2,944 kamikaze missions flown against the American invasion fleet. Had there been an American invasion of Japan in 1945–46, kamikaze would have been the principle threat from the air. A pilot on Okinawa defending against kamikaze, Samuel Hynes, now a distinguished war and cultural historian, wrote: "The true end of the war for the men I was fighting against was not victory but death." But unlike the banzai attacks early in the war, these suicide missions traded few lives and little material in trying to buy time for Japan near the end of the war.

The Divine Wind—the kamikaze—was a storm that saved Japan from a thirteenth-century Mongol invasion. At the end of World War II, the pilots of the same name hoped to forestall a similar invasion or at least to bloody the Americans to the extent that they would lose interest in a landing or allow the Japanese to sue for peace on more advantageous terms. It was a strategy designed to enhance the terms of peace, not to win the war. But above all, the kamikaze were recruits in a great game—soldiers awaiting orders, soldiers prepared to die for the emperor.

Like today's Islamic bombers, the young Japanese pilots who flew these last missions were notable for their outward lack of martial prowess. Many were mediocre high school students with literary pretensions. Besides the image of leather helmets and white scarves, they also left behind haiku that sings the song of sacrifice. Verse such as,

O my soul, if you do not get killed,
you are going to die, anyway.
This is a death pool in front of you

could easily be found among the papers of a kamikaze pilot, except that it is from an Arabic poem quoted often by bin Laden.

THE ASSASSINS:
"propaganda of the deed"

The word *assassin* derives from an Iranian Islamic sect that existed from the eleventh to the thirteenth centuries. These people killed their enemies and themselves in moments of frenzy. In Arabic the word means "hashish smoker." Marco Polo and others told about fanatics who prepared for martyrdom as if it were a rock concert. In many ways, bin Laden is heir to the traditions of Hasan, a grand master of the assassins, who in the eleventh century "commanded a chain of strongholds all over Iran and Iraq, a network of propagandists, a corps of devoted terrorists, and an unknown number of agents in enemy camps and cities."

Suicide bombers take their inspiration from anarchists of the late nineteenth and early twentieth centuries who dreamed of worlds without hierarchy or authority, and found their targets among the governments or royal families in Europe or America. In *The Proud Tower* Barbara Tuchman describes their belief in something called the "propaganda of the deed":

> The thinkers in press and pamphlet constructed marvelous paper models of the Anarchist millennium; poured our tirades of hate and invective upon the ruling class and its despised ally, the bourgeoisie; issued trumpet calls for action, for a "propaganda of the deed" to accomplish the enemy's overthrow. Who were they calling? What deed were they asking for? They did not say precisely. Unknown to them, down in the lower depths of society lonely men were listening. They heard echoes of the tirades and the trumpets and caught a glimpse of the shining millennium that promised a life without hunger and without a boss. Suddenly one of them, with a sense of injury or a sense of mission, would rise up, go out and kill—and sacrifice his own life on the altar of the Ideal.

Almost forgotten today, the Anarchists killed an American president, the empress of Austria, and a Russian tsar.

Playing the Great Game

Ironically, today's suicide bombers share few of the tactics of the Afghan guerrillas, who for several hundred years have fought their invaders from the country's forbidding redoubts. The disaffected legions that bin Laden has trained inside Afghanistan are not Afghans but Arabs—Saudis, Algerians, Syrians, etc.—who have been recruited to the cause of martyrdom from the violence and despair of either the Palestinian struggle or their sense of inequality within their own societies.

In the Afghan wars of the nineteenth and twentieth centuries, of which there have been many in the Great Game of the world's empires, Afghan rebels rarely adopted the strategies of suicide warfare. Instead they used the rugged landscape to bleed their invaders, as a British advisor to Afghan forces wrote of the Russian war: "It is a nightmare as fighting territory. It is a natural fortress . . . they move from one village to the next, where they have bases stocked with food . . . they carry very little and cover ground much faster than a Western force could. . . . In the Hindu Kush don't expect to appeal to the Geneva convention."

An American officer with a similar experience inside the country observes: "A 'good' Afghan battle is one that makes a lot of noise and light. Basic military skills are rudimentary and clouded by cultural constraints that no matter what, a warrior should never lose his honor."

What suicide bombers do borrow from the Afghan guerrilla traditions is the need to blend into the surrounding landscapes, be they in the Hindu Kush or the New York financial district. In the fallout from the World Trade Center, an English newspaper published a profile of bin Laden's childhood, "Portrait of the Terrorist as a Young Man."

The article included a photograph of the youthful Osama with some of the his fifty brothers and sisters, in which most are wearing the bell bottoms and large-collar shirts that could have been worn by the Osmond family. His first trip to Sweden was made on a private jet that apparently had a Rolls Royce in the cargo bay. His family fortune had come from contracts with the Saudi royal family, itself awash in American petrodollars. His family was not unknown in the West, where several members of the bin Laden clan had done business in oil—including deals with a prominent U.S. political family, in which both the father and the son had dabbled in oil and politics.

[September 2001]

Giving My Regards
to Broadway

As a short introduction to what I hope will be the first of many columns under the heading "Letters of Transit," I will tell you that I was born in Manhattan at mid-century and, after coming of age on Long Island, I settled in Brooklyn, a compromise for someone whose first twenty-six years straddled both sides of the East River. I went to school in Pennsylvania and New York and worked first in magazines and then in banking. During the 1980s, I spent my downtime either riding my bicycle across the Brooklyn Bridge or, when vacation and money allowed, journeying to frontiers—ones that mixed political and sentimental education.

On one trip I traveled overland from the Korean demilitarized zone to the Khyber Pass in Afghanistan, describing an arc along the contours of the Cold War. For our honeymoon, my wife and I made an improbable crossing from Argentina's Dirty War to the repression in South Africa, hardly one of the itineraries sketched in *Bride's* magazine. A year later we managed to thread our way from Amman to Jerusalem, at the outbreak of what became known as the first intifada.

Despite the sense of darkness at noon in these destinations, I often found voices of political tolerance. In South

Africa, I had the good fortune to meet Alan Paton, the author of *Cry, the Beloved Country*. In Peshawar, the Casablanca of the latest Afghan war, I got to know Abdul Haq, an Afghan leader in the Russian resistance, who, this past October was killed by the Taliban as he tried to rally a fragmented rebellion either to the exiled king or perhaps to the pretenders at the CIA.

Back at my desk in New York—whenever one of these countries broke into the headlines—I would match the desperation of the evening news with the optimism of those I had met. Paton, for example, had said he was "not hopeless" about South Africa's future, and he was right. In Buenos Aires, my friend Horacio Mendez Carreras had hoped that laws, not guns, had the best chance of success against the Argentine junta. In 1983 Haq had said the Afghans could beat the Russians.

In 1991, my wife and I moved from Brooklyn to the Swiss countryside near Geneva, exchanging the D train, egg cream, and the New York Botanical Garden for lives best understood as passages from *Heidi*. We enrolled the children in a local Swiss school, took French lessons, and tried as best we could to live what the French call the provincial life.

My new office, at a Swiss bank, overlooked Lake Geneva, and instead of traveling for the day to Cleveland, Chicago, and Dallas, I now found myself searching for flights to Rome, Budapest, and Moscow.

In the early 1990s, anyone traveling around Europe on business looked East with the expressions of innocence and expectation that President Woodrow Wilson had drafted into the Treaty of Versailles. But beneath the hope of a duty-free Europe lay a darker reality.

For much of the decade, Moscow remained mired in gangland. After I went prospecting in the Balkans for truth, justice, and the American way of sales, the cities that I visited had follow-up calls from NATO and the Strategic Air Command. When evoking the juxtaposition in Europe of civilization and its discontents, the historian Barbara Tuchman quoted from Edgar Allen Poe:

> *While from a proud tower in the town*
> *Death looks gigantically down.*

It was on television from my own tower in Geneva that I saw death looking down from the World Trade Center. At my desk I spoke on the phone with a friend trapped in a nearby building (he survived), and in the days that followed I read and heard the accounts of survival and disappearance much as if Argentina's Dirty War was unfolding in New York or as if the city had inherited the fatalism so redolent at Panmunjom.

I had worked for seven years in the shadows of the Trade Center. Despite the television and news magazine coverage, I found it impossible to visualize the abyss. I knew it was a Hades of smoke and death, and that everyone knew someone who, in turn, knew someone who was lost. But from Geneva it was as remote as the battle of Coral Sea or Crécy until, a few weeks after the attack, I flew to New York.

The business rationale for the trip was flimsy, and my New York friends said it was impossible to get close to Ground Zero. But I persisted in heading downtown.

Past City Hall, my first impression was of the trenches of World War I, as some streets near Broadway are lined with wooden tunnels, like the paths of glory that laced the earthworks at the Somme or Verdun. Explaining to the police that I wanted to learn the fate of my friend Betsy Chun who ran the World Trade Art Gallery (she lived), I passed through a checkpoint and peeked into the void through a construction stockade, a view of hell as seen through the lens of a pinhole camera.

The skeletal frame of the Trade Center evokes the dome at Hiroshima, and through the dust and noise I expected to find a surrealist clock, suspended in time at 8:56 A.M. On the edges of the plaza, the surviving buildings are ripped apart, Beirut's nihilism draped on the mannequins of Brooks Brothers.

I read a number of Xeroxed tombstones, flyers of the missing pasted to subway staircases. They could easily have been verses from Greek tragedy; they recounted last sightings on Wall Street or at doomed elevator banks, as though the River Styx that day had been a tributary of the Hudson.

The handbills were like those normally put up for lost cats and dogs, except that here what had gone missing was the innocence of American isolation—that which President Washington had conferred in his farewell address, delivered a few steps from where I stood contemplating mortality.

Only once before had I seen similar street posters to martyrdom, but they were in Peshawar, in the underworld between Pakistan and Afghanistan.

[2001]

Amateur Hour

When I moved to Europe, I joined a company that each year sponsors a pro-am golf tournament for charitable causes. Since 1991, this grand tour, with me in tow, has visited such hallowed ground as Gleneagles in Scotland and Deauville in Normandy. Although many of my drives remind me of a remark that followed one of Garrison Keillor's tee shots, "That'll teach them not to bring their Cadillacs," I sometimes find myself in a famous foursome. If, as the English writer Geoffrey Moorhouse says, golf is the last sport played by gentlemen, this is largely thanks to the current Masters and British Open champion, Mark O'Meara, known also as Tiger Woods's best friend. Several years ago when I played with O'Meara, who has the same soft touch with strangers that he has around the green, he was more a caddie than a pro to his amateur partners. He lined up our putts, searched the rough for our errant drives, and hit his own shots seemingly as an afterthought. Only back in the clubhouse did any of us realize that he had shot a course record 64.

During the round, O'Meara's wife, Alicia, joined us, and I

asked her how they had met. As a college golfer, he invited her to watch him play a sport about which she knew nothing. On the first hole, a par four, he had an eagle two, holing out his fairway iron. At the second, he had a birdie. By the third hole, he knew they would marry because, when he made par, she asked (as only a wife can), "What's wrong?"

I learned golf as a nine-year-old from a friend's grand-father, "Dad" Seamon, who considered it a necessary life tool—corporate finance then as now being a dismal science, he thought we were better off on the links than prepping for business school. My friend Nick and I honed our game at various Long Island public courses where those who filled out the foursome tucked tees and unfiltered cigarettes behind their ears. When asked today where I play most of my golf, I still answer "Christopher Morley," where a bad approach on the first hole rolls toward the expressway.

My clubs were a mixed bag, an odd lot of forgotten irons. But I never followed them with a proper set and after college let my golf go fallow. At my first few pro-ams, I played with clubs cadged from pliant caddie masters. Ambivalent about leveraging a buyout of Ping irons or Taylor Made woods, I showed up at my third pro-am with a set pulled from the rack at Wholesale Depot in Bangor, Maine. Ever the gentleman, O'Meara greeted me on the practice tee. "I see you have new clubs," he said cheerfully, too gentlemanly to add, "I thought Rawlings only made baseball gloves." Sure that my problems off the tee, in this age of titanium, related to the weakness of my capital expenditure program, I handed O'Meara my discount-house driver and then watched a half-dozen range balls disappear over the Scottish horizon, a feat of arms that would undoubt-edly dampen the spirit of any Callaway salesman.

One consequence of playing with pros is that many feel obliged to correct my Christopher Morley swing, much as before Sunday school my mother would fuss with my necktie or paste down my hair. I use the stance of O'Meara, the grip of Steve Elkington, the backswing of Brian Gunson, the putting stroke of Bill Rogers, and the follow-through of Peter Townsend—much as I once put together a Little League swing from scrutinizing those of Mickey Mantle and Ted Williams. Under such influence I should have a stroke as seamless as the disciples of the Dutch masters. But during most rounds my head swims with advice about the position of my shoulders, hips, and hands, and by the back nine I am again in dancing class, with sweaty palms, trying to learn the fox-trot.

Among other professionals, my favorites include Steve Elkington and Mark Calcavecchia. An Australian, Elkington brings to the golf club the charms that Crocodile Dundee dispatched with his boomerang. The only problem in playing with Elkington, a man of grace and humor, is that he comes with a gallery. Announced on a loudspeaker at the first tee in Deauville, I felt as if I were addressing the ball in front of the Million Man March, which may explain why my drive barely carried the women's tee. Calcavecchia, the winner of the 1989 British Open, is like a character from a Henry James novel, bringing American insouciance to a game that often feels as confining as an English drawing room. The first year I played with him in Bordeaux, Air France had lost his luggage. Unfazed, he played in sneakers and with borrowed clubs. But he scored under par. The next year we were again in the same foursome, and, as I had not played at any time in between, my best "shot" of the day was to note that while I do not play a lot of golf, when I do, at least it's with Mark Calcavecchia.

[1998]

War's End on Okinawa
In Search of Captain Robert Fowler

Nothing except a battle lost can be half
so melancholy as a battle won.
　　　—The Duke of Wellington, 1815

For the past fifteen years, I have been collecting books about the battle of Okinawa and reading about the fighting in longer histories of the Pacific war. I have also heard many stories set among its ridges. From before the war and into the occupation, my father served as a combat infantry officer in the U.S. Marine Corps, commanding C company, First Marines, through some of the worst campaigns, including Guadalcanal. Before the First Marine Regiment landed on Okinawa, however, he was sent stateside, along with others who had fought in three earlier campaigns. But many of his stories about the war touch on Okinawa, where, in particular, his close friend Robert Fowler was killed and many other First Marines were killed or wounded.

Before leaving for Okinawa, I asked a number of C company Marines about the fighting, receiving answers about the face of battle that suggest its portrait is best painted in the agonies brushed by Goya. "I saw one of my men fall," wrote John Wilkerson. "I missed him later that day and I never learned his fate." He also recalled a close encounter with the enemy: "We were about three feet apart. He looked me dead in the eyes for a split second. My first bullet hit him two inches above his right eye." John Pido, who also served with C company, remembered: "I'm seventy-five now, and fifty-five years ago, June 9, 1945, I was shot through the face, jaw, and neck while with the First Marine Division." Emil Buff spoke for many when he recalled randomly:

> My mind is more a sea bag than a filing cabinet... as kamikaze pilots continued to introduce their god to our fleet, we who knew him would soon take refuge in ours... the lead teams, stretched far too thin for the ground they covered, were pinned and bleeding.... Smoke was thick, could find no one ... the smoke drifted and stung eyes... trail now slick with mud ... was on a hospital ship that night...

To see Okinawa for myself and to follow the last footsteps of Robert Fowler, I flew to Naha, the capital, after a business trip to Hong Kong. As the plane descended into Naha International Airport, it passed over Ie Shima, the small island where, several weeks into the campaign that began on April 1, 1945, the war correspondent Ernie Pyle was killed. Before he was struck by a Japanese machine-gun bullet, he wrote: "In Europe, we felt that our enemies, horrible and deadly as they were, were still people. But out here I soon gathered that the Japanese were looked upon as something subhuman or repulsive; the way some people feel about cockroaches or mice." The battle for Okinawa lasted for two months after Pyle was killed. During the eighty-two days of fighting, an average of almost three thousand soldiers and civilians were killed daily.

The airport at Naha is inland from the blue waters of the East China Sea, where the largest naval task force in history landed an American army of almost six hundred thousand men. Russell Davis, a marine in the invasion forces, recalls: "We were going 'up' again. . . . We were outbound for Okinawa by way of Ulithi," where he saw "the greatest gathering of ships in the history of the world . . . . In such an army, the great Spanish Armada would have been run over and never sighted." But despite the size and power of the American fleet, the seas turned red wherever the waves of kamikaze planes washed over the American bows.

ONE QUARTER OF OKINAWA: *"a standing army"*

Thanks to my friend, George Feifer—whose book, *Tennozan*, is one of the best histories of the battle on Okinawa—I was met at the airport by Alex Kishaba, a man in his early forties, the president of the Ryukyu American Historical Society. Landing at Naha has the feel of stepping into the Hawaiian sunshine, and Alex's round, warm countenance, dark hair and complexion made other connections between these islanders and those of Polynesia. Walking to his parked car, we formed an immediate bond—sharing a mutual admiration for George and his history, and discussing that day's tour of battle.

The battle for Okinawa was fought along a ten-mile front, with Naha the western anchor of a fortified Japanese line that cut across the island to the east coast. With the marines on the right and army divisions to the left, the American Tenth Army attacked from the north, encountering about one hundred thousand Japanese entrenched between low, razor-backed hills that line the Okinawan landscape. By the end of June, the six-hundred-thousand-man American force drove the last Japanese soldiers into the sea off the southern coast. But first they had to gain the Japanese trenches and fortifications east of Naha, and that was a struggle of World War I desperation played out with World War II weaponry.

Leaving the airport to head toward the peace museum, Alex and I drove south on Highway 7, along a stretch of urban sprawl—suggesting to me that one way Okinawans tried to forget the war was to cover the front lines with nondescript apartment blocks and motorbike shops. Once clear of the congestion, we drove on narrow roads through land Feifer describes as "an ancient patchwork of tiny fields, sparely inhabited mountains and thousands of sharp ridges and rises." The cliffs break the landscape as if they were whales of granite, and as we drove south, Alex associated many of the humpbacks with desperate battles. Often we passed small Shinto burial shrines, which in the fighting became Japanese pillboxes that poured fire against the Americans, who, in response, laid waste to many sacred family treasures.

We stopped the car near a wooded knoll where the American ground commander, General Simon Bolivar Buckner, was killed—the highest ranking U.S. general to die in combat in World War II. According to H. C. Merillat, a family friend and a Marine Corps correspondent who served throughout the battle in Buckner's headquarters, the general was a "handsome" man who inherited from Ulysses S. Grant tactics that pushed forward each day on all fronts. Toward the end of the battle, he had gone forward to observe a marine regiment, was marked by his entourage as an important officer, and was killed by a shell fragment, which, I have read, prompted a massacre of nearby Japanese prisoners.

About 225,000 people died in the fight for Okinawa, of

which some 120,000 were civilians. Many were Okinawans impressed as laborers into the Japanese lines; others were squeezed between two industrial armies. A few committed suicide. Feifer writes: "Still, the majority of civilians did not choose death but were killed by starvation, disease, individual Japanese cruelty and, most of all, indiscriminate American firing."

Near the Buckner memorial we peered into one of Okinawa's many caves, deep crevices that hid well-armed Japanese soldiers, camouflaged gun emplacements, and, often, cowering Okinawan civilians. It prompted Alex to tell the story of his mother's family, which during the battle hid in one such cave. In their advance south, Americans sealed hundreds of caves; sometimes after warnings shouted in Japanese, sometimes not. In this instance, the cave was attacked with satchel bombs and smoke, and, miraculously, Alex's mother (then a child) survived. Her eight brothers and sisters and parents did not, which may explain the cliffside we passed later where Okinawan nurses chose suicide over American captivity.

All war memorials in Japan are called peace parks, and this one, near the island's southern cape, is surrounded with concentric circles of marble, where the names of dead American or Japanese soldiers and Okinawan civilians are engraved—similar in manner to Washington's Vietnam Memorial. To Alex's discomfort, the peace museum and shrines cost twenty-five million dollars—more grist for the pork mill. Inside are galleries of political correctness, arranged to wean the samurai inheritance from innocent school children, plus some more conventional cabinets of battle. We had tea with the director, Mr. Seiji Hokarna, a man of simple elegance, and then wandered through an exhibition of the American occupation (1945–1972), in which the portraits of the U.S. military governors had the impassive expressions of Roman proconsuls.

Before leaving the museum, Alex and I hiked up a long

hillside, which was lined on both sides with oriental gardens and shrines, dedicated by each of the Japanese prefectures that lost men in the battle. Each has delicate shrubbery, rock gardens, or altars of Shinto elegance. A steady line of tourists, all Japanese or Okinawan, were paying their respects to the departed spirits. Farther on, we came to the southern coast of the island and looked down on a necklace of rocky, forbidding beaches. In earlier times, American whaling ships plied the waters off these shores, where the last survivors of the Japanese Thirty-second Army died from their own despair or at the hands of American riflemen. In a cave that overlooks the sweep of the Pacific, General Mitsuru Ushijima, the Japanese commander, and his second, General Isamu Cho, committed ritual suicide—faithful to Melville's expression in *Moby-Dick* about the "impenetrable Japans."

SHURI CASTLE: *"straight ahead into the sausage machine"*

In the car Alex had an official army history, complete with regimental maps. During the day we were trying to retrace the steps of the two marine divisions, the First and the Sixth, and those of Robert Fowler. But only a visit to the Shuri Line brings into focus the relentless American tactics on Okinawa, as recalled in *Tennozan*: "There was no other way for Buckner but straight ahead into the sausage machine."

Japanese strategy was to allow an American landing, but then to defend a fortified line across the island from Naha to Shuri Castle, and then to the eastern coast. Colonel Yahara devised the interlocking fields of fire and fortifications, also described by Feifer: "The Japanese had carved the limestone and coral of each commanding hill there into a kind of land battleship... A network of trenches, galleries, caves and tunnels—some complexes almost two miles long—featured the added advantage of exits at both ends and sometimes flanks of the hills." The objective was not victory, but to bleed the Americans, who might then waver in their determination to invade the home islands or lose heart for the war.

At the center of the line was Shuri Castle, which was rebuilt after the war, although the independent kingdom of the Ryukyus has never been restored. Alex and I parked near the imperial grounds, where ponds, lily pads, and cherry blossoms cover battle works as formidable as anything that plugged the line at Verdun. The castle is now part of a local university, and it brought to mind not just the heart of the Okinawa battle, but the comedy of errors that was the mission of Commodore Matthew Perry to push the Japanese door open.

As recounted in George Kerr's history of Okinawa, Perry used the port at Naha as a staging area for his visit to Yokohama. The next delegation of Americans to call at Shuri was the First Marine Division in May 1945, and on that occasion, too, Shuri remained a remote kingdom. Russell Davis, serving in the First Regiment, describes an early glimpse of the castle: "Beyond the edge of the wall, the ridge ended. There was a long roll into the valley below. Far across the valley, beyond low hills and one east-west escarpment, was Shuri itself. . . . Off beyond a coastal flat near the China Sea, Naha—largest city on the island—smoldered like a city dump."

In the same attack, E. B. Sledge, a marine infantryman whose memoirs the writer Paul Fussell describes as "one of the finest to emerge from any war," remembers the Shuri Line as: "the worst area I ever saw on a battlefield. . . . I shudder at the memory of it . . . each time we went up, I felt the sickening dread of fear itself and the revulsion at the ghastly scenes of pain and suffering among comrades that a survivor must witness." It echoes a line in Davis: "The thought of dying in the mud was a terrible one that haunted my dreams," if not a line from Siegfried Sassoon's "Suicide in the Trenches": "The hell where youth and laughter go."[1]

Despite the large number of marines and soldiers on Okinawa, the sharp end of the battle was seen by relatively few frontline infantrymen. According to Feifer, "it was only within rifle range of the enemy where the world went mad, where life was so unlike anything previously known, that those just a quarter of a mile behind could not easily imagine it." But the numbers of dead and wounded along that battle line were some of the highest in World War II.

American casualties at Okinawa were 7,613 killed and 31,807 wounded. Another 26,221 left the lines at some point with battle fatigue, most in the assault against Shuri. In Sledge's unit, 485 Marines served at some point with K Company, Fifth Marines, and only a handful walked off the island without wounds. 107,539 Japanese soldiers and impressed laborers were also killed. A marine captain, Robert Sherer, who served under Robert Fowler, told Feifer: "The only glory was in surviving, in staying alive."

Sugar Loaf: *"the hell where youth and laughter go"*

Toward dusk Alex and I drove the short distance from Shuri to the hill known as Sugar Loaf, which, in the currency of blood, was the most expensive piece of real estate acquired

---

[1.] Sledge made the analogy between Okinawa and the trench warfare of World War I when he wrote me a letter on September 14, 1982, shortly after *With the Old Breed* was published: "In writing W.T.O.B., I often thought how similar much of the experience around Shuri, Okinawa, was to that which I had read in Sassoon, Frank Richards, Owen, and Blunden of their World War I experience. These conditions on Okinawa, some of the most awful imaginable, resulted from the rain, mud, and near-impregnable Jap defensive positions we faced. Unless our tanks could support and move with us (and they could not in that mud), those Jap defenses simply stopped us, and resulted in the Shuri Stalemate. Thus it resembled the Western Front in WWI. This has rarely been mentioned as far as I know, because journalists and war correspondents or photographers never came anywhere near the front line during that period on Okinawa." Sledge died in 2001.

during World War II. We had to park in a field off the side of the road, and gazed into the darkness at a low hill that is now covered with a water tank. It felt more like a New Jersey sub-urb than a Pacific island. As James Hallas, the author of *Killing Ground on Okinawa: The Battle for Sugar Loaf Hill*, a vivid account of the encounter, writes: "The remote spots men died for 50 years ago are now—preposterously—covered with McDonald's hamburger franchises, Dairy Queens, Kentucky Fried Chicken outlets, pawn shops and used car lots." Later I complained to a marine veteran of Okinawa, Richard Whitaker, about such a desecration. But he was more philosophical:

> Yes, I agree, the water tank on Sugar Loaf Hill is disturb-ing. However, one must remember that as far as the Japanese and Okinawans are concerned, the events of the spring of 1945 are bitter memories that are best left forgot-ten. The Japanese gave Sugar Loaf their best shot and so did the Sixth Marine Division. We prevailed. The water tank is understandable.

Feifer estimates that the battle for Sugar Loaf ranged over an area the size of "six football fields." One veteran recalled: "What made Sugar Loaf such a stunner was its seeming insignif-icance . . . it wasn't a mountain, it wasn't even a hill." Another called it "a little lump in the ground . . . it looked like a plowed field." But it was one of many little round tops that the marines and the army had to take, and each time they took one slope, they came under raking fire from interlocked positions, such was the genius of the Yahara defensive system. In less than a week, almost three thousand marines were dead or wounded on ground that today is paved with the paradise of convenience.

By one calculation, the marines made eleven concentrated attacks against Sugar Loaf. But rarely did they see the enemy, which fired machine guns and mortars from concealed posi-tions. "They were almost shapeless forms," a veteran recalled.

Another remembered: "Men were clinging to the hill as men would cling to a reef in a heavy surf." In Sledge's description, "The place was choked with the putrefaction of death, decay and destruction . . . every crater was half full of water, and many of them held a Marine corpse . . . Men struggled and fought and bled in an environment so degrading I believed we had been flung into hell's cesspool."

Sledge recounts the world of the First Marine Division, in the line to the east of the Sixth Marine Division. My father's comrades-at-arms, C company of the First Marines, were hard against the ramparts of Shuri Castle. But in the marine regiments given the luckless task of directly attacking Sugar Loaf, the newly formed Twenty-second and Twenty-ninth, several of the frontline companies were commanded by my father's former lieutenants.

Captain Maurice F. Ahearn, who led F company, Twenty-second Marines into the jaws of Sugar Loaf, was wounded but refused to be evacuated. "Yes, that sounds like Mike," was my father's remark when he heard this account. They had served together on Guadalcanal and Cape Gloucester, as each had with Robert Fowler, who during the struggle for the Shuri line moved up from command of F company, Twenty-ninth Marines, to S-3 of the Second Battalion. The Twenty-ninth eventually seized Sugar Loaf on May 19, and Captain Sherer credits Fowler for devising the strategy that allowed the Marines to envelope that and the surrounding hills: "The strategies that enabled the 2nd Battalion to seize and hold Sugar Loaf were undoubtedly formulated by Captain Fowler."

Another member of the Second Battalion at Sugar Loaf was William Manchester, whose memoir of the Pacific war, *Goodbye, Darkness*, must be among the most controversial of the war. In an article I wrote about Guadalcanal, I complimented Manchester's writing, echoing later sentiments expressed by Feifer: "the book's puzzling inaccuracies do not invalidate some of the best descriptions in English of the fighting on Okinawa and in other Pacific campaigns." But in response, I received a number of letters from other veterans, dismissing Manchester's accounts as war stories. Still, he can write graphically, as when he describes Sugar Loaf:

> I realized that something within me, long ailing, had expired. Although I would continue to do the job, performing as the hired gun, I knew that banners and swords, ruffles and flourishes, bugles and drums, the whole rigmarole, eventually ended in squalor. Goethe said: "There is no man so dangerous as the disillusioned idealist."

ROBERT FOWLER: *"the USMC never had a better officer"*

It was largely to track down a passage in Manchester's memoir that I had gone to Okinawa. He had known my father's close friend, Robert Fowler. But his account of Fowler's death on Okinawa had drawn angry responses from other historians, Feifer among them. In his descriptions of Sugar Loaf, Manchester writes:

> My father had warned me that war is grisly beyond imagining. Now I believed him. Bob Fowler, F Company's popular, towheaded commander, had bled to death after being hit in the spleen. His orderly, who adored him, snatched up a submachine gun and unforgivably massacred a line of unarmed Japanese soldiers who had just surrendered.

Until the book was published in 1980, my father had never known how his close friend had died.[2] It pained him

---

[2.] Nor had other members of C company known the story, as is reflected in a letter that I received from Guadalcanal veteran Ed Foley: "That part of your letter that really hit me, where it hurts, was your recounting the death of Lt. Fowler. I had asked repeatedly about his death and they answered: 'Oh, he got killed in one of the battles.' He was my platoon lieutenant, who had earned my lasting respect, as had your dad. He emulated your dad with his style of command. He was a leader, but still one of the troops."

further to imagine his death as the cause of a massacre. Now in his eighties, many of my father's regrets about the war focus on the loss of Robert Fowler. "I always thought," he says, "that if he had stayed with me, I could have gotten him through." He also speaks of war as a lottery. After four years of the worst combat in the war, Fowler's luck ran out—the last engagement his battalion fought was its last battle of the war.

After the war, my father paid his respects by visiting Fowler's parents in Hartford. They were undecided whether to have their son's body returned to the United States or to leave him overseas. Wanting to spare his parents further grief, my father told them that "Bob would have wanted to be buried in the Pacific." His grave was later moved to the Punch Bowl war cemetery near Honolulu. On my first trip to Hawaii, to pay tribute to my father's lost friend, I found Fowler's headstone in a tranquil, volcanic valley that sits among that island's tropical peaks.

From Lieutenant Colonel Jon Hoffman, a Marine Corps historian with access to the archives, I had with me on Okinawa a sketch of Robert Fowler's life and military career. In my father's recollection he graduated from the University of Michigan in 1941, having grown up in Hartford. Then Hoffman's notes pick up the story:

He was a reserve captain whose "date of appt/enl" in the Corps was 7 February 1942, in Philadelphia, PA. It says he had prior service, so he may have enlisted before that and was merely commissioned in 1942. He was born 16 April 1920 in Milwaukee, Wisconsin. He was married and his legal residence in 1945 was in West Hartford, CT. He was wounded by shrapnel on 15 April 1945 and returned to duty the same day. (It says wounded in the spine, but obviously it was not very serious.) He died of a gun shot wound to the chest on 12 June 1945, and was initially buried in the 6th Marine Division cemetery on 13 June. A Navy chaplain wrote the condolence letter to his family. In March 1948, Fowler's foster father authorized his interment in the Punch Bowl cemetery in Hawaii. (His wife may have remarried since 1945.)

To retrace Robert Fowler's last steps, I had several sources, in addition to Manchester and several official Marine Corps histories. I had letters from marines in the two companies in which he served during the war, including correspondence from Robert Sherer, who was with him when he died. I also had Feifer's history, in which one of the narrators is Richard Whitaker, who, by chance, served in Fowler's F company, Twenty-ninth Marines. Whitaker was with Charles Oates, Fowler's orderly, when the alleged massacre occurred.

From Manchester, I had thought Fowler died at Sugar Loaf. But a letter from Sherer places his death almost a month later, on the Oruku Peninsula. Marines from the Sixth Division, including Fowler's 29th Regiment, made an amphibious landing onto that peninsula—on a small-scale, opening a second front that Buckner's critics wanted sooner and with more troops. Certain army and marine officers believed that a marine landing below the Shuri line could have rolled up the Japanese from the rear, breaking the stalemate. But Buckner was reluctant to divide his forces, and the landings on the peninsula only leapfrogged along the coast and flanked a portion of the Japanese lines.

The fighting at Oruku (where the Naha airport is now located) lasted little more than a week but still cost almost two thousand casualties. An official Marine Corps history of Okinawa describes the fighting around Easy Hill:

> During the day the 29th Marines broke through the hard core of the enemy defense that had been holding it up for a week. . . . By 15:40, 1/29 had overrun the center of resistance, permitting 2/29 to move up on the left. Company F moved out from Oruku to seize Easy Hill, immediately south of the village—the last strong point in the zone of the 29th Marines.

Sherer's letter to me picks up the story:

> The death of Captain Bob Fowler, S-3, 2nd Battalion,
> 29th Marine Regiment, 6th Marine Division, on June 12th,
> 1945, to this day lacks cogent explanation as to the reason for
> his presence at Easy Hill on Oruku Peninsula, Okinawa. . . .
> I do not know the reason that Captain Fowler approached
> Easy Hill as the mopping up was in progress. . . . He did
> not wear a steel helmet but a fatigue cloth baseball cap. He
> was armed only with a shoulder-holstered .38-caliber pis-
> tol, not a Marine issue weapon. At a distance of about 50
> yards from the base of Easy Hill he was observed to have
> been hit by either rifle or machine gun fire.
>
> Why was he forward with hostile action in progress,
> particularly since he was so easily identified as a leader by
> his dress and arms? I doubt that Bob had been ordered for-
> ward and can therefore only reason that his motivation was
> of the highest desire known to a Marine—that of being
> with the men of the Company that he formed, trained and
> led into combat until he was ordered to a greater responsi-
> bility, the S-3 Operations Officer of the 2nd Battalion.

Of Manchester's account of the massacre, Sherer adds
dryly: "I cannot confirm his version in *Goodbye, Darkness.*"

Three versions of a massacre that followed Bob Fowler's
death have circulated, each involving his runner, Charles
Oates, who in most accounts had gone "a little Asiatic," in his
pursuit of a Japanese kill. Manchester's account implies that
the slaughter happened immediately after Fowler's death. Feifer
and Whitaker describe another incident, but it happened several nights later and may or may not have related to Fowler's
death. Sherer wrote me that on the day that Fowler died,
Oates had killed a prisoner who was trying to escape:

> This incident may have been the source of Bill Manchester's
> account but based on hearsay it grew in numbers and actual-
> ity. I do not deny that there was a company-wide passion of

anger and grief from the death of Captain Fowler. Bob was all that you and your father knew him to be. Fox Company, under his leadership, was a family.

After the fighting on Okinawa, Sherer wrote letters to both Fowler's widow, Mary, and his parents, to the latter praising the way that Fowler had been devoted to Oates. Sherer describes Oates at length: "He was so grief stricken over Bob's death that he was determined to have vengeance on every Jap he could find and sought to go on every patrol from this reason." Oates was found dead a week after Fowler was killed. No one was with him when he died.

By all accounts, Captain Fowler had acted as a father figure to the troubled Oates. Their bond included a pact that each would get the other's personal effects should they die in the combat zone. To Oates then went Fowler's revolver, with its Western holster, similar to the one my father wore. According to Whitaker, as recounted in Feifer, Oates had Fowler's weapon at his side when several days later he and Whitaker were on watch together. Three Japanese approached a hut where they were alternatively sleeping and standing guard. Wearing only loin cloths, the Japanese could have been soldiers out of uniform, trying to slip through American lines as civilians. They also could have been on a suicide mission. Or they could have been unarmed. Oates waited until the Japanese were within a range that was point blank and then shot down all three. Whether he was a brave marine fulfilling his mission or this was Manchester's exaggerated massacre, in memory of his lost friend, are questions of war and revenge as old as the stories of Achilles and Patroclus. Homer tells us:

> *Achilles led them now in a throbbing chant of sorrow,*
> *laying his man-killing hands on his great friend's chest:*
> *"Farewell, Patroclus, even there in the House of Death!*
> *Look—all that I promised once I am performing now:*
> *I've dragged Hector here for the dogs to rip him raw—*

and here in front of your flaming pyre I'll cut the throats
of a dozen sons of Troy in all their shining glory,
venting my rage on them for your destruction!"

In *Master and Commander*, Patrick O'Brian writes that "a serving officer in an active war has an intense rather than a lasting grief." But I sense it might have been the opposite for my father. After returning from Okinawa, I sent my father the letters about the death of Bob Fowler, and he responded:

> The correspondence you sent, as to the details of Bob Fowler's death, shed final clarity on a matter that had troubled and eluded me all these years. From it, I see that he died exactly as I would have imagined could well have happened, having seen him act with similar, spontaneous bravery quite often on Guadalcanal and Gloucester. The USMC never had a better officer!

OKINAWA'S LEGACY: *"invasion was too high a price to pay"*

Leaving Sugar Loaf, I asked Alex if we could drive past the memorial known as the Garden of Remembrance. I had recalled a newspaper article that described its dedications when some of the U.S. veterans who attended had refused to mix with their Japanese counterparts, fifty years after the peace.

We lacked base clearance to visit the Sixth Marine Division memorial. All we could do was peer through a chain-link fence, at the low obelisk, similar to those Civil War memorials in New England village centers. Alex pointed out that the few U.S. monuments rest on borrowed ground, and perhaps on borrowed time—implying that when the bases revert to Okinawa, the monuments would be returned to America.

We ate dinner in a small restaurant, exchanging stories of our families and work. I then spent a restless night in one of

Naha's few commercial hotels, in a windowless room that could well have been one of Okinawa's forgotten caves. Awake at odd hours with jet lag, I flipped through my books and wondered whether Bob Fowler's death was as needless as the civilian casualties at Hiroshima and Nagasaki. Many histories, such as Fussell's and Feifer's, make the connection between the desperate fight in the Ryukyus and the atomic bombs. Feifer has a quote from Ian Gow: "The experience of Okinawa convinced them that invasion was too high a price to pay," implying that the fates of Hiroshima and Nagasaki were sealed along the Shuri Line.

In his essay, "Thank God for the Atom Bomb," Fussell looks back toward Okinawa from ground zero: "The degree to which Americans register shock and extraordinary shame about the Hiroshima bomb correlates closely with a lack of information about the Pacific war. In much the same spirit, Feifer writes: "It is difficult to comprehend such [casualty] figures and to remember the strains of 1945. Focusing revulsion on the bomb is easier. But if a symbol is needed to help preserve the memory of the Pacific War, Okinawa is the more fitting."[3]

[3.] During the writing of this article, I made a few attempts to locate Robert Fowler's widow, but I gave up after the trail went cold in 1945. My father had not met her when he visited Fowler's parents after the war, although he did remember giving his friend a seventy-two-hour leave in 1942 in order for him to get married. The Marine Corps archive didn't contain any promising leads either.

About the time the article was published, the Columbia College magazine, in its class notes section, published a short profile of my father, mostly about his work in the last twenty years as president of the Association of Macular Diseases. The class correspondent started the profile by writing: "I received an inquiry out of the blue from the Maryland state archivist: 'Is the Nikolai Stevenson of the Class of '40 the same as the major with same name who was a tank commander on Peleliu in September 1944? My father-in-law wrote a paper about him.' Checking with Nick, the answer was a qualified yes—not a tank commander, but second-in-command of the First Battalion of the First Marine Regiment and an infantry officer overseas, including Peleliu, for two-and-a-half years."

Some weeks later, through a Web site listed in the profile, my father received the following e-mail:

Dear Nick,

I trust you remember me from Columbia College where I was a member of the Class of 1939. I just learned your whereabouts and marine history from the Class Notes in the May issue of "Columbia College Today." My wife, who also read the Class Notes, asked me to inquire if you might have known her first husband, Robert Fowler, who was with the First Marine Division on Guadalcanal and New Britain as a Lieutenant and later as a Captain with the Sixth Marine Division on Okinawa where he was killed in action.

Fowler came from Hartford, CT. He and my wife were classmates at the University of Michigan. He was called to active service immediately after Pearl Harbor and went right into the First Marine Division. Perhaps you knew him from personal recollections, historical writings, official records, contemporaries, or whatever. If so, we would be delighted to know any thing you wish to pass on.

My father answered this letter by calling Ed Biele, and speaking with his wife, the former Mrs. Robert Fowler. In December 2003, she wrote to me the following letter:

With a great deal of pleasure I shall write a little about Robert's schooling and what I knew about his becoming a Marine.

Robert was a day student at a prep school in Windsor, Connecticut. It may be there he became intereted in Dartmouth. He often mentioned Dartmouth to me but did not say why he ended up at the University of Michigan. Robert and I were both in the class of 1942. Pearl Harbor occurred about two weeks before Christmas break. During the holiday he received orders to report to Quantico. He returned briefly to Ann Arbor to collect his belongings. The University awarded him a degree porthumously.

Mr. Fowler encouraged Robert to enroll in a summer session at Quantico. I think he went every summer beginning in 1939. Mr. Fowler was a lieutenant in the army during World War I and saw a lot of action. He was disturbed about the state of things in Europe and thought Robert should be prepared. The peace time draft began September 1940. It is a good thing Robert went to Quantico when he did—he ended up being where he really wanted to be. I remember so well how happy he was to be a Marine.

I have enjoyed having these memories reawakened.

The Fowlers embraced Edward and our children. We were all family.

In December 1966 Edward and I visited Robert's grave. We took some flowers with us and paused for a long time at its beauty—it was stirring. We took pictures of it for the Fowlers.

In the late 1960s Ibelle and Lemuel visited us in Seattle. Not too long after that they both died. There were no surviving relatives on either side. Being in my 80s, I'm probably the only one around who remembers them.

Sincerely,

s/ Mary Biele

Field of Schemes

By age twenty-five Jim Bouton, who struggled to play even high school baseball, was an all-star, had won twenty games for the New York Yankees, and had pitched in two different World Series, winning two games in 1964 against the St. Louis Cardinals. He was a teammate of Mickey Mantle, Whitey Ford, Yogi Berra, and Roger Maris. Like the current Yankee pitching coach, Mel Stottlemyre, who was a rookie in 1964, Bouton was a great Yankee hope to bridge the dynasties of Casey Stengel and Ralph Houk to others who would carry pennants to the Stadium in the middle and late 1960s. But both Bouton and the Yankees dissolved in 1965. He developed a sore arm—he describes the pain in his tendon akin to that of a toothache—and lost more games than he won. Neither Bouton nor the Yankees fared much better in the years that followed. In 1968 he was traded to the minor leagues, if not to oblivion.

By good fortune, both for books and baseball, Bouton's new minor-league club morphed into the Seattle Pilots, a team that lasted only one season, 1969. That year for the Pilots, and later for the Houston Astros, Bouton pitched with some distinction as a knuckleball reliever—the heat having left his fastball. But his real contribution was the locker-room diary he kept, which was published in 1970 as *Ball Four* and which more recently the New York Public Library named one of its Books of the Century. The initial press run was five thousand. But after the commissioner of baseball tried to ban the book—Bowie Kuhn charged Bouton with the equivalent of blasphemy and baseball heresy—*Ball Four* sold five hundred thousand copies in hardback and another five million in paperback. For the first time baseball fans could wander the locker room and ride the team bus, something football readers had sampled in George Plimpton's *Paper Lion* and Jerry Kramer's *Instant Replay*. But those accounts were written in the language of hagiography. By contrast, Bouton filled the bases with Holden Caulfields.

Among the adolescents that Bouton describes loose in the nightclubs of New York is Mickey Mantle, who in the pages of *Ball Four* hits home runs while hungover and leads ballplayers to hotel roofs, in search of uncurtained windows and attractive women—a recreation known to those in the trade as "beaver shooting." (Bouton later wrote: "Think of a ballplayer as a fifteen-year-old in a twenty-five-year old body.") Bouton recalls breaking in with the club in 1962: "One of the first big thrills I had with the Yankees was joining about half the club on the roof of the Shoreham at 2:30 in the morning. I remember saying to myself, 'So this is the big leagues.'" He told his roommate on the Pilots, Gary Bell, that "you could win a pennant with the guys who've been on that roof." "Pennant, hell," Gary said. "You could stock a whole league."

Bouton understands baseball's hierarchy, observing correctly that "if Mickey Mantle had written *Ball Four* he would have gotten away with it. A relief pitcher on the Seattle Pilots has no business being a deviant." But because he had tarnished the reputation of, among others, Mickey Mantle, he was cashiered from baseball. To be sure, he remembers Mantle pushing "little kids aside when they wanted his autograph, and the times he was snotty to reporters." But Bouton, better than most biographers, captures Mantle's warmth, boyishness, and sense of humor. "What we do know, though,"

Bouton writes, "is that the face he showed in the clubhouse, as opposed to the one he reserved for the outside world, was often one of great merriment."

For a long time a rumor circulated in New York that Mantle would not attend Old Timers' Day at Yankee Stadium if Bouton were present. But before Mantle died (he had quipped: "If I had known I was going to live this long, I would have taken better care of myself."), he and Bouton had a warm reconciliation—further proof that while *Ball Four* broke literary form in 1970, by the mid-1990s, it was as quaint as wool uniforms and the suicide squeeze. For example, it reveals the players' view of other players, including the stars: "Talking about Yastrzemski not hustling recalled one of the great non-hustlers of all time, Roger Maris. Rodg always went to first base as though he had sore feet." A tone of puckish teasing runs throughout the anecdotes—similar to what you would hear in a golf foursome. Bouton writes: "In the bullpen Talbot revealed an awful truth about Joe Pepitone. He has two different hairpieces. He's got a massive piece, which he wears when he's going out, and a smaller one to wear under his baseball cap. He calls it his game piece."

While celebrity Yankees, like Mantle, Maris, and Pepitone, make cameo appearances in *Ball Four*, the heart of the book describes the expansion of the Seattle Pilots, which had as many memorable crewmen as one of Herman Melville's whaling boats. The manager, Joe Schultz—"short, portly, bald, ruddy-faced, twinkly-eyed"—is a genial Ahab who weaves allusions to Budweiser into many of his sentences. He screams at a pitcher: "For crissakes, Gelnar, you'll never get them out drinking Dr. Pepper." He trades the soon-to-be rookie of the year, Lou Piniella, with the words: "Lou, you're gonna have to pound Bud somewhere else." The pitching coach is the former New York Giant, Sal Maglie, aka Sal the Barber: "He's got those big evil-looking eyes. . . . He still looks like he'd knock down his grandmother." Pitching wisdom is distilled into the perpetual advice: "Smoke 'em inside." One day, leaning into the Pilots' bullpen, "a young girl asked one of the guys if he was married." "Yeah," he said, "but I'm not a fanatic about it." When some of the Pilots are filling out a questionnaire from the team publicity department—"What's the most difficult thing about playing major-league baseball?"—Mike Hegan responds: "Explaining to your wife why *she* needs a penicillin shot for *your* kidney infection."

Despite the book's camp-bus humor, the baseball commissioner said Bouton had done the game a "a grave disservice." Dick Young called him a "social leper." The literary criticism of Pete Rose was more direct. He stood on the steps of the dugout, the next time the Cincinnati Reds faced Bouton, yelling: "Fuck you, Shakespeare."[1] But the threat posed to baseball was not the revelation about Pepitone's game piece or that "Yastrzemski has a bit of dog in him." Instead the book "revealed, in great detail, just how ballplayers' salaries were 'negotiated'... how owners abused and manipulated players by taking advantage of their one way contract"—the so-called reserve clause under which professional baseball, with anti-trust exemption from Congress, operated like the Texas Railroad Commission. Although it was not Bouton's intention, *Ball Four* loaded the bases for Marvin Miller and the Players' Union to drive in the million-dollar runs that came with free agency.

Although baseball wanted to be through with Jim Bouton in 1970, he still had more innings left, both with his knuckleball and his pen. He retired from the Houston Astros after

---

[1] Bouton played against Rose in the minor leagues, in the late 1950s, and while they are not friends, he believes Rose got a bum rap from the baseball commissioner. "I think his lifetime ban for betting on baseball was cruel and unusual punishment. . . . Today we know that compulsive gambling is an addiction, just like alcohol or drug addiction, and denial is part of the illness. Accordingly, Rose should have been treated the same as baseball's drug users; a one-year suspension and rehabilitation with Gamblers Anonymous." But by banning him for life, Bouton writes, "baseball is saying, in effect, that gambling is worse than drugs. How do kids make sense out of that?" At least when they bumped into each other at a sports banquet, Rose admitted: "You know, I never read your fucking book."

the 1970 season and then worked as a New York sportscaster, covering some of the same players who had panned his book. For love of the game, he continued to play independent- and minor-league baseball on summer weekends for such teams as the Teaneck Blues, the Portland Mavericks,[2] and the Englewood Rangers. In 1978, he convinced Ted Turner to let him bang the professional drum for another season. At age thirty-nine Bouton (the same age as Turner) started several games for the Atlanta Braves, winning one in September—his last victory in the majors. During this time, he also appeared in a Robert Altman movie, invented "Big League Chew" (bubble gum that is shredded like tobacco), and traveled the country as a businessman, motivational speaker, writer, and inventor. Sometimes he would call on his old teammates, such as Steve Hovley, known on the Pilots as "Orbit" for his intellectual bent. Among other subjects, they touched on religion. Always insightful, Hovley remarked: "Religion is like baseball: great game, bad owners."

In a new marriage, with his children grown, Bouton moved to the Berkshires in the 1990s, his only connection to baseball being occasional starts for Mama's Pizza and the Saugerties Dutchmen. For Bouton "being there" is never as exciting as "getting there." Amateur baseball stirred memories that had never left him: "The real experience of baseball was the bus rides and the country ballparks and the chili at 3:00 A.M. with a bunch of guys chasing a dream." He once proposed a "non-contrived reality show" about players struggling to make the Birmingham Barons, a White Sox AA affiliate. In *Ball Four*, he describes being sent to the minors:

[2.] In 1977, Bouton earned $300 a month, playing for the Portland Mavericks in the Class A Northwest League. He nicknamed them "the dirty dozen of baseball," in part because they sang "Happy Trails to You" whenever the opposing pitcher was lifted from the game. Once an umpire came over to the Mavericks' dugout and told them to knock it off, that they had too much class for that. To which one of the Mavericks responded: "Oh yeah! Who says?"

There's nothing like walking into a minor-league clubhouse to remind you what the minors are like. You have a tendency to block it. It was cold and rainy in Tacoma when I went there to meet the Vancouver club and the locker room was shudderingly damp, small and smelly. There's no tarpaulin on the field, so everything is wet and muddy and the dirt crunches underfoot on the cement. The locker stalls are made of chicken wire and you hang your stuff on rusty nails. . . . There's no batrack, so the bats, symbolically enough, are stored in a garbage can. There's no air-conditioning and no heat, and the paint on the walls is peeling off in flaky chunks and you look at all of that you realize that the biggest jump in baseball is between the majors and Triple-A. The minor leagues are all very minor.

Since 1892, minor-league baseball in the Berkshires has been played at Wahconah Park in Pittsfield, Massachusetts. Both Casey Stengel and Lou Gehrig played at Wahconah. In one of his many comebacks, Bouton had a tryout there for the Texas Rangers. The roof and the toilets leak, and the seats are wooden benches. But like Fenway Park and Wrigley Field, it is a connection to baseball before Astroturf, domed stadiums, steroids, corked bats, and the San Diego Chicken. And it is the oldest minor-league park in America, which may explain why Pittsfield wanted to tear it down.

Before Bouton got involved, the local political establishment tried to spend eighteen million dollars (that it didn't have) to build a new stadium in Pittsfield. By chance, the lot selected for the new ballpark was owned by the local newspaper, the *Berkshire Eagle*, which ran a series of editorials equating the proposed stadium with a new birth of freedom and the chance to revive the city's sagging economic prospects. Not feeling a spare eighteen million dollars in their pockets, the voters of Pittsfield turned down the proposition to build the ballpark, but that did not stop either the mayor, the newspaper, their benefactors at General Electric, or the Parks Commission from trying to revive the new stadium public works.

In his introduction to *Foul Ball*, which brings to local politics what *Ball Four* brought to baseball, Bouton writes: "A historic ballpark soon to be abandoned, a government that ignores its citizens, a newspaper at war with its readers, the curious involvement of General Electric, and the shots are being called by a guy in Denver?

"It was about this time that I began taking notes."

The result is the diary of the political campaign to save Wahconah from the wrecker's ball and to bring to Pittsfield a locally owned baseball team that cannot be moved to another city when the owners find bigger subsidies in other pastures. In the introduction, Bouton writes: "You are no doubt familiar with America's most costly hostage crisis, perpetuated by the owners of professional sports teams: 'Build us a new stadium,' they warn, 'or you'll never see your team again.'" As an alternative, Bouton and his faithful—he calls them the "Marching Veto Warriors"—offer "100 percent private funds to restore a public ballpark to house a 100 percent locally owned baseball team. Pittsfield would get a renovated landmark and a professional baseball team, at no cost to the taxpayers. We'd even sell stock to local investors so no one could ever move the team out of town." At a public meeting on the subject, he implores: "Wahconah Park should be a working museum . . . the Museum of Minor League Memories."

Playing Robin to Bouton's civic Batman is Chip Elitzer, an engaging local investment banker who can both count and write.[3] Together with Eric Margenau, who owns several teams,

---

[3.] Their relationship can be glimpsed in an exchange prompted by nervousness over public speaking.

This reminded Chip about the most difficult speech he ever had to give.

"I was working for Eugene McCarthy," said Chip. "And I had to tell an all-male college crowd that I would be speaking instead of Jill St. John. Two-thirds got up and walked out."

"Why only two-thirds?" I said.

they draft plans to save Wahconah Park and to purchase a minor-league franchise that would be locally owned. Bouton and Elitzer file petitions, write letters, appear on radio, and testify before the city council and the Parks Commission, ignoring friendly advice that the political establishment "has been 'touched' on this new stadium issue." Other than a majority of the voters, no one around city hall is listening to their request for a long-term lease and locally owned baseball. "It was like trying to have a conversation with animated robots at Disney World," Bouton says of his encounters with the old guard. To anyone who has ever championed a hopeless local cause or circulated an unanswered petition, this Bud's for you.

Against such a coalition of the wishful is the usual political lobby, who, in Bouton's account, sound similar to those running a major-league baseball team, or at least the Seattle Pilots. Batting leadoff in this starting lineup is the mayor, Gerald S. Doyle, Jr.: "Doyle, tanned and fleshy with a balding dome, settled into his swivel chair, looking somehow retired. His style, as exhibited this morning and at the Bousquet meeting last week, is a combination of regular-guy affability and unjustly accused fury, creating the overall impression of a pugnacious maître d'." Bouton and Elitzer collide with an establishment that is suspicious of outsiders beyond the reach of smoke-filled rooms. They ask themselves: "What's worse than a lame-duck mayor with a chip on his shoulder? A lame-duck mayor with a chip on his shoulder who needs powerful friends."

Among the mayor's friends is the *Berkshire Eagle*, the local newspaper, hardly one of those beacons of independence so often profiled when the mythology of the American press touches on local papers. Not only does the *Eagle* own the land on which the state-funded stadium will be built (without fear or favor?), but it is part of MediaNews Group of Denver, which invests $250,000 in a promotion company, Berkshire Sports & Events, as Bouton observes, "to convince local voters that it was in their interest to spend $18.5 million, mostly from the public trough, for a new minor-league park." When

Bouton speaks to the publisher of the *Eagle* about saving Wahconah Park, he is told: "The guy you have to convince is my boss in Denver."

Why such a fixation on a new stadium? One tantalizing possibility is that the location selected, that owned by the *Berkshire Eagle*, was part of an old junkyard where in the 1940s and 1950s, General Electric and others may have dumped waste contaminants, including PCBs. Thus having a field of dreams instead of a waste site would save local interests millions in clean-up costs: build it and the Environmental Protection Agency will stay away.[4]

For the Bouton-Elitzer plan to work, they had to get a thirty-year lease for Wahconah from the city, with the condition that they would purchase a franchise from one of several minor leagues playing in New England. They pledged to invest $250,000 in Wahconah upgrades prior to opening day, 2002, and they unveil plans to maintain the stadium's turn-of-the-century charm with improvements such as a "Taste of the Berkshires" food court and what they called "Not-So-Luxury Boxes." Omitted from the plans were some of the minor-league promotions that Bouton saw in his playing days, such as "Bladder Buster Night," where the beer was free until someone went to the rest room, or Diving for Dollars, where fans scrambled for one thousand dollars in single bills scattered around the stadium.

An ally summarized the dilemma of the Bouton-Elitzer proposal: "You can't get a lease without a team, and you can't

---

[4.] During their campaign Bouton and Elitzer are told what everyone knows about Pittsfield: "This city is marinating in PCBs." In 1998 it reached a settlement with General Electric to clean up some of the PCB waste disposal sites in and around Pittsfield, a GE city where Jack Welch worked for many years. Critics of the settlement with GE, which was negotiated by Mayor Doyle, among others, said that Pittsfield should have gotten double the amount agreed to fund the cleanup. Bouton records a conversation with Elitzer on GE's dumping:

"Their calculation was that they'd never have to pay that much if they ever got caught," said Chip.

"They figured correctly," I said. "And that explains why Pittsfield has to turn out its street lights and Jack Welch has $900 million."

get a team without a lease." Elitzer's response stresses the importance of flexibility: "Pittsfield has an unprecedented opportunity to do what no other community has done before—take control of its baseball destiny. [Pittsfield has had seven teams in the last thirty years.] Instead of having a league or team owner dictate to the city who will play there or what terms must be met for them to stay, Pittsfield can . . . ensure that an all-Berkshire group will negotiate with both leagues to secure the best possible deal for the city." But he was up against the heirs of Huey Long who knew that "the time has come for all good men to rise above principle."

Bouton, Elitzer, and their many supporters lobbied to have an open forum to debate the merits of the proposals for Wahconah and, later, to have the question on the November ballot. Bouton raised the public hearings with a Parks official:

> "Speaking of that," I said, "whatever happened to the public hearings you said they were going to have?"
> "I spoke to Cliff [Nilan, head of the Parks Commission]," said Mellace, "and he said, 'I don't want to have to talk to everybody and defend what we're doing. Everybody's just going to have to live with it.'"
> Sounds like a slogan for Pittsfield . . . "Pittsfield: Everybody's Just Going To Have To Live With It."

At a city council meeting convened in the shadows, the council voted against putting the question of Wahconah's lease on the November ballot. Of what Satchel Paige might have called a "hurry up" session, one local politician told Bouton: "The council meeting last week was really about the abdication of democracy, not the ballpark." Bouton reflects: "This is democracy in action, advise and consent, Pittsfield style: The power structure *advises* the council what it wanted to see happen, and asked them to play ball or else. Once the council *consents*, which can take all of fifteen minutes, the matter goes to the lower chamber—DelGallo's or The Brewery—for enactment by people like the mayor or the commissioners."

At about the same time, the *Berkshire Eagle* criticized Bouton and Elitzer for their "continued divisive mentality," prompting one of Bouton's few piques of anger in a frustrating political battle:

> The mayor says "the fix is in." The City Council President says he's getting "an unbelievable amount of shit" from new-stadium councilors "and others." A mayoral candidate says state officials told him "the city was lying about not having to put up money." A state senator says he "knows" decisions are being made at a bar. And the Parks chairman is going around telling people we're "out" before the Commission has voted.
>
> And Chip and I are somehow responsible for "this continued divisive mentality"?
>
> Well, too bad. "Everybody's just going to have to live with it."

The umps, however, were in the bag. Instead of granting the Bouton group a thirty-year lease for independent, locally owned baseball in Wahconah, the mayor and his pals on the Parks Commission gave the field to Jonathan Fleisig, the owner of the Massachusetts Mad Dogs, despite his lack of a comprehensive plan to develop Pittsfield baseball. Bouton describes his presentation to the Parks Commission: "Watching Fleisig that night was like watching a man at his own funeral . . . speaking from notes, Fleisig gave a presentation that is hard to describe, although the word 'rambling' would be a good place to start." But he was "a place holder for the new-stadium guys." Two years later, as I write this, he is re-negotiating with Pittsfield for the additional subsidies that he will require to keep baseball in Wahconah.

Whatever the outcome in Pittsfield in the years ahead,

109 minor-league stadiums have been built since 1985 with taxpayer dollars. Bouton writes: "The amount of public money spent on sport stadiums over the past fifteen years is estimated to be in excess of $16 billion. And that's just what is visible." In most cases stadiums are built to attract a team from another city or to keep an existing franchise on location, but, according to Bouton, other threads link these projects, which all play the game of "hide the subsidy."

In Bouton's research, those who favor new stadiums tend to be local oligarchs: the law firms, the banks, the politicians, the contractors. Invariably, if there is a door-to-door campaign, it is to oppose a new stadium, the proposals that rarely make it to any ballot. The consensus is that a public vote on the issue would go against new building. No matter what team owners say about putting up new-stadium money, nearly all the finance for these ballparks comes from public sources, although the shell game of land swaps, zero-coupon bonds, state grants, match funding, and the like usually makes it difficult to trace the flow of funds.

In Bouton's view, local newspapers nearly always support new stadiums, because, like the *Berkshire Eagle*, they are part of vertically integrated "media" conglomerates that have side bets in real estate, cable television, radio, and sports. (For example, the *New York Times* owns 17 percent of the Boston Red Sox, who have discussed a new Fenway Park.) In most cases neither the team owner nor the league puts up any new-stadium money. But Bouton believes the reason that so many stadiums get built with other people's money is because the opposition gets "worn down" while the sentimental support of a local team touches a cord of civic pride, under which the costs are buried. Only in San Francisco, thanks to a loyal opposition, were private funds raised for a new ballpark.

A great many of these conditions were present in New York when former mayor Rudolph Giuliani put forward plans to build new stadiums for both the Yankees and the Mets, at an estimated cost of $1.6 billion. At the time, post-September 11

New York had a budget deficit of $4 billion, and Giuliani had already given both Messrs. Steinbrenner and Wilpon, the owners of the Yankees and the Mets, the gift of a $100 million for minor-league stadiums—one in Brooklyn and the other in Staten Island. When someone had the temerity to complain to Mayor Giuliani about why a vote had not been held on the proposed major-league ballparks, he responded, "Because they would have voted it down."

Bouton also believes that new-stadium economics trickle wealth only into the pockets of the team owners. Once the construction is completed, those employed around baseball fields, other than the players, tend to earn the minimum wage—selling hot dogs and beer, cutting grass, and parking cars, not exactly the stuff on which economic revivals are made. "The only people, besides the team owners, who want new stadiums are politicians, lawyers, and the media," Bouton concludes. "Politicos like to swagger around a palace—and stadiums are the modern palaces—the bigger the better, especially for mayors suffering from stadium envy. They like to watch games from the owner's box in full view of the TV cameras and hang out in the clubhouse with the players. This is in addition to the usual perks, kickbacks, and patronage that accrue to politicians on big construction projects."

Seen through Bouton's eyes, baseball appears as a feudal guild, a restricted trade manipulated so that a few appointed nobles maintain their designated fiefs. Of the office of the commissioner, he writes: "Since he is hired and paid by the owners and not the players or the fans, he should more accurately be described as the Person in Charge of Protecting the Financial Interests of the Twenty-Six Business Groups Which Make Profits from Baseball."

The current commissioner, Bud Selig, was the owner of the Milwaukee Brewers, which he created after buying the franchise of the bankrupt Seattle Pilots. He supports the ban on Pete Rose for his financial indiscretions, but when Selig had to divest his ownership in the Brewers, he put the team in a blind trust, albeit one run by his daughter. He also presided over the condemnation of the Montreal Expos, who were purchased by the owners' guild at a distressed price and who are now entertaining offers to move to a new city, provided the package includes a new stadium. When they turned down the possibility of the city of San Diego owning the Padres, Selig and the other owners also made it clear they will not tolerate a community-owned team in the major leagues. Who do you blackmail if the fans own the team?

While *Foul Ball* is mainly a book about minor-league politics, it is possible to glimpse, both in it and the updated edition of *Ball Four*, Bouton's attitude on the modern game of baseball. He deplores the way baseball thrives on a series of ugly confrontations—between players and owners, between one team and another. "Baseball has become a cheaper game, designed for unknowing fans accustomed to gross action over subtle beauty." He remembers the respect once accorded players on visiting teams, not to mention modesty in achievement. At times he finds baseball "cartoonish." When he started playing, he recalls that: "a homer was just a homer—not a religious experience."

Nor are the minor leagues thriving, despite all the new ballparks. When Bouton signed with the Yankees in 1958, New York had eleven minor-league teams, and he played in a system that moved him from Auburn, New York, to Amarillo, Texas. Now the Yankees have only six minor-league affiliates, as the major leagues rely more on college baseball to stock the professional pond. Modern players come to the game more prepared for the major leagues, and they have the benefit of well-funded programs. But college baseball has made the game, in Bouton's view, "more corporate." As a game of rival corporations, baseball loses some of the character it drew from sandlot America. Gone are the days when a scouting report consisted of the advice to "smoke 'em inside." Or the times when Bouton was told "the word on Tim McCarver of the Cards was that Sandy Koufax struck him out on letter-high fastballs," which as Bouton later reflected, "is great advice if you can throw letter-high fastballs like Koufax could."

When *Ball Four* was published in 1970, I purchased the hardback edition for $6.95, a lot of money for a high school sophomore to spend on a book. That summer and throughout high school I read it endlessly, flipping back and forth across the diary entries. I wish I had spent as much time in high school with Shakespeare or Henry James as I did with the Seattle Pilots. But *Ball Four* was the perfect coming-of-age account for anyone who grew up between the salad days of the Yankee dynasty and the fog of Vietnam and Watergate. In the same vein, *Foul Ball* reconciles baseball's faux nostalgia—as expressed in Baltimore's Camden Yards or the stereopticon of Ken Burns—with what Howard Cosell called "the ugly business of carpet-bagging."

Another pleasure of *Foul Ball* is to catch up with Jim Bouton after thirty years and not to find him, as is the case with former Yankee Fritz Peterson, shuffling cards in a casino. At one point his wife complains that he's spending too much time trying to save a run-down stadium. "It's such a long shot," she says. He answers: "My whole life is a long shot." His mentor, Yankee pitching coach Johnny Sain, used to tell him "not to be afraid to climb those golden stairs." Now Bouton has moved from challenging hitters to busting one inside on a cozy political establishment. He does it with language that lays bare the extent to which town democracy is played on a field of schemes. But in using baseball to write an important book about local politics, he does credit to the editor of *Ball Four*, Leonard Shecter, who said before he died: "A guy could make a living just telling the truth."

[2004]

Beatrice Stevenson Stanoyevich

1889-1980

I finished college in 1976 and returned to New York, a city my grandmother loved. She lived on Fifty-seventh Street, worked on Madison Avenue, worshipped in this church [St. Bartholomew's Church, New York City] and went often to the New York Public Library guarded by lions. She grew up in New York—along lower Fifth Avenue—and although she was fascinated by the world and by travel, she never really wanted to be anywhere else. Here were the things she loved: her family, her job, many of her students, her friends, and the books she enjoyed reading.

In New York, my grandmother (whom we called Bahmie) and I often ate lunch together. We talked as friends: about the world (Could I please explain why Iraq had attacked Iran?); about the family (Nothing delighted her more than that Julie was studying in France.); about history (Did I know that our ancestors had landed at Plymouth Rock?).

My grandmother loved conversation: the play of words,

the power of the imagination and the mind. She read the newspaper daily, especially the dispatches from abroad, and even past the age of ninety followed current events more devotedly than most people I now know—even in the magazine world. By all rights, this was a time in her life when she could have rested, taken it easy, basked in the sun. But instead she preferred to be part of the debate, to think and to reflect on those issues that shape our lives.

I always felt free to bring friends to these lunches, and she welcomed all. We were her students, and the seminar was in session. But it was Bahmie, perhaps more than the rest of us, who remained a student her entire life. At a time when academics were a male domain, she earned a degree from Wellesley and a doctorate from New York University. As the executive secretary of the Institute of World Affairs, she worked with students all her life. She liked students—their restlessness and their ideas. When the Institute was not in session, she organized round-table discussions in New York, Geneva, and Palm Beach. She lived a life that Aristotle probably had in mind when he wrote about education, politics, and the public good.

As a young boy I did not know Bahmie well. She could seem almost forbidding at times. It was with Grandma Gray that I shared the affections one normally associates with a grandmother: I would watch Grandma cook, she would watch baseball with me. It was only later, and theoretically after my character had formed, that I began to know Bahmie well. But as I see my life today, it appears almost to be a mirror of hers.

In the 1930s, she worked as an editor at the *North American Review*, a magazine similar to today's *Harper's*.

With her encouragement I studied abroad and at several schools of international affairs. Just this week I bought a globe at a map store that she took me to as a small boy. If she wanted anything, it was that the generations would renew themselves.

Over our lunches, I think what delighted her most was

that the family traveled. She was the navigator—the family's Prince Henry—and she considered all our trips somehow related to the trips she had made as a young woman. She possessed and admired the traits that make travel interesting: an ability to speak foreign languages; a knowledge of culture, history, and people (she was an anthropologist by training); a sense of who you are and where you are.

I am sure that when she traveled, her best qualities emerged: patience, curiosity, a keen wit, and a tireless interest in what other people were doing. She never really stopped traveling; in later years, although she rarely strayed far from home, she would receive my father's postcards, and respond to them with the delight of someone on her way around the world.

In 1976, for Christmas, she gave me a book about Vienna, and wrote in the inscription: "I value it greatly because it unites you and me in thoughts." I was there in 1975; she was there in 1914.

Vienna: the city of dreams. Much like her own life, it embraced the old world and the new. She was a contemporary of both Habsburg and Freud. I can imagine her sitting in cafés discussing Russian politics or, maybe, in less guarded moments, romance and love. There is almost a fatalism about Vienna, a sense of tragedy that is based upon a knowledge of the past. She understood this, and it was in Vienna that she witnessed something that stayed with her for the rest of her life. If I may, I would like to read from a letter she sent to me while I was living there. I received it on April 20, 1975:

In reply to yours of April 6th, I can write my experiences of being in Vienna, 1914. It was a very eventful period of my life. As the daughter of a New Yorker, who worked for the Mutual Insurance Company, I was privileged to travel with my mother to Europe. Passing thru Paris, we came by train to Vienna. We stopped at the Grand Hotel, then at the corner of the Oper Ring and Kartner Strasse.

One day as my mother and I made purchases in Kartner Strasse the shopkeeper whispered to my mother that the South Slavs were showing war dispositions. We consulted our men friends who said that in case war broke out, Austria would stand with Germany to fight.

With this anxiety arising, my mother said we should pack to go. August 4th was to be our departure. When we reached the railroad station, there was high excitement. As we approached the departure gate, a railroad employee notified our Austrian friend conducting us that "the ladies should return to their hotel for the French were armed to prevent our train from starting." So we returned to the Grand Hotel and saw the pride and glory of Austria's armed might riding by on their magnificent horses. In the lobby tearful wives were saying good-bye to their heroes.

Then came the Battle of Tannenberg and victory of the Germans over the Russians! Shouts of victory!

Meantime we were reassured financially because the Mutual Life Insurance of New York had its own cable under the Atlantic Ocean—not destroyed as the Atlantic Cable had been.

With autumn came a mission from U.S.A. It lodged at Hotel Bristol across the Ring Strasse. So I was advised to go consult it. The commander of the mission said: "Young lady, tell your mother that when we say the word, you must go!"

So we packed and went to Berlin, awaited instructions and boarded a night train to Holland. We arrived at Rotterdam 3:00 A.M., then took a train to the dock to cross the Channel to England.

In that parlor car, sitting opposite my mother and me, were two English-speaking gentlemen. As I overheard their conversation, for the first time in all those war weeks, I heard the English and French side of the fighting. It was like a bolt from heaven.

Such is the nature of Publicity!

So, I tell all of this, because you are in Vienna!

Lovingly,

(s) Bahmie

Like the Viennese, she understood that there is tragedy in life, but unlike the Viennese she rarely complained. She was able to adjust to both ancient and modern ways—it was her fate to see that war begin—but in both worlds she remained cheerful and optimistic that man could learn from his past mistakes.

I wonder if it is possible for me to convey here today the strength of her faith, how strong it was, how it lives on today. How easy it would have been to live through such days—she watched an Austrian boyfriend march off to war and be killed—and then despair forever about the human condition. The narrator in *All Quiet on the Western Front* says of his generation, which was also Bahmie's:

> We will be superfluous even to ourselves, we will grow older, a few will adapt themselves, some others will merely submit, and most will be bewildered;—the years will pass by and we will fall into ruin.

But this was not her fate. Her faith was stronger. She did more than adapt. She flourished. It is this faith that sustains us today. We shall miss her beyond words, but we shall go on.

Delivered in New York City, January 1981

All Aboard
the Berlin-to-Baghdad Railway

I, like many others, have spent more than a few weekends away from home, a lull that often feels like the eye of a business-meeting storm. I can remember a stranding in Perth, Australia, where it rained for forty-eight hours. Nevertheless, I have used a few of these long weekends to make some of my most memorable passages.

On one occasion I played hop-scotch between Hong Kong and Tokyo, visiting the American battlefields on Okinawa and then driving from Kagoshima to ground zero in Nagasaki. I remember another weekend in St. Petersburg, on an eternal summer day in a park near the Hermitage, reread-ing *Doctor Zhivago* and then hiring a launch to navigate along the canals that bordered the tsar's shuttered mansions.

Recently I arrived in Istanbul on a Saturday for Monday meetings. The World Cup was in session, so the highways were deserted. I went from the airport directly to a friend's boat, thus entering the Bosphorus at eye-level with the impe-rial palaces that line the waterway between Europe and Asia. We were part of the long procession of tramp steamers, tankers, and ferries that ply the straits—some were taking commuters home while the Russian destroyers were in search of warm water.

This is the Sublime Porte. Pierre Loti, who conjured the enchantments of Madame Butterfly when living in Nagasaki, also lived here: "The sea is at its feet, a sea crossed by thousands of ships and small boats in perpetual motion; and from this sea rises the clamor of Babel, in all the tongues of the Levant; like a long, horizontal cloud, smoke floats over the mass of black ocean-liners and gilded caïques [and] on the multicolored crowds shouting out their transactions, bargaining. . . ."

Only the harbors of Hong Kong and New York can rival that of Istanbul, which I first saw in the summer of 1976, when my father took our family on a Black Sea steamer that sailed overnight from Greece to Turkey. We passed the Hellespont at first light and the Dardanelles at dawn. Then, toward sunset, we approached the minarets and domes that bridge not just Europe and Asia, but Christendom and Islam.

Early on Sunday morning, I went with a car and driver in search of tourist Istanbul, which I had not seen since that summer after I had graduated from college. In front of the Blue Mosque, I bargained hard for ten minutes to pay three dollars instead of the demanded fifteen for a guide, only to find one offered for three dollars in most gift shops. Inside the mosque, the tranquillity of the soaring domes and the richness of the carpets underfoot contrasted sharply with the recent televised images of Islam, in which many of the faithful are either suicide bombers or cave dwellers in the Tora Bora.

When President George W. Bush declared the war against terrorism, he spoke of a crusade. The results of an earlier such endeavor were on display in Hagia Sophia, the seeming Anglican cathedral that fell to the Ottomans in 1453. Various sultans transformed the center of Eastern orthodoxy into a mosque, and even six hundred years later the Arabic script that lines the cathedral heavens seems like a consecration. But a guide said St. Sophia suffered more at the hands of the crusaders, who came to protect it, than it did later under the Ottomans, whose heirs today have the unhappy task of trying to bridge the worlds of fundamental Islam with the chevaliers of George the Lionhearted.

Topkapi Palace was home to the Ottoman sultans, for whom the inner courtyards and gardens were an oasis of luxury and refinement, in a realm that devoted itself to the ruthless conquest of the infidel. A number of sultans cultivated tulips—not to mention the flowering of the harem.

Topkapi was also witness to numerous scenes of debauchery. During the Mongol invasions, the so-called tulip king, Bayezid, fell to Tamerlane, who proved as ruthless as many of the residents who later came to Topkapi. Mike Dash evokes the change of power wonderfully in his splendid history, Tulipomania: "The tulip king was shown no mercy. Tamerlane seized the women of the sultan's harem for himself and forced Bayezid's wife Despina to wait on him, naked, at this table. The sultan he confined within an iron cage, which the Mongols took with them as they traveled. On state occasions Tamerlane had the once-proud Bayezid dragged before him so he could use him as a footstool."

The harem is a series of opulent rooms, covered, as you might expect, with oriental rugs and divans. (Only later did we call them ottomans.) But when not on duty, the concubines lived more like stable horses, in stalls leading to the harem. The shelf life for those currying imperial favors was rarely longer than that of tulips. Unwanted subjects, not to mention political rivals, were pitched into the waters where the Bosphorus meets the Sea of Marmara, a spot that now has a lovely café, on what Pierre Loti calls "the last promontory of Europe." I took a break there to sip Turkish coffee and looked down on the Golden Horn, which Loti writes "is not only an arm of the sea separating the two parts of Constantinople, but also puts an interval of two or three centuries between what is bustling about on one bank, and falling asleep on the other."

As a banker, I am often asked to pay my last respects to the Turkish economy, which alternates between boom and bust, if not bustling and falling asleep. Every few years the banking system collapses, the currency fails, and the West bails out the government as if it were an Arkansas savings and loan. Before my arrival, the International Monetary Fund had given Turkey sixteen billion dollars to salvage a number of failed financial institutions, perhaps with the hope of forestalling another Mongol invasion, this one waving the banners of Islamic fundamentalism.

After my weekend with the Ottomans, I visited a number of Turkish banks. Some operate responsibly, with credit committees that weigh the benefits of exchanging toasters for deposits. The state-owned banks, however, are aligned with political favor, not monetary restraint. When Washington received word of Turkey's pending bankruptcy, it was discovered that some thirty-two billion dollars in so-called "duty loans" had been advanced to customers whose only collateral consisted of electoral expedience.

The run at the banks broke the house of cards on which the government has funded its social agenda of secular Islam. Turkey dreams of assimilation with the European Union to compliment its NATO membership. But despite the cosmopolitan trappings of Istanbul—I stayed in the Hyatt and drank French wine at dinner—Turkey also inhabits an oriental world: it has a population of sixty-seven million, of whom 98 percent are Muslim and twelve million are Kurds. Its borders with Greece, Bulgaria, Iraq, Iran, Armenia, Georgia, Russia, and Ukraine are tense. Once hoping to lure the Ottomans into an English alliance, Queen Victoria awarded the sultan the Order of the Garter, which is still on display in Topkapi's museum. Two years later, the sultan responded with what are known as the Bulgarian atrocities.

Today Turkey has the most to lose in any Allied attacks against the regime of Saddam Hussein: first, it trades contraband Iraqi oil; second, the liberation of Baghdad will trigger demands for an independent Kurdish state, which would inevitably make a claim against southeastern Turkey. Needed foreign exchange earnings from tourism would disappear, and an already fragile governing coalition would face even greater challenges from Islamic parties.

If the wars of the Ottoman succession dominated so much of the nineteenth and twentieth centuries—think of the charge of the Light Brigade and NATO's liberation of Kosovo—then those of the twenty-first century may turn on whether Turkey looks to Brussels or Mecca for its calls to the faithful.

The thought of war on the Turkish frontier also reminds me of the Gallipoli peninsula, which I first saw in 1976 on our passage through the Straits. In 1915, French, English, and ANZAC forces landed there to capture the Dardanelles, occupy Istanbul, and knock Turkey out of the German alliance. Winston Churchill was among the sponsors of the landing, which cost 265,000 Allied casualties in hills that overlook what remains of the walls of Troy—yet another imperial excursion in Asia Minor.

The father of secular Turkey, Mustafa Kemal, known as Atatürk, helped repulse the Allied invasion, at one point commanding his soldiers (as if they were boarding buses in Jerusalem): "I am not ordering you to attack. I am ordering you to die." At Chunuk Bair and other contested hilltops, the Allied assault failed. A side effect of these battles, as one historian has written, was that it produced in Turkey a "changeover from a form of national consciousness to a type of brutal chauvinism."

On the day that the Allies landed, so optimistic to roll back the tide of Islam, the Turkish government began its genocide of Armenians, which claimed 1.5 million lives. It was a holocaust of exhaustion, as the Armenians of central and eastern Turkey were marched into the desert to wither and die. A witness to this tragedy was the U.S. ambassador to Turkey, Henry Morgenthau, who later wrote that these caravans of death could be seen "winding in and out of every valley and climbing up the sides of nearly every mountain," to unscheduled stops on the Berlin-to-Baghdad railway.

Leaving Istanbul on this trip, I passed what is left of Constantinople's city walls that were breached when the forces of Mahomet stormed the St. Romanus gate. The only witnesses to such a chapter in history are the decaying fortress walls and gypsy tent villages that fly their talons of drying laundry. In 1453 the city was a Christian island in a Moslem sea. Only some renegade Venetians and Genoans shored up the defenses, which eventually crumbled. The crusaders had long since departed for Europe. Survivors of the battle were taken to St. Sophia where, before they were sacrificed, they had to witness its conversion to Islam.

[2002]